The Ethos of Pluralization

Borderlines

A BOOK SERIES CONCERNED WITH REVISIONING GLOBAL POLITICS
Edited by David Campbell and Michael J. Shapiro

Volume 1 William E. Connolly, *The Ethos of Pluralization*

The Ethos of Pluralization

WILLIAM E. CONNOLLY

BORDERLINES, VOLUME 1

 University of Minnesota Press

Minneapolis

London

Published by the University of Minnesota Press
111 Third Avenue South, Suite 290
Minneapolis, MN 55401-2520

Book design by Will Powers.
Set in Sabon and Officina types
by Stanton Publication Services, Inc., Saint Paul, Minnesota.
Printed in the United States of America on acid-free paper
Second printing, 1996

Library of Congress Cataloging-in-Publication Data
Connolly, William E.
        The ethos of pluralization / William E. Connolly.
            p.   cm. — (Borderlines : v.1)
        Includes bibliographical references (p.   ) and index.
        ISBN 0-8166-2668-5 (hardcover : acid-free paper)
        ISBN 0-8166-2669-3 (pbk. : acid-free paper)
            1. Pluralism (Social sciences)   2. Democracy.   I. Title.
        II. Series : Borderlines (Minneapolis, Minn.) : v. 1
        HM276.C67   1995
        321.8—dc20   95–13777

It is important to resist that theoretical gesture of pathos in which exclusions are simply affirmed as sad necessities of signification. The task is to refigure this necessary 'outside' as a future horizon, one in which the violence of exclusion is perpetually in the process of being overcome. But of equal importance is the preservation of the outside, the site where discourse meets its limits, where the opacity of what is not included in a given regime of truth acts as a disruptive site of linguistic impropriety and unrepresentability. JUDITH BUTLER

It is at precisely that nexus of committed participation and intellectual commitment that we should situate ourselves to ask how much identity, how much *positive consolidation,* how much *administered approbation we are willing to tolerate in the name of our cause, our culture, our state.* EDWARD SAID

With tremblings of disturbance,
   you may begin to feel:
on the pathways of difference,
    does ethics become real. A DESCENDANT OF JOB

We're tired of trees. They've made us suffer too much.
GILLES DELEUZE AND FÉLIX GUATTARI

Contents

Acknowledgments   IX

Introduction: The Pluralist Imagination   XI
The Condition of Pluralism · Reworking the Pluralist
Imagination · The Ethos of Critical Responsiveness ·
The Pluralization of Pluralism · Mapping the Course

1. *Nothing Is Fundamental . . .*   I
Ontopolitical Interpretation · Ontopolitical Registrations ·
The Ontopolitical Matrix · Strategies of Detachment and
Attachment

2. *The Desire to Punish*   41
The Call to Punish · Pathways of Desire · The Desire of
Dontay Carter? · Desire and Punishment · The Micropolitics
of Desire

3. *Democracy, Equality, Normality*   75
Models of Democracy · Democracy and Equality ·
Democracy and Normalization · Majority Assemblages
and Economic Equality · The Constitutive Ambiguity
of Democracy

4. *Fundamentalism in America*   105
   Fundamentalism · Paradigms of Fundamentalism ·
   The Fundamentalist Political Formula · Liberalism and
   Fundamentalism · Renegotiating Fundamentalisms?

5. *Democracy and Territoriality*   135
   Theory and Nostalgia · The Paradox of Sovereignty ·
   (Schumpeterian) Realism and (Walzerian) Idealism · The
   Democratization of Territorial Security · The Disaggregation
   of Democracy

6. *Tocqueville, Religiosity, and Pluralization*   163
   The Ambiguity of Boundaries · The Civi-Territorial
   Complex · Tocqueville, Thoreau, Apess · Justice and Critical
   Responsiveness · Reconfiguring the Sacred/Secular Duopoly ·
   The Borders of Pluralization

   Notes   199

   Index   237

Acknowledgments

I am grateful to the Center for Advanced Study in the Behavioral Sciences in Palo Alto for a fellowship in 1993–94 that allowed me to complete this book. Life on the Hill is great. Not only were the daily volleyball games a competitive delight, I profited immensely from conversations with Mark Baker, Jamshed Barucha, Jerry Bruns, John Gillis, Bonnie Honig, Arthur Kleinman, Joan Kleinman, Buck Schiefflin, Laura Stoker, Carlos Vélez-Ibáñez, Patricia Williams, and Mayer Zald as this book was nearing completion. Jerry Bruns, Bonnie Honig, and Arthur Kleinman were kind enough to read large sections of this manuscript in early drafts, and I have revised it considerably in the light of their thoughtful commentaries. Judith Butler, Wendy Brown, David Campbell, James Der Derian, Fred Dolan, Tom Dumm, Dick Flathman, George Kateb, Kirstie McClure, Mike Shapiro, and Nathan Widder all commented on particular sections. This book might have been even more kind and gentle had it not been roughed up by this group of wrestlers. Yet, even as we circle around one another we may foment together a productive pluralization of cultural and political theory. Jane Bennett, once again, has stayed close to this manuscript from its inception to its completion, helping me to clarify murky sections and inspiring me to discern more actively points of connection with some of the traditions I resist. I am grateful to her and to the others listed here both for the example of their work and for their willingness to involve themselves so generously in thinking with and against this project.

While each of these chapters has been extensively revised and expanded, shorter versions of four of them have been published previously: Chapter 1 as "The Irony of Interpretation," in *The Politics of Irony: Essays in Self-Betrayal,* ed. Daniel W. Conway and John E. Seery, copyright Conway and Seery (New York: St. Martin's, 1992), used by permission; chapter 3 as "Democracy and Contingency," in *Democracy and Possessive Individualism: The Intellectual Legacy of C. B. Macpherson,* ed. Joseph H. Carens (Albany: State University of New York Press, 1993), used by permission; chapter 5 in *Millennium: Journal of International Studies,* 20, no. 3 (Winter 1991), used by permission; chapter 6 as "Tocqueville, Territory and Violence," *Theory, Culture and Society* 11 (Winter 1994), used by permission. I acknowledge with thanks the permissions.

Introduction: The Pluralist Imagination

THE CONDITION OF PLURALISM

Pluralism, advertised as a diverse, tolerant form of life, is again on the discussion agenda in Europe and America. Its resurgence reflects the contingent confluence of several elements. They include the collapse of communist states, accompanied by the post-Marxist appreciation of energies in civil society exceeding the unity of command economies;[1] the acceleration of population flows accompanying the globalization of economic life, as affluent managers step up the pace of transnational mobility and postcolonials migrate to the centers of former empires; the acceleration of speed in military delivery systems, cultural communications, civilian transportation, disease transmission, ecological change, and political mobilization, accentuating the experience of contingency, porosity, and uncertainty in territorial boundaries and national identities; the eruption of new claims to positive identity among constituencies whose previous identifications along lines of race, gender, sexuality, nationality, class, religion, or irreligion were experienced as injurious or degrading; and the devolution of the individualist/communitarian debate of the 1970s and 1980s in Anglo-American political theory into a set of compromises that reposition many of its participants as conventional pluralists.[2]

These drives to civil society, multiculturalism, return of the colonial repressed, transnational mobility, and pluralist tolerance encounter a series of bellicose responses. The most virulent emanate from fundamentalisms that demand reinstatement of a unified faith, race, reason, gender duality, normal sexuality, nation and/or territory that never was secure. A few examples of such reactions are ethnic cleansing; enforced heterosexuality; racialization of crime and punishment; redogmatizations of divinity, nature, and reason; and intensification of state border patrols.

This correlation between pluralization and fundamentalization is not accidental, for each conditions the other: each drive to pluralization is countered by a fundamentalism that claims to be authorized by a god or by nature. Moreover, any drive to pluralization can itself become fundamentalized. These two drives participate, therefore, in the same political matrix. In the United States, for instance, the struggle between them infiltrates contention over the liberal arts canon, the authority of scripture and reason, the relation of god and nature to dying, the question of abortion, the relation of creationism to evolution, the character of gender, the normal range of sexual desire, the pace and composition of immigration, the role of race in identity, the relation between race and IQ, the policing of territorial boundaries, the lines of division between public and private morality, the sovereignty of the state, the social effects of political correctness, and the politically correct shape of the new world order. These struggles, in turn, churn up old, dyspeptic debates over the role of divinity, nature, tradition, and reason in moral and political life. If, as Nietzsche surmised, the medieval god retreated as the enchanted world of signs over which he presided faded away, he has not returned to take vengeance today. His place, rather, has been usurped by an electronic/media/techno-deity who foments and funds political campaigns of late-modern fundamentalism.

I engage such issues in these essays, asking how the contemporary condition sometimes fundamentalizes contending parties and what might be done to renegotiate and disperse these divisions. But my attention is drawn most actively to the pluralist imagination itself. For the contemporary pluralist imagination, proclaimed as the guardian of diversity and generosity in social relations, remains haunted by ghosts it seeks to exorcise. The American pluralist imagination, in particular, remains too stingy, cramped, and defensive for the world we now inhabit. These stingy dispositions sustain operational standards of identity, nature, reason, territory, sovereignty, and justice that need to be reworked. For crucial presumptions within them both camouflage injuries that might otherwise be ventilated and foreclose admirable cultural possibilities that might otherwise be pursued.

REWORKING THE PLURALIST IMAGINATION

By focusing on the pluralist *imagination,* I do not work hard to locate myself on the contemporary scale of optimism and pessimism. Nor do I gauge too closely the probability that a more generous, pluralizing ethos will actually come into being. The value of such spectatorial stances can easily be overrated. Rather, I seek to refashion the pluralist imagination itself. I give priority to possibility over probability because closures in the pluralist imagination itself help to conceal or marginalize injuries and limits in need of political engagement.

A conventional pluralist celebrates diversity within settled contexts of conflict and collective action. Often diversity is valued because putative grounds of unity (in a god, a rationality, or a nationality) seem too porous and contestable to sustain a cultural consensus. Such pluralist instincts are admirable. Any reworking of the pluralist imagination will draw sustenance from them. But what about the larger contexts within which the pattern of diversity is set? How plural or monistic are they? To what extent does a cultural presumption of the normal individual or the preexisting subject precede and confine conventional pluralism? What conceptions of identity (and difference) are taken for granted in pluralist celebrations of "diversity"? How are subjects territorialized by operational codes of conventional pluralism?

In American pluralist theory from the 1950s to the present these issues are often resolved below the threshold of explicit determination. While demands for close ethnic or religious unity are resisted, many pluralists bound diversity by the territorial state, the normal individual, and monotheistic or monosecular conceptions of morality. For example, when secularism is advanced as an alternative to monotheism in public life it often retains a unitarian conception of morality remarkably close in structure to that supported by the Christian faith that originally spawned the space of the *seculere.* Moreover, conventional pluralism is a state-centered ideal: outside the warm, protected spaces of the normal individual and the territorial state, conventional pluralists project a lot of abnormality, anarchy, and cruelty in need of exclusion or regulation. Inside these boundaries prevail a set of general presumptions about the terms of national security, the basis of gender difference, the normality of heterosexuality, the source and scope of rights, the monotheistic or monosecularist basis of morality, the shape of the economy, and the generic character of justice, reason, identity, and nature. Stark definitions of the outside contain the range and reach of diversity on the inside, and vice versa.

This matrix not only sets the context within which plurality is appreciated; it also fixes stringent limits of reasonableness within which new claims to diversification are judged. Social *pluralism,* you might say, is often presented as an achievement to be protected, while the eruption of new drives to *pluralization* are often represented as perils to this achievement.

My reading configures the dissonant relation between pluralism and pluralization as the constitutive tension of pluralist politics itself. The paradoxical politics of pluralist *enactment*—through which new, positive identities are forged out of old differences, injuries, and energies—does require preexisting pluralism as one of its supporting conditions. For preexisting pluralism provides new movements with funds of difference from which they proceed, subterranean connections from which responsiveness to them might be cultivated, and cultural continuities upon which new negotiations might build. But the culture of pluralism also engenders obstacles to new drives to pluralization that must recurrently be challenged. How to reconfigure and renegotiate the constitutive tension between democratic pluralism and pluralization is the central question of this study. The theories appraised here are selected largely because of the ways they negotiate or obscure this tension.

The most serious shortcomings in conventional pluralism are difficult to articulate. You might say, though, that the conventional understanding first misrecognizes the paradoxical relation between a dominant constellation of identities and the very differences through which the constellation is consolidated and, second, misrecognizes new possibilities of diversification by freezing moral standards of judgment condensed from past political struggles. These two patterns of misrecognition install an unconscious conservatism at the center of the pluralist imagination. The first deflects appreciation of how the campaign to propel a new possibility of being into an established pluralist constellation encounters resistance from fragile identities shaken by movement in those differences that give them meaning. The second insinuates a conservative presumption into pluralist judgment by implicitly treating the congealed results of past struggles as if they constituted the essential standard of reasonableness or justice itself. These two pressures, then, turn the pluralist order against itself. Contemporary theories of identity, tolerance, diversity, and justice contribute to this effect when they slide over constitutive opacities, ambiguities, and paradoxes in these very practices.

While the constitutive tension between pluralism and pluralization is potentially productive, the conventional imagination gives too much privilege to the former over the latter. This imbalance does not result simply from conservative inertia. Rather, misrecognition of the paradoxical character of identity\difference relations and of the complexities of political judgment installs it at the center of the pluralist imagination. Presumptions within these understandings must be reworked in order to reshape the pluralist imagination.

THE ETHOS OF CRITICAL RESPONSIVENESS

If you come to terms with the ambiguous relation between new movements and congealed standards of political judgment and between hegemonic identities and the intrasubjective and intersubjective differences in which they are inextricably implicated, you might strive to cultivate an ethos of critical responsiveness to political movements that challenge the self-confidence and congealed judgments of dominant constituencies. You might, that is, translate the pluralist appreciation of established diversity into active cultivation of generosity to contemporary movements of pluralization. This cultivation of generosity is not a simple matter of applying the existing moral code fairly and consistently. For the introduction of a new possibility of being out of old injuries and differences contains a paradoxical element: the drive to recognition precedes consolidation of the identity to be recognized, and the panic it often induces in the self-confidence of established identities tempts them to judge the vulnerable entry through disabling identifications already sedimented in the old code. Such a bind sets up the new entrant to be repudiated even before "it" becomes crystallized in the institutions of law, marriage, work, investment, the military, religion, and education. And this repudiation is often expressed in a language of fairness and normality grounded in misrecognition of the binds involved in the enactment of a new identity out of old injuries. "Why should They be treated any differently from Us?" If the risky, disruptive politics of enactment is, as I contend, indispensable to identification and redress of social injuries, one of its conditions of possibility is cultivation of an *ethos of critical responsiveness* to social movements seeking to redefine their relational identities. Another way of putting this is to say that the recurrent disjunction between the injuries suffered by particular constituencies and the barriers to their rectification posed by cultural *codes* of morality and normality requires mediation by an *ethos* of critical responsiveness never entirely reducible to a code.

The key challenges to a pluralist culture are first to cultivate critical responsiveness to new movements of pluralization and then to negotiate modified relations of coexistence as new identities cross the magic threshold of enactment. For, again, at its most fragile point a new possibility of being both disrupts the stability of established identities and lacks a sufficiently stable definition through which to present itself. This is because to *become* something new is to *move* the self-recognition and relational standards of judgment endorsed by other constituencies to whom you are connected. Identities are always collective and relational:[3] to be white, female, homosexual, Canadian, atheist, and a taxpayer is to participate in a diverse set of collective identifications and to be situated in relation to a series of alter identifications. Hegemonic identities depend on existing definitions of difference to be. To alter your recognition of difference, therefore, is to revise your own terms of self-recognition as well. Critical responsiveness thus moves on two registers: to redefine its relation to others a constituency must also modify the shape of its own identity.[4] In that sense critical responsiveness is always political. It is a political response to the politics of identity\difference that already precedes its intervention.

The call to critical responsiveness becomes more complex yet when you recall, as traditional pluralist theory reminds us, that some putative movements to enactment eventually undermine the conditions of future pluralization. That is one reason why the ethos of responsiveness must grind critical edges. These complexities grow when you distinguish critical responsiveness from a therapeutic response, or paternalism, or pity, or certain types of Christian charity and secular community, where you respond humbly and warmly to the other to prepare it to convert to the universal identity you already represent. The ethos of critical responsiveness pursued here does not reduce the other to what some "we" already is. It opens up cultural space through which the other might consolidate itself into something that is unafflicted by negative cultural markings.

We can see, then, how the pressures to pluralization and fundamentalization so readily track one another. For those generally on the receiving end of pluralizing movements are pressed to accept revised terms of self-recognition so that cultural space for the redefinition of difference can be opened up. Critical responsiveness and fundamentalism, then, represent two contending responses to the same movements of difference. Tolerance does not quite split the difference between them. For this latter disposition is too often anchored in misrecognition of identity\difference relations. That is why proponents of tolerance are so often shocked by "prejudice" or fundamentalism. This recurrent expression of surprise is rooted in prior misreadings of the relation of connection and strife between alternative identities. If fundamentalism recognizes the entanglements of identity with difference in its rage against difference, and if critical responsiveness recognizes these entanglements in its cultivation of an ethos of pluralization, tolerance is an underdeveloped form of critical responsiveness grounded in misrecognition.

Critical responsiveness is an indispensable lubricant of political pluralization. Since it is neither entirely reducible to a preexisting moral code nor (uncontestably) derivable from a transcendental command or contract, it challenges some popular conceptions of what morality must look like. There is unavoidable risk, uncertainty, and ambiguity in the cultivation of critical responsiveness, just as there is transcendental selfishness in the attempt to force each new claim to identity back into the disparaging identifications it struggles against. For to demand comprehensive criteria of judgment before a new movement becomes consolidated is to suppress the paradoxical element in the politics of enactment, while the refusal to apply a fixed set of criteria to new movements risks allowing a putative movement of pluralization to consolidate itself into a powerful form of fundamentalism. An ethos of critical responsiveness must run this risk, up to a point. It depreciates the sharpness, clarity, and certainty claimed by highly coded moralities in order to cultivate respect for a politics of pluralization that exceeds the reach of any closely coded morality. Indeed, militant invocation of a fixed code is one of the most virulent forms preemptive strikes against difference assume today. Such preemptive strikes, delivered in the name of morality itself, form the hard core of political fundamentalism. They sometimes emanate from surprising places.

What shape does an ethos of responsiveness assume? The key may be to turn disturbance of what you are into critical responsiveness to what you are not. For where the politics of enactment and critical responsiveness intersect, irreducible differences acquire softened edges and refined relational possibilities. Sometimes contending constituencies become through these engagements more alert to traces of the other in themselves. Each may come to acknowledge these traces as differences it regulates to *be* what it is, recognizing thereby a certain affinity with the other it resists or engages across the space of difference. It might even come to feel that it is implicated in a set of differences that help to define it *and* inhabited by diffuse energies, remainders, and surpluses that persistently exceed its powers of articulation. It may, thereby, affirm a certain indebtedness to what it is not while reconfiguring dogmatic interpretations of what it is. A new respect might emerge for drives by the other to break out of injurious definitions, even as those drives destabilize and denaturalize the identity of established constituencies. And new challenges might emerge to those identity-maintaining mechanisms that automatically translate the difference that disturbs into immorality and abnormality.

This may be what the descendant of Job meant, suggesting that the most important ethical bond is that formed between constituencies engaged in intensive relations of interdependence and strife. This is not the bond that ties you to your prior identifications. *That bond of identification is ethically important too* (I know from experience some will skip this clause). But *unfettered* by other influences the politics of moral identity all too readily transcendentalizes violence against the other in order to shower superiority on itself. This is how morality and selfishness so often forge a transcendental alliance. An ethical connection, however, flowing across fugitive experiences of *intrasubjective* and *intersubjective* difference opens up relational possibilities of agonistic respect, studied indifference, critical responsiveness, and selective collaboration between interdependent, contending identities, allowing these options to compete more equitably with bland universalism, obliviousness to the other, denigration of it, or implacable opposition to it. The cultivation of this first set of possibilities is crucial to a viable ethics of engagement.

The current world (dis)order transforms pluralism from a diffuse body of understandings into a dissonant problematic. In this setting questions of identity and difference, nature and culture, morality and politics, retrospective judgment and prospective responsiveness are thrown up for renegotiation. My sense is that conventional pluralist theory has not proceeded deeply enough into dominant presumptions within Euro-American culture about the character of the state, the nation, identity, responsibility, morality, monotheism, secularism, and sexuality. We pluralists thus need to rework, *and to render ourselves available to reworkings of,* the pluralist imagination: so that it comes to terms with paradoxical relations of conflict and interdependence between identity and difference; so that it extends the terms of horizontal pluralization to include among its sites sexuality, (non)theisms, gender, the shape of the household, and the relation of the living to their own prospect of death; so that it verticalizes pluralism, as it were, by honoring modes of political identification and action that exceed the state as well as those pitched at or below the state; so that it appreciates the problematical character of retrospection in political judgment by interrupting the drive to judge every new development through the moralization of congealed codes; and so that it reshapes "the political" to honor the politics of disturbance, the politics of enactment, and the politics of social movements across state lines. Such a pluralization of pluralism does not depreciate the politics of governance through a state apparatus. Rather, it nudges the latter into critical relation with other dimensions of politics also essential to maintenance of the constitutive tension between pluralism and pluralization. Nor do such refashionings of the pluralist imagination supplant classical pluralist theory. These ventures, rather, draw upon traditional theory while reconfiguring some of its dimensions.

THE PLURALIZATION OF PLURALISM

Critical attention to the questions posed here, predictably, will seem to some to reduce the pluralist imagination to a shambles, draining public life of a matrix of common meanings, citizenship, national identification, state action, and democratic accountability. Attention to these issues seems to me, however, to refine possible lines of agonistic respect and critical responsiveness between diverse constituencies and, thereby, *to multiply lines of connection through which governing assemblages can be constructed from a variety of intersecting constituencies*. You do not need a wide universal "we" (a nation, a community, a singular practice of rationality, a particular monotheism) to foster democratic governance of a population. Numerous possibilities of intersection and collaboration between multiple, interdependent constituencies infused by a general ethos of critical responsiveness drawn from several sources suffice very nicely.

Some theorists may be wary of these possibilities because they remain blinkered by the terms of debate between "individualism" and "communitarianism." But neither of these traditions is good at characterizing how action in concert can be mobilized among a populace crisscrossed by multifarious lines of identity, difference, connection, indifference, and opposition. The individualist seeks to minimize such modes of action while the communitarian demands a strong cultural consensus as its necessary basis. Neither is appreciative enough of the positive connection between a democratic ethos of responsiveness cultivated by numerous constituencies and creative formation of representative assemblages of political action. For possibilities for democratic political action are enhanced when diverse, interwoven constituencies resist becoming frozen into contending claims to intrinsic identity or exclusive morality. There are some general dispositions that must course through the cultural world of multifarious differences and connections. But the discourses of reason, individualism, contract, nation, nature, and community are not that good at articulating them. So it is misleading in the extreme to pit "the politics of community" or "the universal" against "the politics of difference." Such a juxtaposition first reduces the essentially *relational* character of difference to the bland idea of diversity among independent identities and then convicts "theorists of difference" of a defect haunting communitarian and individualist theories. For some individualists and communitarians *do* misrecognize the paradoxical character of identity\difference relations. The ease with which many paint this simple contrast between the politics of community and the politics of difference provides an index of that misrecognition.[5]

There is no identity without difference. Everything, my friends, depends upon how this paradoxical relationship is negotiated.[6] The stronger the drive to the unified nation, the integrated community, and/or the normal individual, the more powerful becomes the drive to convert differences into modes of otherness. And the more implacable the cultural drive to convert difference into otherness the less feasible it becomes to build majority assemblages of democratic governance that can actually govern a diverse populace.

The biggest impetus to fragmentation, violence, and anarchy today does not emerge from political engagement with the paradox of difference. It emerges from doctrines and movements that suppress it. Specifically, it arises from totalistic identities engaged in implacable struggles against those differences that threaten their hegemony or exclusivity. Such culture wars do not reflect too much diversity, difference, or variety; they express contending demands to control the exclusive form the nation, state, or community must assume.

But what, more specifically, does it mean to say that pluralism must be pluralized along several dimensions? Consider the dimension of "the political" itself by way of illustration. A pluralizing culture embodies a *micropolitics* of action by the self on itself and the small-scale assemblage upon itself, a *politics of disturbance* through which sedimented identities and moralities are rendered more alert to the deleterious effects of their naturalizations upon difference, a *politics of enactment* through which new possibilities of being are propelled into established constellations, a *politics of representational assemblages* through which general policies are processed through the state, a *politics of interstate relations*, and a *politics of nonstatist, cross-national movements* through which external/internal pressure is placed on corporate and state-centered priorities.

These conjunctions of *sites* of action with *types* of combination do not exhaust the possible modes of politics. The set is designed, rather, to pluralize the modes through which we recognize and mobilize the political today. By comparison to traditional versions of pluralist theory, this hybrid set constitutes a significant pluralization of the political. I will contend, as well, that each knot in this tangle *today* contributes to a pluralizing culture ethically responsive to constitutive conditions of contemporary life.

What, though, is the relation of pluralization to territory? Doesn't pluralism itself require definitive boundaries? If it does not, what could distinguish it from atomism, chaos, anarchy, nihilism, or, in the words of Hegel (a largely unsung hero of the classical pluralist imagination), a "heap of sand"? We might approach this question by thinking about what it means to territorialize something and what the ambiguous effects of territorialization might be. *Territory,* the *Oxford English Dictionary* says, is presumed by most moderns to derive from *terra. Terra* means land, earth, soil, nourishment, sustenance; it conveys the sense of a sustaining medium that fades off into indefiniteness. People, you might say, feel the claim the land they belong to makes upon them. This experience of belonging to a place, as long as it does not exclude other identifications, and as long as it incorporates the disruptive experience of earthquakes, tornadoes, floods, and firestorms into the experience itself (this essay is being written during a year in California), can play a positive role in the cultivation of care and critical responsiveness. But the form of the word *territory,* the *OED* says, suggests something different from the sustenance of *terra. Territory* derives from *terrere,* meaning to frighten, to terrorize, to exclude. And *territorium* is "a place from which people are warned." *Territorium* seems to repress the sustaining relation to land that it presupposes. Perhaps a modern territory, then, is land organized and bounded by technical, juridical, and military means. Perhaps the experience of land as sustenance is both presupposed and repressed by the modern organization of territory. To occupy territory, then, is both to receive sustenance and to exercise violence. To become territorialized is to be occupied by a particular identity. The advantage of this nomination is that it discloses strains of terror in the ambiguous logic of territorialization.

Territory is sustaining land occupied and bounded by violence. By extension, to territorialize anything is to establish exclusive boundaries around it by warning other people off. A religious identity, a nation, a class, a race, a gender, a sexuality, a nuclear family, on this reading, is constructed through its mode of territorialization. Multiple territorializations are indispensable to pluralization, even though they never lose entirely those edges of exclusion that enable particular modes of being.

How might an advocate of critical pluralization, then, stand with respect to the logic of territorialization? One approach, common in traditional pluralist theory, is to fix the normal individual and the territorial state as the explicit or implicit limits of cultural pluralism. But these very presumptions elide distinctive issues of the late-

modern time: they overlook the globalization of dangerous contingencies outside the control of any single state such as the greenhouse effect, ozone depletion, acid rain, soil depletion, and air pol-
lution; and they deflect attention within the territorial state from
new sexualities, gender diversification, refugees, new linguistic communities, legal and illegal immigrants, competing pressures to de-
nationalization and renationalization, and so on. So it might prove
more productive to *modify the ethos* in which territorialization occurs and to *pluralize the modern territorial imagination* that, to exaggerate just a little, maps a nation onto a state, the nation-state
onto preexisting subjects, the subject onto the citizen, and the citizen
onto the nation-state as its highest locus of political allegiance.

In these essays I keep returning to two questions, asking how to
foster an ethos of reciprocal forbearance and responsiveness in relations between interdependent, contending identities and how to pluralize lines of territorialization so no single line becomes overcoded.
This involves me above all in the modulation of traditional ground-
ings of morality in a universal identity or the presumption of natural
design, and in a cautious reworking of the boundary of pluralism in
the contiguous geography and centered civilization of the territorial
state. The first modification challenges the traditional, contending
moralities of command and communion with a generous ethical sensibility grounded in appreciation of the fugitive abundance of being.
The second construes the territorial state to be one among several
sites of political action and identification in the late-modern time.

These modulations implicate me in debates both with critics of
"postmodernism" who contend that it cannot sustain a positive ethic
and with some of its defenders who insist it must not. My sense is
that some defenders of both traditions reduce the possibilities of
ethics to the options of contractual morality, command morality, or
teleological morality. The modernists find these options to suffice;
the posties find all three perspectives to harbor too many violences
and exclusions. There is much to be said on behalf of the latter judgment. But it may be possible to articulate a conception of ethics that
conforms to none of these moral conceptions. The course I pursue
appreciates the emphasis on "virtue" in teleological theories while
resisting the metaphysics of intrinsic purpose within which teleological virtues have been defined and cultivated historically. The ethos of
critical responsiveness introduced in these pages lodges itself in the

underpopulated space between the teleological and command traditions. It pursues an ethic of cultivation rather than a morality of contract or command; it judges the ethos it cultivates to exceed any fixed code of morality; and it cultivates critical responsiveness to difference in ways that disturb traditional virtues of community and the normal individual. It does not present *itself* as the single universal to which other ethical traditions must bow. Rather, it provides a prod and counterpoint to them, pressing them to rethink the ethics of engagement and, crucially, to rework their relations to the diversity of ethical *sources* that mark a pluralistic culture. Such a post-Nietzschean ethic resists oligopolistic control over the currency of morality while affirming the indispensability of ethics.[7]

MAPPING THE COURSE

This book consists of a series of interlocking essays. Two are published here for the first time. The others were initially written for specific occasions. While I have significantly expanded and reworked the previously published essays, I have also retained signs of the particular occasion in which each was presented. Moreover, I find it impossible to sustain the flow of each essay without retaining some repetition between them. My hope is that a brief review in one essay of a central theme in another adds something to the earlier presentation or places that theme in a different context. These essays, partly for that reason, can be read in any order, depending on whether your first concern is with, say, the ontological positioning of critical pluralism, the relation of micropolitics to macropolitics, the relation of economic equality to cultural pluralism, the relation of cross-national movements to statist politics, the relation of international relations theory to political theory, the relation of normalization to the politics of identity, the cultivation of a responsive ethos, or the role of the politics of enactment in a pluralizing culture. If I am on the right track, it turns out that each of these questions feeds into the others. And you may have to read the whole book, eventually. Perhaps it is best, therefore, to provide a preliminary map.

"Nothing Is Fundamental . . ." locates a set of contemporary political theories on an "ontopolitical matrix" that enables comparisons between them and the fundamental perspective governing this book. Once the matrix is set, it is easy to see how and why disparate, contending theories on the matrix are moved to offer complementary critiques of the type of perspective elaborated here. This chapter pays attention to the ontological dimension of political thought, drawing upon Nietzsche and Foucault to suggest how relative neglect of this dimension by many thinkers on the matrix contributes to reductive readings of post-Nietzschean thought. And it sets the agenda for the orientation to ethics expressed in these essays, suggesting that an ethic responsive to the fugitive flow of surplus and difference in dominant constellations is likely to be more sensitive and generous than a morality grounded in a putative command, an original contract, a fixed conception of utility, the presumption of the universal subject, or attunement to a putative purpose in being. This suggestion, however, is qualified by the judgment that in a pluralizing culture the *sources* as well as the *mandates* of ethics will be marked by plurality: the key *ethical* question is what kinds of relation bearers of each contestable orientation strive to enter into with their competitors.[8]

"The Desire to Punish" is an exercise in micropolitics. I argue that contemporary categories of agency, responsibility, crime, and punishment are porous forms readily infiltrated by a drive to revenge against culturally marked constituencies whose very being threatens the self-certainty of established identities. These predispositions readily become activated when criminal violence escalates, particularly when the agents of criminal violence are members of cultural minorities, especially when those minorities are either gay men or young African-American males in the inner city. The question becomes, then, how to work on the self and local social forms such as the family, the school, the neighborhood, the court, and the media to strain the spirit of revenge from categories of criminal judgment that are both indispensable and problematical. The idea is not to perfect categories of agency and responsibility whose diverse and ambiguous genealogy probably renders them unsusceptible to perfection. Taking the Baltimore trial of a young African-American carjacker and murderer of urban whites as its point of departure, this essay disperses the terms of debate between the model of crime grounded in the theme of the responsible offender and the model grounded in the theme of social determination. This dispersion proceeds by exploring the flow of desire crossing and recrossing this unstable division. When we come to terms with elements of contingency in the formation of a pattern of desire, with variable patterns of imperiousness in the logic of desire, and with how drives to abstract revenge can readily infiltrate the structure of desire, we may be in a better position to drain the spirit of revenge from operational categories of agency and responsibility, doing so by practicing a micropolitics of the self upon itself and the social aggregate upon itself.

The objective of this micropolitical experimentation is not to drain every ounce of revenge from desire. The objective is to drain the spirit of revenge from operational practices of judgment and responsibility, doing so to open the possibility of a macropolitics that addresses anew the sources of criminality and the role of the desire to punish in the social production of racial identities. If, as Etienne Balibar contends, the cultural marker of "class-race" identifies "populations . . . collectively destined for capitalist exploitation," it also marks the same constituencies as available targets of accumulated desires for social revenge through the legal rubrics of crime, agency, and responsibility.[9]

It may be pertinent to recall how micropolitics is not a new practice, transported into "life-worlds" previously innocent of it. Micropolitics goes on all the time. The macropolitics of state fascism, for instance, drew much of its support from a series of resonating microfascisms:

> But fascism is inseparable from a proliferation of molecular focuses in interaction, which skip from point to point, *before* beginning to resonate together in the National Socialist State. Rural fascism and city or neighborhood fascism, youth fascism and war veteran's fascism, fascism of the Left and fascism of the Right, fascism of the couple, family, school and office; every fascism is defined by a micro-black hole that stands on its own and communicates with the others, before resonating in a great, generalized black hole. . . . What makes fascism dangerous is its molecular or micropolitical power, for it is a mass movement . . . American film has often depicted these molecular focal points; band, gang, sect, family, town, neighborhood.[10]

The micropolitics considered here provides a counter to microfascisms, microfundamentalisms, and the points at which they resonate. It is not pursued in the interests of "political correctness," a phrase that embodies a recent success in the micropolitics of the right. For "political correctness" was introduced initially by one faction of the American left to chide another for its tendency to essentialize the identity from which its interventions proceeded. It was then appropriated and inverted by fundamentalists of the center and right to mark any movement that challenges presumptions of correctness in the dominant cultural constellation, particularly those that press privileged constituencies to modify themselves to open space for pluralization in the domains of race, gender, sexuality, and canonical texts.[11]

The micropolitics pursued here supports the macropolitics of pluralization. To work upon the desire to mark constituencies available for punishment is one essential preliminary to rendering "whites" more responsive to "black" drives to pluralization. The importance of micropolitics in a variety of domains might be registered through the suggestion that American post-World War II liberalism controlled visible sites of macropolitics while it ceded a lot of micropolitical ground to other forces in churches, families, neighborhoods, clubs, corporations, armies, and schools. As a result, liberalism has slipped from providing the matrix in which national debates are organized to becoming a defensive partisan in the debates that occur.

"Democracy, Equality, and Normality" moves onto the terrain of macropolitics. Through an examination of C. B. Macpherson's "models of democracy" it endorses a conception of democracy in which identity is understood to be a relational formation laced with contingency, the demand for a unified social consensus is understood to serve the politics of normalization, economic equalization is understood to provide one condition of multifarious pluralism, and the politics of representational assemblages is understood to provide the best way to promote patterns of economic equalization most compatible with a pluralizing ethos. I concur with Macpherson on the significance of economic equalization to a democratic ethos. I admire how he acknowledges the contestability of central "postulates" informing his thinking. But I attenuate somewhat the extent to which he would equalize, and I modify the ways in which he would do so. Most significantly, I dissent from his ideal of democratic unity. And I recast the form his commitment to democratic action in concert assumes.

"Fundamentalism in America," playing off Tocqueville's study, *Democracy in America,* charts sources and effects of various drives to fundamentalism today. If fundamentalism and pluralism represent two contending responses to the same contemporary condition, it

seems pertinent to ask where they intersect and where they discon-
nect. After modifying the conventional definition of fundamentalism
to include the refusal to acknowledge the contestability of your own
fundaments or to resist violences in the exclusionary logics of identity in which you are implicated, and after addressing a few conventional paradigms of fundamentalism, including the fundamentalism
of the nation, I engage strains of fundamentalism running through
certain versions of American liberalism. If it is possible to renegotiate patterns of fundamentalism—there are no guarantees that it is—
reconstitution of the fundamentalist strain within liberalism may be
a strategic place to start. For religious fundamentalists are onto
something when they charge that the ideals of the neutral state, the
veil of ignorance, and the secular individual all embody a "secular
liberal bias" misrecognized by supporters of these principles. The
doubtful claim to liberal neutrality, combined with a tendency in
some quarters of liberalism to dismiss out of hand perspectives that
contest presumptions in the liberal matrix, pours fuel on those fundamentalist fires of revenge liberals campaign against. Liberalism, at
its best, contends not only against these tendencies in others, but also
against them in itself.[12]

"Democracy and Territoriality" connects pluralist theories by
Paul Ricoeur, Joseph Schumpeter, and Michael Walzer to a theory of
international relations grounded in the territorial nation-state advanced by both Walzer and John Herz. None of these perspectives
adequately appreciates the positive role a "vertical" pluralization of
political movements can play in compromising the state as the final
site of political identification or in calling into question state-
centered priorities of "the new world order." During a time when
the drive to renationalize Euro-American states generates a deadly
danger to pluralization, and when everything from corporate transactions to disease transmission and criminal networks has become
globalized, the formation of nonstatist, cross-national movements
becomes crucial to the ethos of pluralization. Schumpeter, Walzer,
and Herz converge not only in drawing a boundary of boundaries
around the state. They also converge in setting severe restrictions to
possibilities for pluralization within the state through, respectively,
the logic of political rationality, the theme of shared understandings, and the ideal of the nation. Ricoeur joins these three in overcoding the border of the territorial state. But Ricoeur, by reworking

and relocating a paradox in political founding identified by Rousseau, also establishes a launching pad from which more plural practices of territorialization might proceed.

Most contemporary American appreciations of pluralism draw sustenance from Tocqueville. "Tocqueville, Religiosity, and Violence" draws several of the themes previously considered in this study into a critical engagement with Tocqueville. It rethinks the question of boundaries through reconsideration of the Tocquevillian pluralist imagination. To do so, it is necessary to confront the incredible violence situated at the vital center of the Tocquevillian world, for the Tocquevillian/American "civi-territorial complex" requires the elimination of the American "Indian" (Tocqueville's term). This massive violence cannot be deemed immoral by Tocqueville because it is taken to flow from the civilizational conditions of morality itself. Pursuing this issue, we may gain a deeper appreciation of both how Tocquevillian pluralism could authorize currents of fundamentalism in contemporary America and why the classical pluralist imagination requires refashioning today.

Tocqueville's appreciation of nomadism in democratic politics contributes to a reworking of the pluralist imagination. But his paranoid panic over those indigenous "nomads" incapable of agriculture, civilization, Christian monotheism, and, hence, democracy in America compels him to turn against the insight he articulates. After addressing this Tocquevillian retrenchment, after then exploring alternative lines of possibility in nineteenth-century relations between "Indians" and "Whites" identified first by Henry Thoreau and then by William Apess (the nineteenth-century Pequot who became a leader of the Mashpee rebellion), we turn to the politics of enactment as one of the correctives to the elements of stinginess and exclusion in Tocquevillian pluralism. The politics of enactment forms a pivot upon which a vibrant culture of pluralization turns. It functions best if it builds upon nomadic disturbances to entrenched identities already introduced by Tocqueville and if it encounters an ethos of critical responsiveness crystallized out of accumulated memories of previous practices of political enactment.

One possibility of enactment may be particularly pertinent today. Tocqueville recognized the profound interdependence in America between the Christian experience of the *sacred* and *secular* presentations of nature, reason, and morality. Subterranean connections between these two contending cultural forces persist today. But today we may be on the verge of a movement to reconfigure that relationship, a movement drawing sustenance from recent drives to pluralization in the domains of gender, sexuality, immigration, dying, and privacy. The hope is to *pluralize the contemporary sacred/secular duopoly control over the cultural currency of morality.* If and as such a movement crystallizes, the possibilities of cultural pluralization may improve on several related fronts. Existing sacred/secular barriers to an ethos of critical responsiveness would become more mobile and porous. Finally, if Tocqueville overcodes the boundaries of pluralism, the question of the boundaries to pluralism must nonetheless be addressed. The last sections return to that topic.

These essays strive to render the contemporary pluralist imagination susceptible to reworking. They do not assess the probability that such an enriched imagination might assume a larger presence in contemporary politics. It is easy to be pessimistic today, partly because a series of promising possibilities have opened up in several sectors of life. These expansive possibilities generate a bimodal cultural response: they encourage critical pluralists to struggle against unnecessary injuries inscribed in cultural monism while they mobilize cultural conservatives to defend established closures more stridently. Perhaps it is pertinent, though, to bypass the spectatorial temptation to bet on the future as if it must pass by like a reel of film. Perhaps a fruitful task for the political intellectual is to interrogate unconscious dimensions of the political imagination through which contemporary possibilities and impossibilities are delineated, doing so not to vindicate a new mood of pessimism or optimism but to contest transcendental violences lodged in contemporary moralities of god, home, rationality, territory, and country. And to support admirable possibilities of political enactment through which to redress the injuries.[13]

1

Nothing Is Fundamental . . .

ONTOPOLITICAL INTERPRETATION

Onta, the really existing things; *ontology,* the study of the fundamental logic of reality apart from appearances. These determinations are both too restrictive and too total for what I have in mind. For example, the *logos* in *ontology* already suggests a fundamental logic, principle, or design of being. But it can and has been urged that the most fundamental thing about being is that it contains no such overriding logic or design. "Ontopolitical interpretation" may come closer, then. *Onto,* because every political interpretation invokes a set of fundaments about necessities and possibilities of human being, about, for instance, the forms into which humans may be composed and the possible relations humans can establish with nature. An ontopolitical stance, for instance, might strive to articulate a law or design set into the very order of things. Or it might deny the existence of a law or natural design while still identifying a profound stability of human interests that persists across time. Or it might deflate this theme of stable human interests while striving to draw us closer to a protean abundance that enables and exceeds every socially constructed order. To say either that something is fundamental or that nothing is fundamental, then, is to engage in ontopolitical interpretation. Hence, every interpretation of political events, no matter how deeply it is sunk in a specific historical context or how high the pile of data upon which it sits, contains an ontopolitical dimension.

2 · NOTHING IS FUNDAMENTAL

Political interpretation is ontopolitical: its fundamental presumptions fix possibilities, distribute explanatory elements, generate parameters within which an ethic is elaborated, and center (or decenter) assessments of identity, legitimacy, and responsibility. But this dimension is today not often an explicit object of critical attention in the human sciences, at least in the United States. How could this be?

I cannot answer this question with the assurance it demands, but a few considerations do seem pertinent. First, there is a widespread sense, itself in need of explanation, that with the (purported) demise in modern philosophy of Aristotelian teleology and Christian doctrines of creation, the human sciences have finally moved into a position to take the world as it is. While these traditional perspectives offer conceptions of the fundamental order of the world and how humanity is placed in this order, modern, secular perspectives are often thought to escape the realm of ontopolitics. On this secular reading, a social ontology is a speculative conception of the world and, fortunately, also a dispensable dimension of social explanation. Few practitioners, of course, assert these conclusions so bluntly. Rather, they insert them into critical characterizations of defunct and self-indulgent perspectives described as "metaphysical," "speculative," "impressionistic," "creationist," "religious," "fundamentalist," "teleological," "essentialist," "foundationalist," or (even) "interpretive," implying through these formulations that no corollary set of fundamental projections circulates through the perspectives they advance. Such a demeaning characterization of the other, one that exempts the narrator entirely from the negative characterization, may even contribute something to that reactive fundamentalization of religious and nationalist perspectives so disconcerting in contemporary life.

A second, more sophisticated, rationale for neglect of the ontopolitical proceeds through argument by elimination across a vast expanse of Western history. One challenging presentation is offered by Hans Blumenberg.[1] Earlier cultures, Blumenberg asserts, were sunk in cosmologies that projected unfounded assumptions about an intrinsic purpose in nature, treating words and events as divine signs of fundamental harmonies to which humanity must strive to become attuned. But various versions of this perspective defeated themselves historically as they tried to perfect themselves. What remains after these indulgent schemes have been peeled away is an austere, scaled-down perspective of a world without intrinsic purpose, indifferent to human concerns, available for human disposition of it through technical organization. Through this progressive elimination, the way has been cleared for "the self-assertion of reason" to establish itself in the modern age. Institutionalization of self-assertion in the practices of science, technology, industry, and state action, indeed, constitutes Blumenberg's definition of the modern. The modern perspective is neither caused by the defeat of its predecessors nor in a position to prove the truth of the presumptions guiding it. But it has established itself as an indispensable set of operative presumptions for the organization of life. And nothing in the previous perspectives suffices to bring it down.

Modern secularism is "legitimate" because none of the historically available alternatives can either prove their primacy over it or undermine its operational presumption to legitimacy. We do not need to think restlessly about ontological issues anymore, except to endorse the "minimal" ontology of a relatively pliable world susceptible to technical dominion. The most pressing need is to ward off those recurrent, dangerous waves of nostalgia to return to one of the historically vacated positions, and, even more importantly, to fight the insidious temptation to treat fundamental *questions* posed by earlier perspectives as if they must be answered somehow within the new framework.

A third, related justification for ignoring the ontopolitical expresses confidence that the most basic conflicts, problems, and issues facing contemporary life do not flow from the fundamental presumptions of modernity itself. So, even if modern practices express an overlapping, contestable set of ontological or metaphysical assumptions (the two terms move close together here), the most pressing contemporary issues of politics, psychology, and ethics do not require us to make these presumptions explicit objects of reflection. Our disagreements do not reach this deep. John Rawls advances such a position when he says, in recent revisions of his theory, that the theory of justice is political, not metaphysical. That is, the way justice as fairness builds upon a more basic, overlapping social consensus allows it to avoid explicit defense of its most fundamental starting points. It invokes a broad set of understandings and convictions (they would be called preunderstandings by Heidegger) central to American culture and the culture of a few other liberal states. We can take these as our starting point. Richard Rorty presents a version of this thesis when he treats the implicit understandings of "rich, lucky, liberal states" as the background from which his own political reflections proceed.[2]

These three considerations help to explain neglect of the onto-political dimension. But do they vindicate it? What if some common presumptions of our time (that is, elements in the overlapping consensus) contain dangerous demands and expectations within them? And what today is the basis of this faith in argument by historical elimination? Blumenberg himself acknowledges that previous social ontologies of the West were defeated not simply by the accumulated weight of internal difficulties, but also by unexpected challenges posed by new perspectives that seemed alien and unthinkable to defenders of the dominant position. Classical "paganism" (a term coined by those who were victorious over it) succumbed more to the new, unexpected challenges posed by Christianity and less to independent disturbances posed by experience of its own aporias. Perhaps modern defenders of "ontological minimalism," then, retain so much self-confidence because they have yet to engage alternative perspectives that both break with the traditions they (purport to) have left behind and contest a set of fundaments they implicitly endorse. What if the ontological minimalism of modern secularists looks minimal only by comparison to the Christian/teleological traditions to which they contrast themselves? What, to condense these questions, if the points of ontopolitical convergence in late-modern nation-states turn out to be exactly the domain in need of reassessment today?

Recent and contemporary thinkers as diverse as Nietzsche, Heidegger, Arendt, Foucault, Taylor, Irigaray, Deleuze, Williams, and Derrida think—though to different degrees and on different registers—that this is exactly the case. They suspect that self-denying ordinances vindicated in various ways by "nonfoundationalists" such as Rawls, Rorty, Habermas, Benhabib, Walzer, and Blumenberg express a refusal to engage questions most important to the late-modern time. They contend that every detailed interpretation presupposes answers to fundamental questions of being, and that this is indeed one of the territories of modern discourse that requires critical reflection. Some on this list strive to loosen the hold of metaphysics on thought while acknowledging that it can never be broken altogether; others labor to modernize an old metaphysic until it becomes suitable for contemporary life; yet others strive to articulate a positive ontopolitical stance that breaks with the onto*logical* traditions of (as seen from their perspective) Plato, Descartes, Rousseau, Kant, Hegel, Habermas, and Rawls. But all concur initially in calling these various pretenses to nonfoundationalism, ontological minimalism, antiessentialism, and overlapping metaphysical consensus into question. I concur.

Before turning to the substantive issues posed by this latter crew, it might be appropriate to consider how the prevailing perspective in the social sciences, at least until very recently, has been able to bypass the debate just summarized. There is a particular presumption—let us call it the primacy of epistemology—that unites most American social scientists, shielding them from this debate. To give primacy to epistemology is to think either that you have access to criteria of knowledge that leave the realm of ontology behind or that your epistemology provides neutral test procedures through which to pose and resolve every ontological question. "Epistem*ology*," on this usage, does not include every philosophy concerned with the question of truth. Heidegger, for instance, was concerned with the meaning and role of truth, claiming that the most fundamental issues are posed by the problematical relation of the truth/falsity pair to the "untruth" they conceal, rather than by contrast between the true and the false.[3] Modern "truth" is a mode of revealing that enables judgments of correctness and incorrectness within its frame. But every historical regime of revealing also conceals. It conceals possibilities of being that cannot be brought into a particular way of life without confounding its basic principles of organization. "Untruth" is deeper than truth and falsity, then: untruth is that which cannot achieve sufficient standing within the terms of discourse of a time without stretching contemporary standards of plausibility and coherence to their limits of tolerance. Untruth is the foreign not up for debate or reflection within a temporally constituted register of the true and the false; its very *absence* enables the historically constructed division between the true and the false to sustain itself.

So "truth" changes its place and standing in Heidegger's orientation, one that seeks to engage the untruth of a particular time through responsive engagements with historical modes of being imperfectly commensurate with it. In Heidegger's thought, then, giving primacy to the question of truth does not mean giving primacy to epistemology. It means exploring those historical conditions in which the question of truth became reduced to the pursuit of reliable criteria of knowledge.

Those who do give primacy to epistemology as a method of representation may be optimistic or pessimistic about its prospects for success: they may be skeptics or optimists with respect to the prospects for knowledge. In giving primacy to epistemology, in this sense, they insist that the first or most fundamental issue is not "What are the various ways in which truth has been construed within alternative modes of life and how could these different ways be drawn into a larger conversation with each other?" but "How can we devise a neutral method that shows human subjects how to represent perspicuously the objects to be known?" The primacy of epistemology short-circuits ontological issues by assuming that once the right procedure for attaining truth as correspondence or coherence or consensus is reached, any remaining issues will either be resolved *through* that method or shown to be irrelevant. The primacy of epistemology thereby treats the ideas of subject, object, representation, and knowledge as if they were already fixed in their range of application. The attraction of this perspective resides in its claim to bypass issues that might otherwise contaminate, derail, or confound the operational self-confidence of the human sciences.

The primacy of epistemology turns out itself, of course, to embody a contestable social ontology. The empiricist version, for instance, treats human beings as subjects or agents of knowledge; it treats things as independent objects susceptible to representation; it treats language as primarily a medium of representation, or, at least, a medium in which the designative dimension of concepts can be disconnected rigorously from the contexts of rhetoric/action/evaluation in which they originate. As is now well known, especially outside the human sciences, this perspective has been subjected to powerful challenges, by several thinkers already listed here as critics of the neglect of social ontology in the human sciences and by others such as Merleau Ponty and Wittgenstein. But the primacy of epistemology persists in the human sciences; it continues to screen out the question of ontology.

There are probably larger cultural considerations that help to account for the primacy of epistemology in the human sciences. Charles Taylor, for instance, argues persuasively that the model of agency and knowledge enforced by the dominant epistemological tradition supports an ideal of freedom governing the modern age, an ideal in which an agent is free to the extent it rises above the social/historical contexts in which it is initially set. On Taylor's reading, the power of this cultural ideal of freedom pulls an epistemological tradition supportive of it into being, rather than the other way around. I would add, as a point to be pursued in a later chapter, that these interlocking conceptions of knowledge, agency, and freedom together support a conception of responsibility also in dire need of reassessment.[4]

How is one to proceed in engaging a mode of inquiry that purports to bypass the ontopolitical dimension? Further signs must be probed in these cases: By what means are ontopolitical presumptions implicitly brought into play? Does the narrative and rhetorical structure of the text, for example, covertly spread the very infection the author pretends to cure?

Consider an example. James Q. Wilson's research into crime and criminality treats the criminal as a responsible agent and the causes of crime as grounded in the attitudes of the criminal. But he does not check these presumptions against an alternative interpretation that, say, treats many forms of violent criminality to reflect a perverse politics of abstract revenge against an order that criminalizes actors by ruling them out of efficacy within it. Wilson's conventional definitions of agency, crime, criminality, punishment, and responsibility precede the abundant pile of evidence he collects to amplify his theory. The evidence buries the crucial issues rather than testing them. The fundaments of the study are set below the threshold of debate by textual tropes through which the evidence is selected, organized, and presented.[5]

Or take, on a higher register of theorization, Roberto Unger's theory of democracy and freedom as mastery over the contexts in which we are situated. The theory depends for its reach and confidence on the presumption that the ecological contexts of social practice—including vegetation, soil, ecosystems, and human bodies as well as established modes of technology and social organization—are inherently pliable media susceptible to formation, disaggregation, and reformation by human agents in an indefinite number of ways.[6] This crucial presumption is occasionally defended by comparison to the classical, teleological alternative Unger once endorsed. But it is not defended at all against post-Nietzscheans who share his resistance to teleological theories while actively contesting his presumptions about the fundamental pliability of bodies and things. Ungerian confidence in the basic flexibility of things is first inserted into the vocabulary of plasticity, pliability, transparency, and receptivity governing the text and then driven home by transitive, activist verbs conveying an intrinsic social will to human mastery of pliable objects. The tropology of the text, in this case too, shuffles its ontopolitical dimension into the background.

Or consider a final example. The "thin theory of rationality" governing some forms of rational choice theory does not establish the ontological assumptions that inform it. As portrayed by Jon Elster, it

> leaves unexamined the beliefs and the desires that form the reason for the action whose rationality we are assessing, with the exception that they are stipulated not to be logically inconsistent. Consistency, in fact, is what rationality in the thin sense is all about: consistency within the belief system; consistency within the system of desires; and consistency between beliefs and desires on the one hand and the action for which they are reasons on the other hand.[7]

We can expect, then, conventional ontopolitical presumptions to enter silently into rational choice theory through its very incorporation of the beliefs, desires, and reasons of the agents it studies into its calculus of conduct. Because this model of rationality dehistoricizes conventional contexts of practice, it is highly unlikely that its exploration of inconsistencies in "belief" will venture far beyond the cultural unconscious within which the inquiry is set. (This finding is less true of Elster himself; his substantive model of rationality and historical orientation makes him an explicit participant on this level of discourse.)

So invocations of overlapping consensus, ontological minimalism, nonfoundationalism, and the primacy of epistemology often combine with the political unconscious inscribed in the textual designs of social scientists to screen out interrogation of the ontopolitical dimension of interpretation. How, though, do *critics* of these strategies of concealment proceed? Can they live without assumptions, for god's sake? Again, these critics diverge significantly among themselves in the ethics they endorse, the extent to which they are political, the politics they advance, and the ontopolitics they peddle (or pedal). It is the point at which they intersect that concerns me now. For most concur in giving initial priority not to a disengaged subject in its relation to independent objects, but to historically specific discursive practices within which people are engaged prior to achieving a capacity to reflect upon them. We humans typically respond to and cope with things within previously established contexts of engagement. These contexts help to constitute us and the objects represented to and by us. Representation does occur, then, but these are representations by historically constructed agents such as doctors, gentry, and government agents in the nineteenth century engaged with historically constituted objects such as the commons, monomania, melancholia, vagabonds, hysteric women, colonials, sodomists, and paupers. Representation, that is, occurs within historically particular contexts that fix both the things to be represented and the terms through which representation occurs. Representation always involves the representation of prior representations. This duality, or doubling, eventually confounds representation, not as an indispensable social practice but as a detached, neutral method of accumulating knowledge.

Few theorists who emphasize the significance of the ontopolitical dimension seek a pure method by which to represent the world, though some of them—perhaps Taylor is one and Habermas another—*eventually* formulate models of discourse that bear a family resemblance to the primacy of epistemology. The initial drift of their thinking, though, proceeds in another direction. For to construe a way of life as a set of discursively mediated practices through which things are constituted in the process of dealing with them both undercuts the search for a neutral, transparent mode of representation and acknowledges the steady infiltration of ontopolitical presumptions into established cultural understandings, institutional demands, affectional dispositions, personal identities, social skills, and instrumental resources.

ONTOPOLITICAL REGISTRATIONS

Let me gather together these preliminary reflections, first by summarizing the way this appreciation of the ontopolitical is elaborated by a single thinker on my list and then by exploring alternative directions pursued as other thinkers cross the intersection Foucault helps to define. We shift attention, then, from those who suppress the "onto" in political interpretation to those who diverge about how to engage it.

In *The Order of Things* Foucault claims that the Enlightenment model of representation (the "classical episteme") was transformed at the beginning of the modern period. Foucault seeks to describe and intervene in this process more than to "explain" it, for the very attempt to explain the origin of the modern episteme would draw him more deeply into some of the very presumptions he seeks to render problematical. At the end of the classical episteme, then, which had been marked by a highly ordered model of representation, things began to acquire a greater density and depth. The table of representations of the classical regime eventually collapsed into the revived depths of "life, labor, and language." In the new domains of biology, political economy, and linguistics, these depths exceeded the capacity of scientists to bring the objects of inquiry under the control of representation.

For example, in the sphere of desire: the Marquis de Sade helped to extend the depths of desire, even while he was pretending to construct orderly (classical) scenes representing each desire in its transparency. But each new representation was confounded by the creation "out of an expanse of shade" of new desires not exhausted by previous configurations. After Sade, "violence, life and death, desire and sexuality, will extend, below the level of representation, an immense expanse of shade which we are now attempting to recover as far as we can, in our discourse, in our freedom, in our thought."[8]

Desire now becomes a powerful, mysterious force in human life that moves and disrupts stable patterns of being even as it escapes attempts to explain it by recourse to those patterns. And this effect becomes generalized. In our discourse: every dialogue invokes a set of prejudgments and preunderstandings not susceptible to exhaustive formulation within its frame. In our freedom: every act draws sustenance from an unconscious and preconscious pool that subverts it as an act of freedom. In our thought: every thought is invested by the unthought serving simultaneously as its condition and its limitation. Such formulations are now familiar to those laboring within the fields of psychoanalysis, Marxism, and hermeneutics, but the vicious circles they expressed were shocking to those advancing them at this juncture.

By the time twentieth-century discourse matured (though Foucault would not use this word), this stubborn situation of "man and his doubles" had become a defining feature of the human sciences.

The "transcendental doublet" is a strange, persistent, self-subverting configuration of modern discourse. It has not proven to be either dispensable or transcendable. The transcendental doublet is a being whose role as governing *subject* of action and inquiry is perpetually chased by the compulsion to clarify opaque elements in its desire, perception, and judgment by converting itself into an *object* of inquiry. Each time the results of a new analysis of itself are brought back to the subject it is moved; it never reaches the solid ground it seeks to stand upon. This pursuit itself has become irreducible. The subject ("man") is haunted by an indispensable and unconquerable double—an immense expanse of shade—that repeatedly compromises its sovereignty, transparency, freedom, and wholeness. This shadow provides both a condition of subjectivity and a sign of the impossibility of acquiring the stability the subject presupposes.[9]

Foucault evokes the paradoxical character of this doublet in his portrayal of the

> Other that is not only a brother but a twin, born, not of man, nor in man, but beside him and at the same time, in an identical newness, in an unavoidable duality. . . . In any case, the unthought has accompanied man mutely and uninterruptedly, since the nineteenth century. Since it was never more than an insistent double, it has never been the object of reflection in an autonomous way; it has received the complementary name of that for which it was . . . the shadow: in Hegelian phenomenology it was the *An sich* as opposed to the *Fur sich;* for Schopenhauer it was the *Unbewusste;* for Marx it was alienated man; in Husserl's analysis it was the implicit, the inactual, the sedimented, the non-effected—in every case, the inexhaustible double that presents itself to reflection as the blurred projection of what man is in his truth, but that also plays the role of the preliminary ground upon which man must collect himself and recall himself in order to attain his truth. For though this double may be close, it is alien, and the role, the true undertaking of the whole of modern thought, is imbued with the necessity of thinking the unthought—of ending man's alienation . . . of making explicit the horizon that provides experience with its background . . . of lifting the veil of the Unconscious, of becoming absorbed in its silence, or of straining to catch its restless murmur.[10]

If the typical drive in the modern episteme is to escape or transcend the limitations posed by doubles, Foucault is (often) a happy posit-ivist, ready to pose distinctive ontopolitical interventions that

endorse the paradoxical situation within which interpretation proceeds. Indeed, Foucault suggests that the retreat of the old dogmatism—where limitations in the finite world were to be transcended
through a faith that linked humanity to the infinite—has been accompanied by the advance of a new dogmatism. The new dogmatism, ironically, endlessly renews the circle of finitude in its restless
search for a mode of attunement or transcendence that might still the
quest. The carriers of these tactics typically act as if they have just
become more closely attuned to the purpose of being itself or as if
they are on the verge of perfecting a transcendental argument that
will soon still the oscillation troubling them.

Foucault seeks to awaken thought from this "anthropological"
sleep—a sleep "so deep that thought experiences it paradoxically as
vigilance, so wholly does it confuse the circularity of a dogmatism
folded upon itself in order to find a basis for itself within itself."[11]
The dogmatism of modern thought consists in the terms of its vigilance, in its modernization of the Augustinian imperative to go
more deeply into the self (or language or community) to find a stable ground for itself. Foucault does not endorse the project of progressively drawing the double into the fold of the subject it haunts,
partly because he suspects that the quest for transparency energizing such a project is endless and partly because the single-minded
pursuit of this elusive end as a "regulative ideal" draws (to use a
later vocabulary) the disciplines of a normalizing society into new
corners of life.

If the first group of theorists we encountered seeks futilely to
evade the ontological dimension of discourse, the second group of
contemporaries endorses much of Foucault's preliminary characterization and then searches for ways to reduce the size of the gaps between man and its doubles. These theorists seek to establish a basis
from which a reflective moral consensus can be built. They treat, as
Foucault suggested is typical of thought in the modern period, the
quest for rational consensus, self-consciousness, and freedom to be
intimate allies. And they fear that if no such basis is found for morality, the web holding society together will become unstrung.

Several contemporary thinkers can be seen in this light. Some may
pursue the goal of transparency itself, while others treat the quest as
a regulative ideal that can never be attained fully but must serve as
the highest goal of reflection.

Habermas's earlier attempts to elaborate the conditions of discursive consensus constitute one paradigm of this effort. But that strategy seems perpetually doomed to encounter new dimensions of the unthought yet to be brought into its fold. Habermas's persistent silence about the body, which is simultaneously the text upon which the script of society is written and the fugitive source from which spring desires, resistances, and thought exceeding that script, may be revealing in this regard. He cannot endorse the theme of an essentially embodied subject, advanced by those who seek to uncover an inner *telos* in the body to be brought more fully into the structure of intentionality. Nor can he accept the Nietzschean portrayal of the body as, ambiguously, the site of social inscriptions and a source of energies exceeding and confounding those scripts. The first position would provide him with resources from which a rational consensus might be formed, but its pursuit would approximate the foundationalism his model is supposed to supersede. The second would undercut his quest for consensus, driving him toward the practices of genealogy and post-Nietzschean ethics he opposes so vociferously.

Habermas has recently relaxed his drive for a consensus. But he still has not yet developed, at least to my knowledge, a conception of bodies or embodiment consistent with the model he pursues. He remains silent about the body, perhaps because any position available to him (the disembodied self, the embodied subject, the body as site and nonteleological source) subverts the ideal of discourse he pursues.

Hermeneutics, at least in its pastoral mode, offers another response to the condition of man and his doubles. It strives to work the open circle between preunderstanding and explicit formulation until understanding becomes more closely attuned to a higher direction in being. Such a relationship to being, while it does not render all opacity transparent, strives to enhance the experience of harmony within the "embodied" self and, potentially, between the self and the well-ordered society to which it gives allegiance. This perspective does not seek to close all the gaps between body and identity, desire and intrinsic purpose, knowledge and being; it promises only *to narrow them perpetually*.

The pastoral orientation presents itself through a rhetoric of harmonization, responsiveness, articulation, depth, fulfillment, realization, and community. It draws extensively upon ocular metaphors of

refined vision, in-sight, and light, using the metaphors of illumination, clarity, obscurity, darkness, cloudiness, and distortion, for example, to pursue its regulative ideal of a transparency never fully to
be realized. It is, of course, not alone in using the metaphors of
height, sound, and illumination; it is distinctive in treating them as
media through which "we" become "attuned" to harmonies of being
and a higher direction.

But it remains deeply contestable whether any pastoral hermeneutics responds to an immanent purpose in being or transcendentalizes a contingent organization of life by treating it *as if* it expresses a
communion with being. This issue has practical implications, for
what appears from one side as the means by which attunement is
fostered often appears from another as the terms through which
painful artifices of normalization are enhanced and legitimated. It is
revealing that practitioners of this mode seldom strive to problematize explicitly the narrative and rhetorical structures governing their
own texts. For these provide the divinized media through which the
ontopolitics of attunement, illumination, and elevation proceeds.

The pastoral mode usually draws silently upon a theistic supplement—upon a contestable faith in a god whose will and purpose are
thought to inform the direction of being. The way it deploys ocular
metaphors, reminiscent of biblical usage, constitutes only the most
"visible" sign of that connection. Such a divine supplement may be
indispensable to the aspirations of communion governing the pastoral form. I concur with Foucault, anyway, that a "commentary" of
this sort can best hope to sustain itself through the faith that "below
the language one is reading and deciphering, there runs the sovereignty of an original Text."[12] Subtract that contestable faith, and pastoral hermeneutics encounters Nietzschean genealogy.

Charles Taylor endorses such a hermeneutic project, sometimes
seeking to bolster it with a series of transcendental arguments that, if
they succeed, close up the gaps between man and his doubles enough
to establish a definitive frame within which the terms of "plausible"
debate occurs. He attributes the model of argument he pursues less
to Kant and more to a synthesis of Husserl and Heidegger. He says:

> If we purge Husserl's formulation of the prospect of a 'final founda-
> tion', where absolute apodicity would at last be won, if we concentrate
> merely on the gain for reason in coming to understand what is illusory

in the modern epistemological project *and in articulating the insights about us* that flow from this, then the claim to have taken the modern project of reason a little farther . . . isn't so unbelievable. . . . Reflection in this direction . . . involves, first, conceiving reason differently as including . . . a new department, whose excellence consists in our *being able to articulate the background of our lives perspicuously.*[13]

Taylor (in one of his moods) strives through a descendant of transcendental arguments to provide a perspicuous framework for reflection as such. If these arguments do not establish the human essence, they can rule out several other philosophies contending for acceptance in late-modern discourse. That is the hope.

Taylor effectively challenges the primacy of epistemology summarized earlier. But he then suggests that it is possible, first, to reject the primacy of epistemology quite definitively; second, to provide fundamental "insight" into the essence of human being; and, third, to show Nietzschean construals of being to operate outside the matrix of plausibility supported by these considerations. I do not think Taylor succeeds in these latter ventures. Even his rejection of the Nietzschean stance is based upon a selective reading of it that renders it unattractive to most post-Nietzscheans themselves. His reading of Nietzschean "radicality of will," for instance, seems to me to underplay the role of *amor fati* in Nietzsche's thought and to ignore the nonhuman loci of "will to power" in Nietzsche's philosophy while concentrating misleadingly on its human sites. His construal of Nietzschean philosophy supports his critique, but the very selectivity of that construal protects his own position from more effective contestation.

In general, I share Foucault's doubt that any transcendental argument in the late-modern context can foreclose the terms of ontopolitical contestation as severely as Habermas, Taylor, and others sometimes hope. Certainly, none has succeeded in doing so yet. In the context of man and his doubles

it is probably impossible to give empirical contents transcendental value, or to displace them in the direction of a constituent subjectivity without giving rise, at least silently, to an anthropology—that is, to a mode of thought in which the rightful limitations of acquired knowledge . . . are at the same time the concrete forms of existence, precisely as they are given in that same empirical knowledge.[14]

All these thinkers, though, share the view that a "lived ontology" infiltrates into thinking even before it is articulated closely. They diverge primarily on the degree to which it is possible and desirable to resolve the issue definitively between alternative ontopolitical stances. In siding with Foucault on this question (at least with Foucault as I read him) I am not claiming his stance to be demonstrated by bulletproof arguments—say, by a countertranscendental argument that disproves conclusions Taylor or Merleau Ponty or Unger or Habermas seeks to establish. I only insist that no set of arguments actually delivered (rather than promised for that near future perpetually receding into the next near future) has ruled his perspective out as a viable position on the field of contestation.

Each scheme of interpretation is necessarily invested with an ontopolitical dimension. But heretofore and into that endless "near future" stretching before us, no perspective has at its disposal a consensual, pastoral, or transcendental strategy capable of reducing competitors in this domain to a small set of friendly alternatives. This is the reading I support. Moreover, this is not a plight to be lamented. It provides food for thought and an occasion for rejoicing. It provides a launching pad for pursuit of a political ethos in which alternative perspectives support space for each other to exist through the agonistic respect they practice toward one another. In a world where a plurality of ontopolitical perspectives is credible, perhaps it is ethically laudable for the proponents of alternative perspectives to reconsider the ethics of engagement between contending constituencies. Maybe the drive to the knockdown argument in ontopolitical interpretation is a corollary to the drive to fundamentalism in political life. Perhaps by pondering more closely the irreducible character of ontopolitical contestation we can move the pluralist imagination into domains that have heretofore escaped it.

THE ONTOPOLITICAL MATRIX

If every political interpretation is invested with fundamental presumptions, do the major contemporary alternatives constitute a random set or is there a pattern discernible among the dominant contenders? I want to suggest that there is a pattern, though the perspective from which it is delineated and appraised is itself contestable. Let us call this pattern the ontopolitical matrix of Anglo-American discourse in the late-modern time (Fig. 1). The most visible theoretical positions in that world fit into this frame, and there is a discernible pattern of interaction among them. But the frame is not so fixed that it stops other positions from pushing against these boundaries or interrogating the complementarities among the debating partners.

On this matrix, the categories across the horizontal axis are mastery and attunement; mastery refers to the drive to subject nature to human control and to the susceptibility of nature in the last instance to this ambition, and attunement refers to a strategy by which members of a community become more closely oriented to a higher direction in being and to the more harmonious life it renders possible. The categories across the vertical axis are the individual and the collectivity; the individual refers to the primacy of the individual in identity, action, knowledge, and freedom, and collectivity refers to the primacy of a single social unit such as the community, nation, or state in these respects. The matrix that emerges contains the following ideal types with a few representative figures drafted into the appropriate slots.[15] It looks something like this:

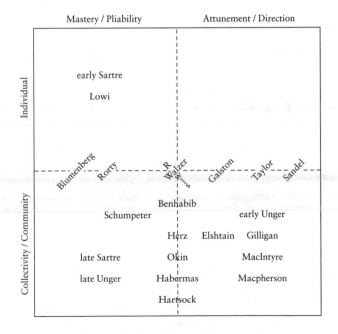

Figure 1. My first and last matrix

It is easy to identify disputes and divergences between positions on the matrix. Consider a few familiar questions. Is freedom to be attained through mastery of nature or through attunement to a higher harmony in being? Is it positive or negative? Is the crucial medium of freedom the individual or some collective unit? Do individuals constitute the collectivity or does the form of the community enter into the very constitution of the self? Is legitimacy grounded in the consent of the distinct individual or in the formation of an order that lifts its members to a higher level of being and freedom? Is a state that honors freedom and diversity to be neutral between competing conceptions of the good life or to be organized around an intrinsic standard of the good? Is rationality instrumental or substantive? Does it emerge from the aggregation of individual and group calculations or from a discourse in which all are altered and elevated by the common good in which they participate? Is knowledge to be gained through representation or through depth hermeneutics? Does the preeminent danger in the late-modern time flow from the residue of traditional restraints on reason and mastery or from the refusal to constrain the modern project of mastery through a more profound communion with the purpose of being itself? And so on.

Whenever a thinker on the matrix finds reason to reject one of these positions, he is drawn as if by a magnet toward one of the alternatives already waiting to receive him. Whenever a thinker finds reason to qualify her position by new considerations, she is moved as if through an internal dialogue to draw one or more of the matrix alternatives into the higher compromise she constructs. The matrix (almost) sets the boundaries outside of which the untruth of contemporary political discourse resides. As time goes by, each matrix theorist is pulled by the logic governing these debates toward the middle, toward a compromise position containing elements from several of the contending alternatives.

Heidegger says:

> Certainly the modern age has, as a consequence of the liberation of man, introduced subjectivism and individualism. But it remains just as certain that no age has produced a comparable objectivism and that in no age before this has the non-individual, in the form of the collective, come to acceptance as having worth.[16]

Taking a cue from him, we might ask, What demands and assumptions bind these disparate positions together onto this checkerboard of mutually defined alternatives? Of course no such delineation itself rises above all ontopolitical determinations, but here I will allow the presumptions governing my analysis of the matrix to emerge through a delineation and critique of affinities and complementarities among matrix debating partners.

Compensatory Ontologies

They share a demand to provide new compensations for the modern "loss" of expressivist/enchanted understandings of the world. Most insist, therefore, that the world must be predisposed to us in the last instance, either by containing a higher direction with which we can enter into closer communion or by being a pliable medium ultimately susceptible to human mastery. Or both. If it does not provide the first compensation, then it *must* offer the second. The absence of both would be, well, "implausible." So we witness theorists such as Roberto Unger moving on this checkerboard from the attunement version of communalism he earlier endorsed to the mastery version of collectivism reflected in his later work, all the while holding constant the underlying demand for a world amenable to consummate freedom, through either communion or mastery. A similar movement along the vertical axis is detectable in Sartre as he opposes teleological perspectives first through an early commitment to individual self-creation and then through a later one to collective self-creation.

The quest for ontological compensation within these contending perspectives can be discerned through interrogating the orientation of each to the human body. In the mastery perspective, for instance, where does the body stand in relation to human agency and nature? With nature or agency? In most presentations this issue is simply bypassed because anything said either way is doomed; any answer will compromise either the conception of agency sought or the conception of nature assumed. In attunement perspectives, on the other hand, the self is generally said to be "essentially embodied," meaning that an inner telos is wrapped in human corporeality or "embodied." The *telos* of the body is presented through the rhetorical structure of texts that celebrate it. Nietzschean countertexts that disturb and unsettle such configurations are treated as insults to the delicate quest for equilibrium. It is as if thinkers who seek to disturb and politicize established patterns of embodiment in the interests of enhancing the possibilities of pluralization are already known by matrix thinkers to be mistaken. Seen from a perspective endorsing neither the mastery view of agency nor the attunement view of embodiment, these two perspectives too often secure themselves through questionable tactics, either by remaining silent about the place of the body in the duality agent/nature they endorse or by failing to engage post-Nietzschean critiques of contemporary theories of embodiment as the last outpost of ontoteleology.

As Nietzsche would ask, from whence does one get the right to issue these "musts"? Who or what says the world owes us this much, so that it must either be predisposed to the human project of mastery or to human attunement to its putative harmonies? Do these two orientations not flow more from a demand for existential reassurance than from the imperatives of historical evidence? And might this covert point of complementarity between these competitors contain exclusions and dangers worthy of interrogation? Is there no more noble way to express "love of the earth"?

The Extension of Discipline

Seen from a perspective pressing against the boundaries of the matrix, the mastery and attunement perspectives together provide too much legitimation for the extension of disciplinary society. They do so through organization of the individual and/or collectivity to achieve mastery over the world and through organization of the individual and/or community to achieve communion with a fictive direction in being. In each case, the mode of organization endorsed is not energetically subjected to self-problematization; the proponents seldom try to flag ways in which the fundaments of each perspective are insinuated into narrative/rhetorical configurations governing the texts in question. This is partly because each position often finds it necessary to defend itself only against other positions on the matrix. Each tends to construe its ultimate standards to be natural, rational, established by common sense, a series of binding transcendental arguments, a social consensus, a set of "shared understandings" or a refined mode of attunement to being; and none of these presumptions is subjected to critical exploration from a genealogical perspective.

Reductions of Politics

While some endorse a robust model of politics for the present, each, when appraised from this contending perspective, projects a regulative ideal of society in which certain essential dimensions of politics have become dispensable. Some do so through treating individual freedom as a private space outside the clash of politics; others through treating freedom as collective action in concert or as communal realization. There is too little emphasis, within this matrix, on the positive value of maintaining contending positions in a relation of restrained contestation, maintaining such relations because no unified model of the world is likely to marshal sufficient evidence to establish its certainty and because an ethic of care for the very differences that make self-identity possible realizes itself best through the institutionalization of relations of agonistic respect between contending perspectives. There is too little attention, on this matrix, to the productive roles the politics of disturbance and the politics of enactment can both play in opening up possibilities of pluralization. Some who do endorse versions of either for the present continue to yearn for a future world in which this will not be necessary. They do not appreciate sufficiently the persistent need to maintain a precarious balance between the politics of governance and the politics of disturbance, not only in the present, but also in the regulative ideal of pluralist politics itself. Hence they so often read those who call for such a *balance* as if they only called for *resistance* or *disturbance*. Others, who do introduce a measure of political pluralism into their ideal, still treat the current shape of the normal individual as the unconscious standard through which to judge the legitimate scope of plurality. They celebrate common sense and shared understandings too eagerly and unambiguously. Still others, while appreciating irony and disturbance, relegate them to the sanctuary of private life.

The Domestication of Contingency

There is a gravitational pull within this matrix to domesticate the experience of contingency in life, either by treating contingency as a type of event susceptible to control because it is not logically necessary or by treating the contingent as an unfortunate falling away from the intrinsic ideal. But the experience of contingency persistently exceeds such theorizations of it. Together, these positions tend to domesticate contingency as the unexpected occurrence, the dangerous or threatening event, the obdurate entrenchments that resist effective intervention, the unavoidable outcome accidental only in the timing of its occurrence, the accidental event that, once it erupts, unleashes dangerous consequences for regions of the earth or the entire planet, and the new possibilities unexpectedly opened up within existing patterns of interaction. Each of these positions—again by comparison to a Nietzschean appreciation of recalcitrance in every cultural formation, untamed energies flowing through every identity, and surprises periodically disrupting every pattern of organization—domesticates the experience of contingency, either through its presumption of world pliability or through its presumption of world directionality.

While one of these orientations appeals to a future of greater organizational scale and another secretes nostalgia for an alleged past of smaller scale and communion, the terms of debate between them tend to deflect attention from the most distinctive and salient feature of the late-modern time: the globalization of contingency. The globalization of contingency refers to a perverse correlation between the drive of dominant states to master contingency in their internal and external environments and the corollary production of dangerous global possibilities that outstrip the capacity of any single state or the interstate system to control them. These new possibilities include the creation of a global greenhouse effect or other climactic/environmental changes—such as worldwide soil erosion or contamination of water supplies—that fundamentally damage the earth as a shelter for human life; crises in the supply of essential economic resources located in foreign lands through crisis or decay in the supplying regimes; the escalation of state and nonstate terrorism into a permanent condition; the production of an international economic crisis within a world economy of extensive interdependence; a nuclear exchange that destroys regions of the world or civilization itself.

It might seem that the contemporary resurgence of attunement/communion theories was engendered by exactly this last set of possibilities, and that they provide the best set of correctives to the mastery problematic. After all, are deep ecology and the ideal of the stable state economy not linked to this perspective? Have they not emerged as responses to that very hubris of modern life that has generated the globalization of contingency? As one who once flirted with this reading, I retain some appreciation for it. But it now seems to me that two considerations cut against it.

First, the existing terms of debate between the mastery and communion perspectives have been elaborated largely within parameters set by debates over the priority of the individual, the small-scale community, and the sovereign state. Thinkers on either side of the horizontal axis can be found populating each of the positions on the vertical axis. But the globalization of contingency exceeds the parameters of the vertical axis. The politics of enclosed territories, while certainly pertinent to these issues, is no longer sufficient to them. What is needed politically, today and tomorrow, is a series of cross-national, nonstatist movements organized across state lines, mobilized around specific issues of global significance, pressing states from inside and outside simultaneously to reconfigure established convictions, priorities, and policies. Such regional constellations require participants who do not bestow *final* loyalty upon the sovereign state, the normal individual, the shared understandings of a culture, or a small-scale community. Each of these loyalties is contingent. It competes with the others and with loyalties to cross-national identifications. For today it is necessary to disturb and challenge—through publicity, exposés, and boycotts and through alliances with beleaguered states and nonstate peoples—a variety of presumptions, understandings, and loyalties inscribed in the nation-state. Those drawn to these unorthodox political combinations aspire to be dissident representatives of a distinctive global time even while they participate in the states that rule them; therefore, they must refuse to be reduced entirely to their status as citizens of a sovereign place. The vertical boundaries of the matrix vindicate a set of allegiances, loyalties, parameters of political action, and organizational forms that must be further pluralized today.

Second, the terms of debate on the horizontal axis are today inclined steeply in favor of the mastery position. If the mastery perspective is challenged only by the attunement alternative, it is almost certain to defeat its favorite debating partner. Proponents of the communion perspective, to put it bluntly, are often effective in conveying what we have lost, ineffective in showing why we should seek to return that lost world today. This is because the modern age defines and institutionalizes its identity to a significant degree through contrast to an earlier legacy of ontoteleological perspectives, and because the communion perspective has been unable to inspire general confidence that there is an intrinsic order of being generally available to us. The experience of modern life—in work, business, travel, consumption, science, communications, military life, and education—is more conducive to faith in the responsiveness of the world to human organization than to belief in a higher harmony in being with which entire societies can commune.[17] *If* attunement were the only alternative, then, the mastery problematic would win by default, as Hans Blumenberg, indeed, thinks it does.

So concern for the environment, the integrity of life, and the self-limitation of states articulated within the confines of the attunement orientation persistently functions to reinstate the primacy of the mastery problematic. Care for the earth becomes a mood of nostalgia for a past that never was. Nostalgia overwhelms imagination. The mastery problematic thus becomes installed in institutional practice, first as dream, then as common sense, eventually as intractable fate.

Perhaps introduction of a position that disturbs both the mastery project and the attunement dissent will eventually be more promising.[18] It would challenge modernist assumptions of nature (things, ecosystems, bodies, desires) as a pliable substratum; it would *accentuate* the modern experience of disturbance, contingency, and undefinability in intrasubjective and intersubjective relations, opening up new possibilities already stirring within these orders. It would *radicalize* the experience of contingency in the formation and maintenance of identities and things; it would thus challenge the modern project of mastery by accentuating the very dimension (the denial of a *telos* in nature) that has heretofore given it advantages over its favorite debating partner. It would call upon hegemonic states to redefine, for instance, their institutional priorities of consumption so that their "vital national interests" no longer place them on a collision course with so many peoples of the world; it would press them to reconstitute their identities and interests (and the *ways* they ground and protect them) so they can coexist over a longer period of time with a larger variety of others on the same globe. It would also, then, oppose the hegemony of the growth imperative and the legitimations of disciplinary society attached to this imperative, all in the name of a more vital appreciation of the contingency of things.

Reductions of Post-Nietzschean Thought

Contenders within this matrix converge upon a common set of reductive, disparaging readings of perspectives challenging their complementary presumptions. The disparagement is applied particularly to "post-Nietzschean" theories—especially those on the left side of a matrix yet to be consolidated—whose renowned contemporary exponents include Judith Butler, Jacques Derrida, Gilles Deleuze, Michel Foucault, Luce Irigaray, Ernesto Laclau, and Chantal Mouffe. Since matrix debating partners tend to converge in their dismissive readings of these perspectives, and since they communicate regularly with each other through the institutionalization of publications, meetings, conferences, rumor mills, and so on, they conclude, understandably enough, that together they have gotten these guys right. It suffices to expose the nihilism, relativism, subjectivism, anarchism, and amoralism of post-Nietzschean thought or, alternatively, its relentless programs of unqualified assertions of self, power, domination, and mastery.

Very few interpretations of post-Nietzschean thought flowing through the matrix construe it to be an alternative perspective through which to reconsider terms of interaction within the matrix itself. Attunement types slide over this reading because they presume that any position challenging the mastery perspective must automatically move to the stance they have already perfected. Mastery types miss it because they too recognize the case for self-limitation only within the terms of an attunement perspective they find to be defunct.

So one encounters readings of Nietzsche as a proponent of "will to power" who would master the earth, or as purveyor of "radical will" who would overturn every form of self-limitation. And he is said to oppose rationality as such because he resists the transcendentalizations, teleological presumptions, and arguments by historical elimination contending for primacy in debates between regimes of thought on the matrix. Finally, he is said to oppose morality because he points to the "immorality of morality" and because he disturbs every attempt to ground morality in something necessary, automatic, or final.

I do not deny that such readings *can* be given of protean texts signed by the name Nietzsche. Every reading draws upon projective predispositions flowing from the reader as well as porous possibilities running through the text. Indeed, the aristocraticism pervading Nietzsche's texts is rewritten by democratic *post*-Nietzscheans who draw sustenance from his challenges to matrix conceptions of identity, ethics, territory, and truth as "stillness." These post-Nietzschean perspectives must be assessed on their own terms, unless it can be shown that the relations of agonistic indebtedness that mark Marx's relation to Hegel, Arendt's relation to Heidegger, Rawls's relation to Kant, and Irigaray's relation to Lacan cannot be replicated by the relations critical democrats establish to Nietzsche. Numerous possibilities reside in the Nietzschean texts, and several inspire democratic reconfigurations of matrix interpretations.

There are many issues to be raised in this context. We must remain content for now to pose only a couple. Many intramatrix critics of Nietzsche and post-Nietzschean thought proceed as though terrible things will happen—such as the disappearance of a stable basis for ethics, or the emergence of relativism, or the breakdown of modern discipline, or the fragmentation of nations—unless strategies are devised to transcend the modern condition of man and his doubles. But both Nietzsche and Foucault, as I read them, think that the more compelling the drive to closure or unity is in a state the more likely it is either to constitute a repressive regime or to foment the very fragmentation it purports to fear the most. For the world is not amenable to such unity. The *initial* need today (and probably in most times) is to detach hegemonic identities to a greater extent from the fixed set of alternatives they already recognize, exciting the experience of discrepancy within established dualities of normality/abnormality, rationality/irrationality, good/evil, and sovereignty/anarchy so that alternative experiences of injury and possibility can be cultivated.

Again, the most powerful contemporary pressures to social fragmentation flow from struggles between contending, dogmatic identities, each hell bent on installing itself as the universal to which everyone and everything must conform. Enhanced appreciation of our own contingency, and of our indebtedness to the differences through which we receive specification, provides an antidote both to the drive to unity and to the social fragmentation such drives often produce. Lebanon, Ireland, Bosnia—to take three recent examples—reflect modes of fragmentation in which some identities insist upon universalizing themselves by conquering, assimilating, or liquidating their opponents. These impulses are closer to calls to universalism and national consensus flowing through the matrix than to the post-Nietzschean sensibility endorsed here.

The post-Nietzschean wager (or operative faith) is that an ethical orientation to life does not depend upon the demand to lock all reverence for life into some universal theistic faith, rational consensus, secular contract, transcendental argument, or interior attunement to a deep identity. It construes these to be diverse theories of an intrinsic moral order, where *order* oscillates between its use as a verb of command (to order) and a noun of harmonious design (the order). From my (post-) Nietzschean perspective these two concepts of moral order too often reflect ressentiment against those persistent, multiple experiences that belie a moral foundation in being. The appearance of such a grounding is too often protected by converting differences that might provide the impetus for relations of agonistic respect among an enlarged set of constituencies into modes of otherness to be marginalized, liquidated, or punished for their immorality. By this means the moralist places a second, transcendental seal upon historically specific identities and priorities already sealed very well indeed, pretending that a critical perspective that challenges them can only motivate conduct if it too is established through one of the very routes it resists.

A post-Nietzschean might pursue an alternative strategy of ethical cultivation, striving to tap into a care for the rich diversity of life that, we hope, already flows through the conventional identities installed upon us. To us, one of the defining characteristics of an *ethical* orientation is cultivation of a critical responsiveness that can never be automatic, deducible, guaranteed, or commanded by some unquestionable authority.

In one crucial respect, then, a post-Nietzschean ethic is closer to the teleological tradition than to the Augustinian or the Kantian traditions. With the former it shares an ethic of cultivation rather than a morality flowing from a categorical command. But, unlike the teleological model of cultivation, it seeks to enhance the possibilities of agonal interdependence between an enlarged set of constituencies thrown together by hook and by crook, rather than to refine a common consensus or to consolidate already fixed understandings.[19] It seeks to translate the late-modern experience of the rich *an-arche* of being into enactment of a more generous pluralism, one that draws multiple and contending ontopolitical dispositions into an enlarged network of intersections.

So both teleologists and post-Nietzscheans pursue ethics of cultivation. And both commend a politics of connectedness. But they pursue these two themes in different ways. Those who pursue a unified or teleological ethic are very likely to miss these points of contact between themselves and post-Nietzscheans, as they concentrate on what to them must seem like the horrendous ("fragmentizing," "divisive," "subjective") effects of its ontoethical bearings.[20]

The post-Nietzschean perspective draws sustenance from an almost always operative attachment to life as a protean set of energies and possibilities exceeding the terms of any identity or cultural horizon into which it is set. This is what Nietzsche means when he says goodness proceeds from abundance rather than a transcendental command. The objective is to thaw out frozen perspectives, to identify arbitrary threats to difference created by the dogmatism of established identities, and to advance accounts of danger and possibility crowded out by established regimes of thought. You draw from this protean care for difference as you move *and* you tap into numerous points of resonance and affinity with others as you proceed.

Post-Nietzscheans cannot prove their case by rising above the level of reason achieved by their opponents; we make it through detailed engagement with assumptions and priorities insinuated as a matter of course into alternative interpretations. We cannot command the motivation to pursue our priorities; we can only tap into counterexperiences and latent dispositions that may be already there in protean form. Of course our own presuppositions acquire the status of quasitranscendentals. But we then seek to problematize these too, acknowledging that our best efforts to state our own presuppositions perpetually fall short of the mark and insisting that the presumptions we do elaborate are also contestable responses to persistent mysteries of existence. We strive to fold a mutual appreciation of ambiguity and contestability into the very structure of social strife and interdependence.

When Nietzsche, for example, dreams of the "spiritualization of enmity," he commends a mode of restrained contestation among friends, lovers, and adversaries who exercise reciprocal respect and self-limitation through mutual appreciation of the problematical bases from which they proceed. "In politics, too, enmity has become much more spiritual—much more prudent, much more thoughtful, much more *forbearing*. . . . We adopt the same attitude toward the 'enemy within'; there too we have spiritualized enmity, there too we have grasped its *value*."[21] (My) post-Nietzscheanism thus presses the spirit of liberalism into domains some liberals have yet to acknowledge to be pertinent; it pushes the politics of agonistic respect into corners that may seem unnecessary or excessive to liberal perspectives nested within the comforts of the normal individual, the private realm, the neutral state, and justice as fairness.[22]

If the post-Nietzschean fails to tap the care she seeks to invest in those ambiguous relations of identity\difference she might try again; or she might reconsider her interpretation of what is happening; or she might conclude that the dispositions needed to confront perceived cruelties and dangers are not forthcoming at this time. Who or what provides the assurance, anyway, that things must come together in the right way, that there is commensurability in principle between a thoughtful encounter with issues and the needed supply of ethical responsiveness, or between an appeal for the spiritualization of adversarial relations and a pool of responsiveness waiting to be tapped? From whence come these musts? Is it not, indeed, possible to be more ambiguous and self-ironic in these domains? Perhaps such modes of self-presentation form pivots upon which the ethicality of care for the strife and interdependence of identity\difference can swing.

The operative faith in a post-Nietzschean problematic, its generally cheerful pessimism, is that interventions it poses may strike responsive chords in some of the constituencies it engages. Its corollary charge is that insistence upon the need to fix a common theistic faith, discover a deep, universal identity, or perfect a set of transcendental arguments prior to ethically informed action fosters either passive nihilism—an inaction born of despair because the world does not provide the moral resources you require—or aggressive nihilism—a repression of those very difficulties and gaps that jeopardize attainment of the transcendental position sought. Do these demands to find a solid ground reflect a futile wish to provide guarantees in exactly that domain of life—ethics—in which such guarantees are impossible? Indeed, where their very attainment would undermine the essence of the ethical bond?

I cheerfully concede that this counterconstrual of the Nietzschean texts in question is a contestable construction. Even this "domesticated" reading (as if Nietzsche were a wild animal) involves me in relations of agonistic indebtedness to Nietzsche, indebted to the fundamental problematic from which to engage the ontopolitical matrix and antagonistic to particular readings of democracy, equality, and so on developed by the author named Nietzsche. Having elsewhere developed the terms of this relation,[23] I merely want to suggest here that such a stance provides an appropriate terrain for exploration among those who would both disrupt established regimes of political thought and cultivate an ethic of critical responsiveness.

I began this section by claiming that several participants on the matrix converge upon a dismissive construal of Nietzsche and post-Nietzscheans. To give plausibility to the counterreading endorsed here I will offer two quotations from Nietzsche. The first refers to one of the numerous pressures he identifies to fix and dogmatize established identities:

> To hear something new is painful and difficult for the ear; we hear new music poorly. When we hear a foreign language we try unconsciously to reform the sounds into words that sound more familiar and homelike. . . . Everything new finds even our senses hostile and unwilling, and more than unwilling.[24]

This does not sound (to me) like a thinker who espouses "radical will," who thinks that the self can create itself out of whole cloth as it sees fit, who anticipates a species of humanity without regularity, or even who thinks that we are the kind of creatures who could successfully master the world. Nor does such an interpretation square with my reading of Nietzsche's ideal of self as work of art. This artwork is explicitly constrained to work within limits set by the many contingencies already branded into the self. It works modest adjustments in the life of a being already shaped by a first and "second" nature beyond systematic remaking. The reading of Nietzsche as theorist of radical will is further cast into doubt upon pondering his presentations of the inertia of language, the drive to regular identity, the irreducible social demands of coordination and order, and the voices of ressentiment in the self that are never completely subdued.

Partial detachment from established modes of realization, insistence, and closure is the first and most difficult task set within a post-Nietzschean problematic. This is the route through which enhanced care for the strife and interdependence of identity\difference can be cultivated. It is hardly likely to be achieved completely. That is one reason why current insufficiencies in transcendental strategies do not worry post-Nietzscheans. We would be more worried if a time arrived when such a strategy was generally said to have succeeded.

It may be that many who read Nietzsche through the goggles of the matrix think that either the self must be grounded in a deep identity or that it must create itself in Sartrean fashion. Since they know that Nietzsche opposed the former thesis, they project onto him the latter wish. They then criticize their own projection as if it were his. But, on my reading, he opposes both of these doctrines.

My last specimen speaks to the sort of care or reverence Nietzsche seeks to cultivate. It is an impious reverence, one that inspires generosity in others because it is not based upon a certain foundation:

> Why atheism today? The 'father' in God is thoroughly refuted, likewise the 'judge' and the 'rewarder'. Also his 'free will'. . . . It seems to me that the religious instinct is growing powerfully but is rejecting theistic gratification with deep distrust.[25]

Here Nietzsche endorses the "religious instinct" while pulling it out of the theistic framework in which it has been set. Nietzsche's invocation of nontheistic gratitude—a theme traversing *Beyond Good and Evil* and *Thus Spoke Zarathustra*—poses a challenge to theistic and secular moralities alike. Its invocation recalls and counters recurrent attempts by modern theists and secularists to devise transcendental arguments to supplement or replace the divine authority (the father, the judge, the rewarder) compromised by the historical dissolution of the expressive world of divine signs. It then slips into that (nearly) vacant space between modern theistic devotion and secular doctrines of rational principle and moral instrumentalism. Such a nontheistic gratitude for the rich diversity of being provides an ethical source from which a modified vision of pluralism might emerge, one in which a larger variety of identities strive to find ways to coexist on the same territory, combining together from time to time to support the general material and spiritual conditions of this very cultural diversity. For it is when a genealogical sensibility is mapped onto the pluralist imagination that both perspectives achieve their highest level of attainment.

STRATEGIES OF DETACHMENT AND ATTACHMENT

Consider two formulations:

> If we reject the progressivist picture . . . the important question . . . is whether or not a given writer . . . believes that, beyond some things that human beings have themselves shaped, there is anything at all that is intrinsically shaped to human interests, in particular to human beings' ethical interests. In the light of that question . . . Plato, Aristotle, Kant, Hegel are all on the same side, all believing in one way or another that the universe or history or the structure of human reason can, when properly understood, yield a pattern that makes sense of human life and human aspirations. Sophocles and Thucydides, by contrast, are alike in leaving us with no such sense. Each of them represents human beings as dealing sensibly, foolishly, sometimes catastrophically, sometimes nobly, with a world that is only partially intelligible to human agency and is itself not necessarily well adjusted to ethical aspirations.[26]

> Nothing is fundamental. That is what is interesting in the analysis of society. That is why nothing irritates me as much as these inquiries—which are by definition metaphysical—on the foundations of power in a society or the self-institution of a society, etc. These are not fundamental phenomena. There are only reciprocal relations, and the perpetual gaps between intentions in relation to one another.[27]

The first formulation resonates with the second. But the first writer, Bernard Williams, is seldom charged with the inability to respond to the world ethically, while the second, Michel Foucault, encountered this charge from almost every neo-Aristotelian and neo-Kantian on the North American continent during the 1980s.[28] Is this because the first is an English analytical philosopher and the second a French genealogist? Perhaps. At any rate, the putative differences between them narrow even further when you engage this statement by Foucault:

> I like the word [curiosity]. It evokes 'care'; it evokes the care one takes of what exists and might exist; a sharpened sense of reality, but

one that is never immobilized before it; a readiness to find what sur-
rounds us strange and odd; a certain determination to throw off familiar ways of thought and to look at the same things in a different
way . . . ; a lack of respect for the traditional hierarchies of what is
important and fundamental.[29]

Both Williams and Foucault are indebted to Nietzsche, whom
each reworks along some dimensions. Both refuse the quest to derive morality from a fundamental order of God, nature, language,
history, or reason. Both seem to cultivate an ethic that responds to
the *absence* of such an order and, simultaneously, responds to the
corollary *abundance* of life over every organization and articulation
of it. They evoke "a care for what exists . . . and might exist." Both
endorse a tragic view of the world while struggling against the
snares it produces rather than resigning themselves to its violent effects. Moreover, both, as I read them, advertise the contestability of
the ontoethical positions they endorse, striving to fold this recognition into the ideal relations they aspire to form with bearers of other
perspectives.

What, then, *is* the difference between them? There is, first of all,
a difference of emphasis. Williams probably identifies a more persistent pattern of human interests than Foucault does, while Foucault
emphasizes how cultural constructions of the self through historically specific forms of science, medicine, economy, education, and
punishment encounter resistances even as they inscribe their effects.
But if you read the Foucauldian "nothing," as it can plausibly be
read, to deny either a divine order of being or a natural order corresponding to human capacities of reason, then this apparent difference begins to narrow. Williams and Foucault converge around the
thought that "there is nothing at all that is intrinsically shaped to
human interests," while they diverge to some degree on the extent
to which human interests remain stable across time. On this score I
locate my hunch somewhere between the most radical reading of
Foucault and the most probable reading of Williams. Between these
two formulations you can identify certain limit conditions—such as
birth, child rearing, and death—that every human and every culture
must somehow engage.[30] The most important thing, though, is to
keep the space between Williams and Foucault alive in our thinking.
For it is likely that every confident articulation of stable human in-

terests in a specific historical context inadvertently naturalizes some contingent features of the present by treating them as if they conformed to the universal as such. And this process of naturalization often unconsciously demonizes those very differences that would otherwise unsettle the experience of stability.

This consideration points to the most significant difference between Williams and Foucault. While Williams advances his contention boldly, and while he connects Greek tragedy to the modern experience of identity, Foucault adds another project to these two themes. Foucault contends both that nothing is fundamental *and* that the pressures of identity, organization, language consolidation, social coordination, condensations of memory, and, perhaps, resentment of a world without intrinsic purpose persistently work offstage to reinstate institutionally embedded presumptions of a fundamental Law or Design of being. To counter this social logic, Foucault pursues critical *genealogies* of how contemporary practices of rationality, subjectivity, normality, madness, criminology, sexuality, medicalization, and gender have been constructed, seeking to deprive these social formations of the aura of a natural design or intrinsic moral order that automatically tends to form around them. His genealogies open us to the play of possibility in the present. Correspondingly, they incite critical responses to unnecessary violences and injuries surreptitiously imposed upon life by the insistence that prevailing forms are natural, rational, universal, or necessary. The idea is to deploy genealogy to loosen up sedimented forms and to cultivate further a care for life (hopefully) already there in protean form—to incite energies on behalf of extending diversity where it is possible to do so.

Neither Foucault nor Williams can offer a formula in advance to separate neatly a good diversity from a bad one; each suggests lines of questioning to pursue and considerations to invoke when something previously treated as natural is now resisted on the grounds that it imposes unnecessary suffering on the differences through which it is organized. Foucauldian genealogy is an essential component in an ethicopolitical orientation that both asserts that the fundaments of being are mobile and that, in the ordinary course of events, social pressures accumulate to present particular formations of life as if they were intrinsic, solid, or complete.

Genealogy delineates the constructed character of contemporary formations of self, morality, convention, rationality, and so on by tracing them back to discrete, particular, contingent elements from which they were constructed. It opens up concealed possibilities residing in the present by the critical historicization of actuality. It thus proceeds in the service of a certain disposition to freedom.

So much on behalf of genealogy. What about its limitations? First, Foucault sometimes acts as if genealogy can proceed simply by bracketing ontological assumptions in established perspectives. That suggestion seems highly unlikely to me. Second, the genealogical enterprise, as advanced by Foucault early in his career, did constitute a refusal to affirm any positive directions or reforms of its own. That self-restriction was posed for ethical reasons, to avoid reimplicating the thinker in the very matrix he sought to disturb. But such a restriction, as Foucault later and explicitly came to see, also limits the positive possibilities. Genealogy, I want to suggest, is necessary but inadequate to a mode of reflection that seeks critical detachment from the contemporary ontopolitical matrix. One reason this is so is that detachment from any particular set of dispositions and presumptions inevitably attaches one to another set. It is hard, indeed impossible, to become detached as such. So it is important to articulate the ideal to which your strategies of critical detachment are attaching you.

Foucault has been accused of denying the extent to which he presupposes those very conceptions of subjectivity, truth, responsibility, and rationality he wishes to render ambiguous. Again, this seems an unlikely charge to press against a thinker who helped to inaugurate contemporary reflection into the aporias of "man and his doubles." But it still may have some salience to certain stages of his thought. Fairly early (1973), he showed confidence in the ability to reduce transcendental presumptions to a bare minimum, though he did not claim to be able to eliminate them altogether:

> I strive to avoid any reference to this transcendental as a condition of possibility for any knowledge. When I say that I strive to avoid it, I don't mean that I am sure of succeeding. . . . I try to historicize to the utmost to leave as little space as possible for the transcendental. I cannot exclude the possibility that one day I will have to confront an irreducible residuum which will be, in fact, the transcendental.[31]

Later on, he is much less confident about the prospect of reducing the transcendental to a residuum and more definite about the need for self-irony here, saying "there is no way you can say there is no truth."[32]

Deconstruction offers a related strategy of disturbance and detachment. It pursues the ambiguity of rationality from within, striving to identify sites of rational undecidability inside perspectives that have been closed up in the name of reason, acknowledging its unavoidable implication in the practices of rationality it seeks to disrupt. One way to read Derridean deconstruction is to say that it seeks to foment the experience of undecidability in areas where the correct decision now seems all too rational or obvious, doing so to render us more responsive to those aspects of alterity that escape current definitions of rationality, identity, and normality. Deconstruction is first and foremost an ethical project.

But deconstruction, too, is both indispensable and insufficient to pose challenges to the ontopolitical matrix. It provides crucial, specific reminders of how limited and ambiguous experiments with detachment are likely to be, challenging the purity of any counterposition that pretends to transcend cleanly the politics of normalization and transcendentalization. But it, too, refuses to pursue the trail of affirmative possibility very far, out of a desire to minimize its implication in ontological assumptions it could never vindicate without drawing upon some of the same media it has just rendered ambiguous.

While I am dependent upon these two strategies of detachment, I pursue a strategy of attachment that stands in a precarious relation of implication and dissonance with them. Let me call it, for the moment, positive ontopolitical interpretation. Such a practice characterizes aspects of Foucault's *Discipline and Punish* and volume one of *History of Sexuality;* it becomes dominant in his later work.

To practice this mode of interpretation, you project ontopolitical presumptions explicitly into detailed interpretations of actuality, acknowledging that your implicit projections surely exceed your explicit formulation of them and that your formulations exceed your capacity to demonstrate their truth. You challenge closure in the matrix by affirming the contestable character of your own projections, by offering readings of contemporary life that compete with alternative accounts, and by moving back and forth between these two levels.

Let the summary offered earlier in this essay serve as an initial specification of the projections endorsed here. By introducing such projections, we can offer affirmative interpretations and positive ideals; by introducing them as contestable, we jostle the sense of closure and necessity governing interpretations on the matrix; by confronting difficulties in our own formulations, we intensify the general experience of gaps between the indispensability of ontopolitics and limitations faced by every perspective purporting to fill this need; by identifying a distinctive set of dangers and possibilities, we move the established terms of debate in this domain; and by reworking the contemporary imagination of diversity, we may contribute support to the pluralization of contemporary life. The idea is to interpret actively, specifically, and comparatively, without praying for the day (or deferring until the time) when the indispensability of interpretation is matched by the solidity of its grounds.

How does this enterprise proceed? We have already seen how the established matrix of political discourse fogs over a set of complementary presumptions about nature, bodies, contingency, ethics, sovereignty, identity, and politics. When an unfamiliar competitor challenges these terms of discourse, the ensuing debates condense some of this fog into a new series of beliefs and counterbeliefs. Of course, only one layer of fog is lifted by such an intervention, and new layers roll in. For these new beliefs are articulated only with respect to the new set of alternatives now placed before us. Nonetheless, new beliefs (and disbeliefs)—susceptible to interrogation, debate, and comparative criticism from a variety of perspectives—have now been formed.

But, it is reasonable to ask, what makes the particular perspective advanced here a timely one to place on the agenda? Why try to lift this layer of fog now, rather than numerous others that persist? I do not have a comprehensive answer to this question. That may be one of the issues doomed to remain shrouded in fog. But part of the answer flows from the internal difficulties previous traditions of discourse have accumulated over the past several centuries. Histories of "Western social ontology" advanced by Heidegger, Blumenberg, Foucault, Derrida, and Taylor are pitched at the appropriate level to review these difficulties and to gain a sense of how this contemporary alternative might solidify itself. Nonetheless, such histories never suffice to explain how new alternatives emerge to challenge established perspectives (they do not show why, say, nominalism actually emerged as the most salient philosophical response in the fourteenth century to the difficulties of Thomism). Western history (itself a dubious category in need of interrogation) is replete with times when a set of culturally indispensable ideas remained intact even though they were full of mysteries and paradoxes. Augustinianism represents one example of this phenomenon, an important one, perhaps, in that it shows how paradoxes and mysteries can be translated into positive resources for the faith that generates them.

One source of pressure for the alternative sketched here resides in the ruptures in contemporary experiences of state sovereignty, global ecology, the internationalization of market relations, and speed in politics. All these changes affect the circumstances through which the individual confronts traditional definitions of itself as a responsible agent, a citizen of a particular state, a member of a democratic society, and a participant in a distinctive global time. These multiple and dissonant experiences provide spurs to recent interrogations of subjectivity, sovereignty, territorial democracy, and transcendental morality. Indeed, these new experiences are rather congenial to the codes of paradox, ambiguity, *différance*, doubles, untruth, life, and nontheistic reverence emerging from post-Nietzschean thought.

The most persistent issue facing critical interpretation today is the ironic relation it assumes to its own ontopolitical projections. We must convert this paradoxical condition (this incoherence, this self-referential contradiction, this presupposition of a standard of truth we ourselves call into question, etc., etc., etc.) into spurs to productive thinking. For this condition/limit of reflection is unlikely to be eliminated. The sense that this ambiguous condition sets the terms within which thought necessarily proceeds today constitutes *our* reverence and spur simultaneously.

We might initially pretend to know, for instance, that being lacks a definite telos, that life both requires identity and exceeds any specific organization of identities, that nature contains diverse energies and forces that exceed attempts to organize it, and that care for the strife and interdependence of identity\difference is cultivated by affirming life to be more fundamental than identity. But these pretenses are problematized in subsequent gestures as we acknowledge that our experiences of contingency in identity, the production of otherness through the dogmatism of identity, and the globalization of contingency through the modern project of mastery flow from an interpretation that competes with others but cannot secure the necessity of its own account.

In the near future perpetually stretching before us, the indispensability and contestability of fundamental presumptions hover over interpretation: the irony of interpretation; the joyful ambiguity of "man" and his doubles; the indispensability of contestable onto-political projections. Post-Nietzschean interpretation draws upon genealogy and deconstruction to expose gaps between its pretenses and the stability of its achievements, even though it takes less pleasure in acknowledging these gaps than it does in identifying them in its competitors. It treats alternative positions—represented all too crudely in this essay by a series of names on a matrix—as competing bearers of projectional interpretation, asking how they fare once the aura of necessity, exhaustibility, or transcendence surrounding them has been attenuated. Asking how it fares, too, as it relieves itself of the obligation to achieve a purity no other perspective attains, and as it moves the established terms of discourse, however modestly, by pressing itself onto the field of debate.

Nothing is fundamental. Genealogy is therefore necessary. For cultural experience of a fundamental order of things keeps reinstating itself in ways that may foster unnecessary injury and violence.

Nothing is fundamental. But *hsu*, in Chinese, suggests that nothingness is also a fullness, as in the proverb "Holding onto emptiness is like grasping fullness."[33] English retains traces of this complementarity between nothingness and abundance, particularly when you consider difference as that which exceeds determinate being without being determinate itself. Differences, resistances, and protean energies flow through the "perpetual gaps" within and between social formations, opening up possibilities for the politics of pluralization.

Nothing is fundamental. A saying that presents itself as a contestable affirmation of the fundamental mobility of things. The affirmation of contestability of this faith affects the character of the relations you pursue with alternative formulations of the fundaments of being. Such a critical reflexivity, if and as it becomes reciprocal across the lines of difference between fundamental orientations, fosters agonistic respect between contenders who share roughly equivalent social power; and it fosters critical responsiveness to difference where power is asymmetrical.

Nothing is fundamental . . . Therefore, almost everything counts for something. An ethic of care for the diversity of life locates itself cautiously between these two statements, presenting this "therefore" as its gift to the protean diversity of life. It acknowledges the need to limit its own self-assertion so that other faiths can count for something too. It suggests that one element in a generous ethic is the recognition that neither it nor its competitors is grounded on something that is demonstrably fixed, automatic, solid, commanded, or necessary. But this means that the ethical disposition one admires the most is never guaranteed. Ethics now trembles as a human possibility without cosmic grounds or pragmatic guarantees. An ethic of care for the diversity of being honors both the indispensability and the fragility of ethics.[34]

2

The Desire to Punish

THE CALL TO PUNISH

What calls for punishment? In a country where rape, murder, mugging, drug wars, and corruption are rampant, the answer seems too self-evident to warrant the question. Crime calls for punishment: to protect the innocent against the criminal in the future, to deter others inclined to crime, to enforce the standard of responsibility upon which civilized social relations rest, to vindicate the conception of justice through which most people live, and, though less often today, to rehabilitate the offender. Of course, these five sources (protection, deterrence, responsibility, justice, and rehabilitation) do not mesh well together. We disagree within and among ourselves over how much comparative weight each deserves. And tremors of uncertainty shoot through each on its own account. We debate (within and among ourselves) the conceptions of self, desire, will, responsibility, injury, and desert through which infractions are defined, guilt is assessed, penalty is assigned. Some of us even wonder why "serving time" is the paradigmatic penalty in a society that otherwise evades finitude and death so adamantly.

If relations between the elements in punishment are unstable and the underlying conceptions grounding each are contestable, why is this cumbersome complex so fervently and widely defended? A chasm opens up here between the fervent desire to punish in a country where crime and punishment have become highly racialized and the persistent uncertainty of the principles governing punishment in general. The desire to punish flows into this seam, freezing it up and breaking down any barriers that get in its way. For the question "What calls for punishment?" can be heard on several registers. If you listen, it is not difficult to hear a call to revenge animating the desire to punish. Revenge against those who rob upright citizens of goods, time, health, dignity, or life itself. And revenge against racially marked urban constituencies whose conditions of existence disturb the practices of fairness, neutrality, impartiality, and responsibility said to govern everyone. These two calls become combined in the same practices of representation. The call to revenge forms the least discussed and most pervasive force in the desire to punish.[1] It infiltrates legal justice, closing up uncertainties within it. It can even be brought against those who interrogate the desire to punish. Think of those punitive responses to the unsettling work of, for instance, Michel Foucault, the thinker who poses the question animating this essay.[2]

Once revenge infiltrates the call to punish, this eminently deniable drive can expand indefinitely. You might seek revenge against entire groups who pose a threat to your security. Or against constituencies whose way of being threatens the security of your identity. You might even seek revenge against the world for not providing the clear and closed concepts of responsibility, identity, merit, and punishment you thought for sure it would come equipped with, though here it may be necessary to find other targets to substitute for the world. Criminals provide paradigmatic substitutes. After all, they are guilty of something, and the state has already decided they must suffer. The call to revenge can be felt in the zeal with which gays or young underclass male African-Americans are punished when the legal opportunity arises. It can be heard in contemporary demands for the death penalty, the termination of furlough policies, longer prison terms, and fixed sentences without parole. In the refusal to allow gays and lesbians to raise children or to participate openly in the military. It is surely discernible in the refusal by the electorate and elected officials to curb police violence against urban minorities, or to seek remedies against corruption, violence, and rape within prisons. For, as even academics know from experience with college administrators, the pleasures of revenge involve making the target suffer, realizing that *you* are the agent of this suffering, and knowing that you have sufficient cover to avoid reprisal or official detection. So today large sections of the American public officially denigrate reports of police brutality and prison violence while gobbling up films and television programs that verify the regular operation of both.

These pressures can be felt inside judicial judgments of crime every day in contemporary America, particularly if you live in a large, racially divided urban center. Consider a case, selected from the *Baltimore Sun* during June 1993, when this essay was being composed. Dontay Carter, an African-American teenager, was convicted of one murder, a series of downtown kidnappings of upper-middle-class white men, and a daring escape while waiting for his case to be brought to trial. Carter forced these men into the trunks of their expensive cars and shot them. One died; another survived after being left for dead. After being convicted and sentenced to life in prison with no parole, plus 190 additional years for good measure, Carter, a leader of angry young black rebels in the city, presented a thirty-five-minute statement to the court. It irritated many in the courtroom. Only a few comments are recorded in the news report (while shorter statements by the widow of the deceased and the judge are covered extensively). Still, it is easy to get the gist:

> "Why is it special when a man is killed and he happens to be a white man? . . . What's the media circus for? Because a black man had the audacity to come home from prison and do something to a white man?" [Carter denies killing anyone.] Carter went on to say that putting him behind bars will not address the root causes of crime and to attack what he termed "the cowardly black leaders" in Baltimore City. He talked of the disillusionment he felt as a youth coming to grips with his mother's miserable inner-city lifestyle [the reporter's term]. He even complained that the 13th Amendment to the Constitution outlawed slavery but that "the system" still enslaves black men by labeling them as criminal. He noted that some prison populations are 70% black. Referring to his capture after his January 18 escape . . . Carter said, "I'd have rather died than be pulled out of that apartment and see black people clapping like the police did something good when I've never hurt a black man."[3]

Carter, whose crime dramatized and exacerbated racial divisions in one way, tried to expose the racialization of punishment in another through his statement. Carter might have said more, noting, for example, how only 6 percent of homicides in the United States involve blacks killing whites, while media theatricalization of such crimes engenders the general impression that the percentage is much higher. But, under these circumstances—and not these alone—nobody was in the mood to listen. The desire for revenge by the grieving widow, with four young children, was understandable. She said, "Carter will be remembered, and I quote [from the prosecutor's charge] 'as a monster, most dangerous, diabolical, manipulative and savage killer,' and I will add, he is totally amoral, and evil personified." The term *black* is never uttered. But it lurks within the words that are. At one point during the sentencing ceremony, when she saw Carter look at his watch, the grieving woman said, "You going somewhere, Mr. Carter?" This response formed the vital center of the reporter's article. The judge, clearly aware that prison usually intensifies the character of men like Carter, threw rehabilitation out of consideration, characterizing Carter as an agent of manipulation vainly trying to politicize the vicious crime he committed:

> Judge John N. Prevas said the blow to Carter's ego [from the applause when he was captured?] was likely as great a punishment as life in prison. "I think that went right to the heart of his own myth structure and showed him he had thrown away his life on a delusion no one was able to follow except the young men he was able to charm into following him." Judge Prevas described Carter "as someone who sees himself as Moses and Eldridge Cleaver. All I see is Charles Manson and Ted Bundy. . . . You talk about yourself as a leader in a cause. All I see is a devil in a Gucci sweater who only thinks about himself and how you can manipulate your friends. . . . I think you ought to thank Mr. Simms [the attorney who cited Carter's youth as a mitigating factor] for the gift of life, but I'm not sure you're going to enjoy it because it's going to be a long haul."

"Remembered as a monster." "He had thrown away his life on a delusion." "All I see is a devil in Gucci sweater." "It's going to be a long haul." "The heart of his own myth structure." "You going somewhere, Mr. Carter?" An assessment of criminality that invokes conventional concepts of agency and responsibility while also sliding past them to a second set of surreptitious conventions. Carter is both a responsible offender and a racialized monster, a manipulative agent and a black devil arrogantly wearing a sweater designed for yuppie white men. Because he is a killer, none of these implicit associations can be noted. For wouldn't that imply that you are soft on the crime?

If the two designations—responsible offender and (racial) monster—coalesce into an intense desire to punish their object, they are divided by the official form vindication of legal punishment assumes in this culture. An ambivalence circulates through the Carter case, making it both incumbent upon the accusers to cross the line between the two categories and necessary to blur the crossing. "You going somewhere, *Mr.* Carter?" manifests it perfectly. For Carter is there nominated as an unmarked responsible agent susceptible to legal treatment under the category "Mr." only *because* he is also implicitly marked as a racial monster finally brought under the control of the state. That combination would not appear if "Carter" were still on the loose: you can be sure he would not be called "Mr. Carter."

Such ambivalence anchors feelings of outrage against Carter in two sources, each fixing him as a target of attack. The first fixes the target as a responsible offender who deserves what he gets; the second defines him as a dangerous monster who must be destroyed or interned permanently. This double anchor must not be lifted above the water line or Carter will slip away from the murky category of responsible agent susceptible to legal punishment into the murky supplement of the monster who does not deserve the layers of punishment publically demanded.

The call to revenge inhabits the murky spaces within and between these categories; this murkiness within and between must be maintained and concealed if the call is to maintain its implacable standing. This murkiness within and between may be philosophically disturbing, but it is politically potent. If "we" made the line between responsibility and monstrosity too clear and clean we might never be allowed to punish criminals inhabiting minority subject positions with the severity we demand. Philosophers who pretend they have dissolved the murkiness in and between these categories make a real contribution to this effect.

Indeed, a reciprocal desire for revenge circulates through every definition by each party in this case: Carter, the widow, the judge, and the reporter who filed the news report (including the term "lifestyle" applied to Carter's mother). But some of these desires are authoritatively dressed in the categories of law, agency, responsibility, and justice, while others are authoritatively reduced to myth, manipulation, devilishness, and delusion. The muddiness of Carter's world is available for discussion, but murkiness in the world of the judge, the jury, and the victims must not be addressed juridically. Elements in the practice of punishment bearing affinities to those in the practice of crime are divided by an unbreachable political chasm between illegal crime and legal punishment.

The porous category of responsible agency provides perhaps the largest container into which the spirit of revenge is poured in contemporary moral and legal practices. No theory of responsibility without messy remainders has ever been consolidated in the Euro-American West, as a genealogy of the wayward and elusive idea of free will from Augustine through Rousseau, Kant, Hegel, and Rawls readily reveals. But, still, the most compelling practices of merit, desert, and respect within Western cultures require attributions of responsibility to maintain themselves.[4] There are powerful cultural pressures, then, to obscure this tension between the social indispensability of responsibility and the problematical desert or merit of those to whom it is applied. This pressure proceeds above all from those constituencies whose dignity and honor are redeemed through existing presumptions of responsible agency. The practice of responsibility becomes the site of a double bind, with cultural injunctions operating at the second level against probing the bind at the first. But once you begin to contest this double bind, it is not too difficult to discern how the cultural integrity of responsibility in Western cultures has been protected historically through a shifting series of devices. These devices deposit the most disturbing cases into cloudy doubles of the responsible agent, isolating them so that the disturbances cannot recoil back upon the category of responsibility itself. The Augustinian categories of monstrosity, evil, and original sin functioned in this way, as do those shifting and unstable categories of monstrosity, perversity, irrationality, amorality, and insanity in modern life.[5]

It could be that some such set of divisions is both indispensable and deeply problematical in Euro-American culture. But a cultural drive to revenge polices this paradoxical combination, crystallizing the indispensability of responsibility, shuffling its problematical standing into the shadows through production of its doubles, and drawing surreptitious sustenance from both responsibility and its doubles when punishment of an outrageous crime is at issue. The governing injunction: save the categories; waste those who disturb their stability.

Nietzsche, the consummate diagnostician of revenge flowing through the most elevated principles of Western culture, reminds us of how legal attributions of responsibility function in those criminal cases that most shock our sensibilities. No one, Nietzsche says, knows "the degree of his inflammability" without being subjected to extreme pressure: a spouse who flaunts infidelity, repeated and authoritative humiliation, subjection to torture, the call by a loved one to avenge a terrible assault, the wanton murder of your child. "No one knows whither circumstances, pity, indignation, may drive him, no one knows the degree of his inflammability. Paltry little circumstances make one paltry oneself."[6] But those of us in paltry little circumstances regularly pretend that we are not when we judge those who are subjected to extreme pressure or when we assume that they too face only paltry little circumstances. This asymmetry between the experience of ordinary citizens who judge criminal defendants and the experience of many who commit them marks a persistent source of injustice within legal justice:

> The criminal, who is aware of all the circumstances attending his case, fails to find his deed as extraordinary and incomprehensible as his judges and censurers do; his punishment, however, is meted out in accordance with precisely the degree of *astonishment* the latter feel when they regard the incomprehensible nature of his deed.[7]

The desire to punish crystallizes at that point where the shocking, vicious character of a case blocks inquiry into its conditions, repressing examination of uncertainties and ambiguities pervading the very concepts through which it is judged. Where astonishment terminates inquiry, the element of revenge is consolidated. The decision to stop the inquiry at this point rather than the next reflects a call to protect responsibility from the trial of uncertainty everyone fears.

The irony is that astonishment regularly crosses the line between crime and punishment. For today some violent crimes are themselves governed by a drive to revenge against abstract targets marked by signs of race and cultural standing. They express a will to revenge against abstract categories of people rather than against specific individuals against whom you hold specific grudges. A will to revenge concealed through its installation into hegemonic categories of crime and punishment. A will to revenge that finds one of its paradigmatic expressions in the judgment that the right time to listen to the voices of the other never arrives. The agents of violent criminality remain astonished by the circumstances of their lives. And they know in advance that those who are astonished by the crimes they commit will never listen to a delineation of its cultural conditions of possibility. For to listen would be to call into question conceptions of agency, responsibility, and justice through which cultural elites and marginal members of the white middle class vindicate their own integrity and standing. "You going *somewhere*, Mr. Carter? . . ."

The desire to punish, to injure the other who violated your body, spouse, lover, property, or identity, prevails at that point in a moral economy where astonishment intervenes. Punishment, among the many things it does, exacts revenge on the past, and the past is not necessarily confined to the past act of the one punished. Of course, the one sent up the river now has plenty of time to vent feelings of injury and revenge. Revenge through the law offers immediate gratification to the offended and limited protection to others from this particular agent in the future. It also fosters unlikely deterrence, impossible rehabilitation, and persistent injustice. In crime and punishment two contending calls to revenge clash on the streets and in the courts, and each is refueled by the collisions between them.

The contemporary practice of punishment does not fail to serve a function. It merely fails to serve its official ends—such as reducing crime significantly or securing justice or restoring offenders to citizenship—effectively. Its visceral success in exacting revenge explains why all the evidence in the world on behalf of its default in these other respects fails to budge the media, the cops, the courts, or the citizenry. So, the desire to punish intensifies as violent crime escalates, as traditional practices of cultural identity in America become more precarious, and as the place of the United States in the world becomes less secure. We insist that we must be sovereign agents and our state must be a sovereign entity, and the desire to punish targets exactly those ambiguous constituencies whose conduct would otherwise call these modes of agency into question. Whenever the call to revenge takes charge, designing a proportionate response proves less pertinent than mounting an awesome attack on the available target, as the behavior of vengeful spouses, parents, criminals, judges, media, politicians, juries, and voters reveals. This ugly game of substitution continues right into the refusal to pursue the quandary of how to engage the probable *inability* to establish proportionality between crime and the legal response to it.

Is it possible to curtail the call to revenge inside the desire to punish? Or, better, to curtail the desire to revenge from flowing so freely into the practices of responsibility and punishment? That remains uncertain. One beginning, pertinent but insufficient by itself, might be to rethink the etiology of desire, exploring how the drive to punish inhabits the desire of both upstanding citizens and violent criminals and how the very way in which a code of desire becomes consolidated disrupts established conceptions of responsibility. Perhaps it is timely to insert a reflection on desire into two familiar and contending modes of analysis in this domain: into those murky conceptions of agency, will, responsibility, and punishment through which crime is juridically engaged; and into minority reports that reduce causes of criminality to the mechanics of social structure.[8] These latter two models too often form mirror images of each other. A murky, insistent model of individual agency competes with a dense, insistent model of social causality. ("Which *are* you, anyway, Mr. Connolly, a determinist or a defender of free will? A retributionist or a utilitarian? A defender of individual responsibility or an advocate of social engineering? Or do you invoke both in some soft, eclectic combination?") But if both models are moved through a reading of desire resisted by both, it might be possible to rethink the role of social structure and agency in crime *and* its punishment.

PATHWAYS OF DESIRE

The modern bifurcations between the responsible agent and the irresponsible offender and, within the latter category, between the offender as irresponsible agent and as unresponsible delinquent, are too sanguine. They pay too little heed to economies of desire flowing through and across these divisions.

By desire I do not quite mean the need for food, clothing, shelter, or nurturance to survive or flourish. I mean something closer to an organization of energy, beyond those needs, to possess, caress, love, emulate, help, befriend, defeat, stymie, boss, fuck, kill, or injure other human beings, both as individuals and as types. It is highly unlikely that any theorization of desire, today or tomorrow, will capture its dynamic entirely. The flows and fixations of desire are too protean, multiple, contingent, and promiscuous for such a theorization to succeed. No simple model of causality, for example, begins to negotiate this terrain. For any interpretation of desire, once it is received by members of the culture to whom it is applied, may enable and inspire many to modify the shape of desire. Moreover, it is probable that diffuse corporeal energies organized into specific pathways of desire are never exhausted by any particular pattern. So an apparently stable pattern might be scrambled or moved by accidental interruptions, unexpected setbacks, new stimulations. The inability of totalistic theory in this domain is mostly a good thing, particularly if recognition of this inability becomes incorporated into presumptions of agency, responsibility, merit, and punishment authorized by the culture. Recognition of these limits might introduce circumspection and generosity into social judgments drawn, as judgment always is, from particular interpretations of desire and responsibility. An ethic of generosity and forbearance might be cultivated through attentiveness to the uncertainties and vicissitudes of desire. We are a long way from such an attitude today.

A promising theorization of desire will come to terms somehow with several elements diffusely discernible in it: desire is socially constructed out of energies made available by the human organism; its intensities, objects, and valences are contingent to a considerable degree; some contingent desires, once formed, are susceptible to further change, while others are highly recalcitrant to it; the arousal of intense desire often contains an element of competition or rivalry; and authoritative prohibition can help to crystallize the shape and intensity desire assumes. I distill these conditions from the conjunction of personal experience and compelling works of literature. What other basis is there from which to proceed? Augustine's recognition, for instance, that his youthful desire to steal those pears was inflamed by prohibition of the act does not prove a universal connection between prohibition and desire. But it may suggest a general drive, differentially distributed across time and circumstance, to be taken into account somehow in any reading of desire. For a prohibition crystallizes a possibility that might otherwise have escaped your attention, as that first couple discovered at the genesis of being. It may also induce a wish to find out more about the thing that you have not experienced and that others seem hell bent on keeping from you. "Do not desire your neighbor's lover." "Do not continue reading this essay."

Among contemporary theorizations to consider, that of René Girard may be particularly pertinent. First, Girard incorporates several of the elements discussed here into his reading. And, second, the very simplicity and relentlessness with which Girard presses his theory enables one to test it against alternative experiences and possibilities. Girard's conception of desire comes out of his readings of protean myths, such as those of Oedipus, Job, and Exodus. The objective is to show how close, symptomatic readings of myths that continue to command our attention disclose a founding violence at the core of traditional communities, a violence concealed by the community to sustain the moral code unifying it. On Girard's reading, a series of loops connects the dynamic of desire to violence, punishment, morality, and concealment. Thus Job is a victim of his people, retrospectively treated by them to be a profound source of insight into the character of the divine. So are Oedipus and Moses, respectively, with Freud offering a reading of the latter that anticipates the Girardian perspective.[9] Girard claims that his readings vindicate his theory of desire; but it also must be said that his theory of desire gives shape to those readings. It may be impossible to avoid such a (hermeneutic) circularity, but the dogmatism with which Girard presents his interpretations of myth and desire alike does belie the problematical standing such circles bestow upon them.

Girard insists that the self is implicated from the start in the social life that constitutes it, and that powerful tendencies toward arbitrary violence are built into this implication. The organization of desire is the key. "In the traditional view," says Girard, "the object comes first, followed by human desires that converge independently on this object. Last of all comes violence, a fortuitous consequence of this convergence."[10] Social contract theory may explain violence so conceived, and commend a legitimate response to it. But, unfortunately for these theories, desire does not work like that. The very formation of desire—the very crystallization of diffuse energy into particular patterns—involves a triangular relation between a fractured subject (as you might call it), a model, and an object already desired by the model. The key to desire resides in the twofold relation the fractured subject assumes to its model(s). First:

> In all the varieties of desire examined by us, we have encountered not only a subject and an object but a third presence as well, the rival. It is

the rival who should be accorded the dominant role. We must take care, however, to identify him [sic] correctly; not to say, with Freud, that he is the father; or, in the case of the tragedies, that he is the brother. . . . Rivalry does not arise because of the fortuitous convergence of two desires on a single object; *rather, the subject desires the object because the rival desires it.* In desiring an object the rival alerts the subject to the desirability of the object.[11]

Girard's account surely taps into a more general experience of desire in this culture. Variations on this theme are reiterated in numerous erotic and pornographic stories, themselves designed to stimulate desire in readers. The teacher of Emmanuelle, to cite one instance, emphasizes the triangular character of erotic desire in his initiation of this pupil into higher erotic pleasures.[12]

But what enables another to serve as a model through which desire crystallizes? Here we arrive at the tragic moment in the production of desire, as Girard reads it:

When modern theorists envisage man as a being who knows what he wants, or who at least possesses an 'unconscious' that knows for him, they may simply have failed to perceive the domain in which human uncertainty is the most extreme. Once his basic needs are satisfied (indeed, sometimes before), man is subject to intense desires, though he may not know precisely for what. The reason is that he desires *being*, something he himself lacks and which some other person seems to possess. . . . It is not through words, therefore, but by the example of his own desire that the model conveys to the subject the supreme desirability of the object.[13]

The domain of desire is where "human uncertainty is the most extreme," partly because no one selects with foresight the early models through which desire becomes consolidated and partly because models possess limited ability to shape this interaction according to their heart's desire. Dontay Carter did not select his mother (who the judge senses was important to formation of his identity), and she did not select the pattern of desire Carter drew from her and others.

Models appear to subjects to possess something they want (hence the Ur-desire in the crystallization of desire). A model appears to possess a fullness of being the subject lacks; but the model turns out eventually to lack it too. A logic of deceit is built into the consolidation of desire, and, since the consolidation of desire is crucial to the formation of subjectivity, deceit is thus built into the structure of subjectivity. The subject seeks wholeness of being to stem its own uncertainty and incompleteness.[14] Because *nobody* actually possesses wholeness, desire keeps moving. This lack in being is productive of desire, and the element of productivity in the lack, as I will later want to suggest in opposition to Girard, can sometimes be translated into a resource to modify particular demands of desire. The conditions of possibility of desire include the impossibility of attaining the end desire aims to achieve. If it attained its end, desire would stop dead in its tracks.

In Girard's reading, rivalries escalate out of this vortex through contingent patterns of mimesis. For models eventually feel threatened by the privileged status they receive, and by the intense desire of disciples to attain the objects they prize the most. Girard may overplay his hand here, in a way that carries him to the Christology the extremism of his account was driving toward all along. But, still, there is enough here to illuminate the problem we have set.

The final element in Girard's theory is the production of scapegoats to still the escalating patterns of violence that so readily issue from unstable social structures of desire and rivalry. Scapegoats are not produced through simple prejudice; nor do they correspond to official definitions of them. Scapegoats serve as objects upon whose lives comes to rest responsibility for the deceits, revenge, and violence built into escalating rivalries of desire. Sometimes, if a scapegoat serves its unifying role effectively, it becomes memorialized and sacralized. Members of the community, after all, are indebted to it for the union it enables: sacralization of an originary scapegoat conceals the arbitrary violence upon which the moral order rests while memorializing the scapegoat as a hero to whom they are in debt. The community forgets its punishment of the scapegoat to conceal the element of violence in the moral code that unifies it. The judge's reference to Moses and, particularly, Eldridge Cleaver in the Carter case may reflect traces of that disposition. I doubt that Cleaver's judge compared him to Moses at the time of *his* trial.

There are a series of uncertainties, omissions, and opacities in the Girardian perspective that may carry broader implications, particularly for efforts to think about how to modify patterns of desire that have already become installed. Let me consider five.

First, does the relation of subject to model not itself assume the shape of something very much like desire? If so, the triangular character of desire is always already mediated by a predesiring conative mode. Desire is ubiquitous, even while it is susceptible to organization into particular patterns. This modification in the interpretation of desire reminds us that there is a reservoir of energies to draw upon in modifying an existing pattern of desire and identifications.

Second, is Girard's use of the male voice, both for the model and the subject, innocent of implications? Perhaps a certain (culturally precoded) masculinism is already folded into this presentation of desire. Perhaps the model, as presented by Girard, presupposes women more as objects of male desire mediated by male models than as subjects themselves implicated in a variety of possible models, erotic possibilities, and gender dispositions.[15] At another level, too, Girard reinscribes the traditional masculine and feminine in the very terms of relation between subjects of desire and models for desire. He masculinizes the model of desire, who represses the subject seeking to displace him; he feminizes the subject of desire who wishes to achieve a fullness it lacks. But, again, such a characterization first implicitly draws upon a paradigm already installed in this culture and then reinscribes it by presenting it as the explanatory model through which to explain cultural sources of violence.

Third, as already intimated, the modality or *type* of desire manifested by a model may be as important as the object or object class at which it aims. The fatefulness with which the competitive element in desire automatically issues in violence for Girard is compromised by this consideration. Desire may be more or less possessive, more or less caring, more or less combative, more or less reflexive, depending in part upon the models through which it is organized, even though the indispensability of models to the structure of desire increases the likelihood that conflict enters somehow into its structure. This dimension of mobility and uncertainty in the element of desire opens up the possibility of working on desire itself, modestly but efficaciously.

A more basic critique flows from this. The ambivalence in Girardian identification is that the subject seeks to become the model it admires; it must therefore violate the model to do so. But this ambivalence, when you incorporate a multiplicity of available models and variability in the possible relations of subjects to models exceeding the Girardian paradigm, might also move in a direction Girard ignores. Now the mature subject both identifies with models and becomes more ironical about destructive tendencies built into this very mode of identification. For if the subject were to assume the place of the model, one of its sources of desire would dissolve, and the element of love or admiration in this identification would be sacrificed too. This ambivalence, which Girard only figures in one direction, also opens up the subject to possible work by the self on itself. In the most far-reaching sense, it opens up the subject of desire to the possibility of maintaining and honoring the ambivalence of identification itself, by fending off the demand to become those it identifies with, doing so because it comes to recognize that the fullness it projected into others is nowhere to be realized and because what is figured from one perspective as a *lack* of fullness can also be figured as the *abundance* over identity that keeps desire moving. (Does this mean, then, there is hope for teachers in relations with current and former students?)

This juncture, indeed, is where Girard, Lacan, and, say, Levinas, as theorists of desire, meet Nietzsche, Foucault, Deleuze, Irigaray, and, sometimes, Derrida, as those who seek to overcome ressentiment in desire by working on the demand for fullness in the structure of desire.[16] For fullness, were it possible to possess, would destroy the *movement* of desire itself. This apparent condition of possibility of desire, then, is marked by the impossibility of its attainment.

Such a shift in the experience of desire might be said to be one of the aims defining the ideal of self as work of art. The idea, to put it crudely, is to move the self beyond the lack-fulfillment experience of desire toward an experience that affirms an abundance of "life" or "differance" flowing through and over identity, an abundance that enables the very movement of desire. Such an experiential shift of emphasis, crucial to a culture that seeks to draw ressentiment from desire,[17] requires a micropolitics in support of work by the self on the assumptions, relations, effects, and ends of desire. The Nietzsche/Foucault ideals of self as work of art, a self modestly working on patterns of desire already installed in it, are implicated, I think, in this drive to move the subject of desire away from ressentiment.[18] Girard does not mine these possibilities.

Fourth, while Girard typically reads the structure of desire through myths that focus on relations between individual subjects, models, and objects, the triangular structure of desire readily draws collectivities into these relations. For instance, in the contemporary

United States, as Wendy Brown shows, a (partly fictive) "middle class" serves as a model of desire through which many resentments are vented and political grievances are articulated. This can function both to displace class as an overt object of political struggle and to spawn patterns of desire that depoliticize constituencies in subordinate class positions:

> What this suggests is that identity politics may be partly configured by a peculiarly shaped and peculiarly disguised form of resentment—*class* resentment without class consciousness or class analysis. This resentment is displaced onto discourses of injustice other than class but, like all resentments, retains the real or imagined holdings of its reviled subject—in this case bourgeois male privileges—as objects of desire. From this perspective it would appear that the articulation of politicized identities through race, gender and sexuality *require,* rather than incidentally produce, a relatively limited identification through class.[19]

Thus, in contemporary America, the model of achievement and redress presumed by many whites conceals class structure as a source of grievance and presents "blacks" as a racially marked constituency whose demands foreclose otherwise viable possibilities. Correspondingly, inner-city African-American experiences of the gap between these generic accusations and the life possibilities available to many— exemplified by the enormous media attention given to the Carter case by comparison to the more frequent white on white and black on black violence—may actually push selected African-American youths toward the model of criminality attributed to them. If the "imagined holdings" of many whites occur within a political economy incapable of generalizing its animating ideal without reconstituting itself significantly, this painful combination engenders cultural misrecognition of the tragic social conflicts it generates.

The fifth limitation in the Girardian perspective can best be pursued by recalling how pervasive and invasive social interventions into the structure of desire have become in contemporary life and how often these interventions inscribe themselves upon the body. Think about the cultural installation of dietary habits, repetitive modes of training and discipline in the army, the inculcation of fear through the recurrent risk of rape and assault, the consolidation of particular modes of erotic desire through socially managed rituals of repetition, the variety of confessional therapies, the cumulative effects of repetitive performance upon habits of smoking, drinking, pitch and pace of voice, stride, demeanor, posture, eye contact, pleasures, and perception. Planned cultural interventions in these domains often misfire, as the history of discipline in modern prisons attests; but they still generate impressive effects on the structure of desire, as the high rate of recidivism among former inmates suggests. Michel Foucault points us in the right direction when he asserts in response to omissions in otherwise valuable theorizations by Derrida, Lacan, and Girard:

> It is not enough to say the subject is constituted in a symbolic system. It is not just in the play of symbols that the subject is constituted. It is constituted in real practices—historically analyzable practices. There is a technology of the constitution of the self which cuts across symbolic systems while using them.[20]

Foucault concentrates attention on how the symbolic, say, in the relation of a subject of desire to a human model or of a contrite confessor to a commanding god, is mediated by "real practices" that fix dispositional patterns of desire in the self by acting upon the body. To bring out the importance of this mysterious nexus between corporeality and symbolic systems, consider an example Foucault himself offers in another essay. Foucault presents a nineteenth-century French psychiatrist treating a mad patient. The doctor, you might say, seeks to become the new model through which the desire of the disturbed patient is organized. He ushers the patient to a shower room and orders him to recount his delirium in detail. Then the doctor orders the patient to promise him "not to believe" these things "anymore." The patient promises.

> 'That's not enough,' replies the doctor. 'You have already made similar promises, and you haven't kept them.' And the doctor turns on a cold shower above the patient's head.
>
> 'Yes, yes! I am mad!' the patient cries. The shower is turned off, and the interrogation is resumed.
>
> 'Yes, I recognize that I am mad,' the patient repeats, adding, 'I recognize, because you are forcing me to do so.' Another shower. Another confession. The interrogation is taken up again. 'I assure you, however,' says the patient, 'that I have heard voices and seen enemies around me.' Another shower.

'Well, says Mr. A, the patient, 'I admit it. I am mad; all that was madness.'[21]

An authoritative agent with coercive power, a subject under authority, the strategic repetition of orders and cold showers punctuated by the subject's obedient repetition of promises. If the contingent order of desire were constituted only through the play of the symbolic, the authoritative repetition of orders and promises and cold showers need not be brought into coordination with each other. Foucault here illustrates through condensation and exaggeration the significant interaction between authoritative agents, interrogation, corporeal inscription, and symbolic identification in the formation and reformation of desire. The therapy surely does not engender the effect the psychiatrist advertises. But it does exert real effects on its target. And it renders visible through abbreviation a larger series of intersections in the cultural formation of desire. It shows how "real practices" of corporeal inscription "cut across symbolic systems while using them." And attention to the role of institutionally mandated corporeal disciplines in the social organization of desire can also inform adult strategies of self-modification in the organization of desire. Or so Nietzsche, Foucault, and I think.

THE DESIRE OF DONTAY CARTER?

It may now be possible to reengage the desire of Dontay Carter. Such a reading is necessarily hypothetical and risky. While it is designed to dissipate the will to revenge binding together implacable judgments of racial monstrosity and criminal agency, any attempt by someone outside the subject position of the accused risks recapture by the very model that is resisted. But such a risk must be run. For, as we have seen, those in the relevant subject position (convicted criminals) are already marked by the cultural presumptions they might strive to rewrite. And those outside that position are never in a position simply to evacuate the cultural space of criminal judgment. In the domain of crime and punishment, citizens are regularly called upon to interpret and judge crime, either as judges and jurors or unofficially and significantly as newspaper readers, viewers of television talk shows, participants in neighborhood gossip, elected officials, voters, and so on. To leave things where they are is to vindicate existing codes of interpretation and judgment. There is no room for a vacuum in this territory.

Was one of Carter's early adult models, amidst the poverty and misery of everyday life, a brutalizer who had been brutalized in turn? It is possible. Some studies suggest that a majority of men on death row have been brutalized, and many have the brain damage to prove it. Any evidence in this direction would be resisted, of course. For, as recent public exposure of brutalized women who killed their male brutalizers reveals, official recognition of such a fate scrambles conventional categories for the judgment of criminal violence. Still, such a projection, while possible, is surely not necessary. If the setting of Carter's everyday life was one in which the adult experience of class and racial injustice was matched by public demonization of those who tried to rectify it politically, that might suffice to set the dynamic into motion. It is not difficult to imagine a drive to revenge against targets defined by race, gender, and class becoming burned into the desire of the young Carter.

Soon teenage models emerge to support this conversion of previous humiliations into a transcendent identity. Perhaps Carter encounters street models like those John Allen, an African-American stickup man in Washington, D.C., met in a juvenile center:

> I learned . . . it was a place where you fought almost every day because everybody trying to be tougher than the next person. As a kid you pay so much attention to how a dude's supposed to be a bad nigger. . . . So you wanna be like him, you wanna act like him and talk like him. . . . And I changed my walk from supercool to ultracool.[22]

Inspired by these models, Carter pushes to the edge stereotypes whites impose on him. He becomes amoral in public attitude, aggressive in public demeanor, and unpredictable in public behavior. He might demonstrate his elevation above the conventional traps of civility, predictability, obedience, and prudence by demanding signs of deference on the streets, or by attacking someone for no apparent reason. By becoming dangerous Carter carves out space for freedom. He transcends his condition by refusing its humiliations. The new identity acquires sovereignty over Carter through a series of *performances* in response to appearances presented by pertinent *models* in confining *circumstances* that supply those models.

But this pattern of transcendence is also a trap. Any bluff in it might be called by others on the street engaged in similar strategies. At each point in its development, then, Carter is pressed to sustain his image through dangerous action. Or to risk a new round of humiliation. If upper-class whites become the consummate enemy, then, hatred and disdain for them must be displayed through action. Carter is now under pressure to provoke the enemy already known to exist under those thin veils of civility and indifference. If the action does not up the ante of other baaad guys pursuing a similar path of transcendence, Carter may have to defer to them. And experience shows that deference is the worst trap of all: it is a step on the road to humiliation, and humiliation is more intolerable than death itself. Carter's performances escalate. Eventually, the baaad black man steals some yuppie cars, stuffs the white owners into the trunks, and shoots them.

You might think about Carter this way. His early conditions of life foster an ideal of masculine self-assertion. The conditions of school and work available to him demean that ideal, rendering him subordinate, dependent, and angry; that is, they feminize him according to the traditional coding of the masculine/feminine and they then treat this feminization as one of the insults he must endure. To rise above that trap is to become hypermasculinized, to engage in crimes of high risk, violence, and self-aggrandizement. But then to be captured, tried, and imprisoned is to be feminized again, partly by guards whose available outlets for masculine assertion are not that different from his own. The conditions of prison life, in turn, either break him or intensify this hypermasculinity. And many white men, marked by their own drives to competitive masculinity, look forward with silent glee to the long-term struggle Carter must endure. The prison as site of correction is overlaid by the prison as site of revenge.

The headline of the *Sun* report—"Carter Remains Unrepentant at Sentencing"—shows how the pattern of identity and desire reflected in Carter's crimes persists through his trial, conviction, and sentencing. But the messages that headline conveys to many "middle-class" white and black participants in the political economy of work as a career, social standing, and citizenship diverges from the one it conveys to Carter's most significant reference group. The headline shows the former that his dangerous will to criminality continues. It informs the latter that his struggle for transcendence persists against

heavy odds. Carter becomes a model to some in the latter constituency. So the beat goes on. Contending patterns of identity and
revenge across racial lines of division are reconsolidated by the same
headline.

Is any contemporary constituency prepared to appreciate the potential for tragedy built into the formation of antagonistic codes of
desire across these lines of division? To appreciate how the contingent crystallization of desire precedes any subject's ability to read its
implications and, often enough, exceeds its capacity to modify a pattern once its traps become set? Carter may come to form a constituency of one in this respect, after his conviction. For many whites
are possessed by a desire to exact revenge against Carter and his type
that is close to the rage he aims at them. This young killer, aware of
all the circumstances attending his case, fails to find his deed as ex-
traordinary and incomprehensible as his judges and censurers do; his
punishment, however, is meted out in accordance with precisely the
degree of *astonishment* the latter feel when they regard the incomprehensible nature of his deed . . .

Don't I pretend to know way too much about Carter's desire?
Yes. But in instances of crime and punishment it is important both to
construct such hypothetical readings across the lines of difference
and to become attentive to how any such interpretation organizes a
set of murky elements unsusceptible to the full transparency of
knowledge. The risk must be run because violent crime requires
judgment and because the challenge posed to dominant interpretations by this alternative eventually opens the desire of the judges of
criminality to interrogation. It must be run if sterile categories of existing legal practice are to lose their cultural appearance of purity
and impartiality. But the risk of closure in the alternative reading
must then be engaged by recalling how the flow of desire itself renders it resistant to final and authoritative readings.

What Carter was to become was never predictable with confidence at any of the innumerable junctures through which he moved.
An infinite number of events might have intervened to disrupt or
modify this path. Hence, no reliable prediction is possible on the
basis of a formal subject position. But the pattern that actually
emerges in a particular instance might become susceptible to reflective interpretation, *retrospectively*. Through retrospection we both
discern a pattern of desire and engage persisting elements of uncer-

tainty, opacity, and mystery exceeding that comprehension. Both dimensions of retrospection are pertinent to critical reassessment of the call to punish. Violent crime (and many other events too) opens up the necessity of judgment across socially inscribed boundaries; the tricky, unavoidable role of retrospection in judgment opens up room for revenge or generosity to flow into the call to punish; recognition of how these dimensions intersect in judgment reopens both the question of punishment and the etiologies of desire of those who pose the question; and all of these together open up new possibilities of modifying existing lines of division.

The value of Girard's account, once it is rendered more mobile and problematical along the five dimensions we have introduced, resides in its conviction that the labyrinths of desire involve an uncertain social process mediated by contingently available models who themselves do not know quite what they are doing. A particular pathway of desire embodies chance and contingency in its formation. Forgive them, Father (and Mother), for models and subjects do not know quite what they do. Girard accentuates this uncertainty by insisting that it is not what models say but the relation the subject establishes with what they desire that is crucial. In the age of mass media we can add that a model does not have to know you for you to know it. A subject of desire, then, does not exercise sovereignty over formation of its own economy of desire. Once formed by hook and by crook, a particular pattern of subjectification may prove to be fortunate or unfortunate, or some combination thereof. Judgments in this respect will themselves be affected by the pattern of desire from which they proceed. Finally, a pattern of desire judged by its own bearer to be unfortunate in certain respects may or may not be susceptible to modification through tactics applied by the self to the self. Variations along this latter dimension also depend upon contingencies exceeding the prior sovereignty of subjects, as we shall see when we engage the desire of those who interpret, judge, sentence, and punish the Dontay Carters of this world.

DESIRE AND PUNISHMENT

When we modify the structure Girard has imposed, as suggested already, we may be in a decent position to probe affiliations between crime against the state and criminal punishment by the state. It will be tricky, for we seek an analysis that shifts conventional orienta-

tions to crime and punishment without lending itself to a new idealization of violence on either side of this shifting and fragile boundary. Of course, any interpretation that deviates from intensely felt
conventions runs the risk of being characterized itself as a contribution to violence. But one should strive to make such accusations
unconvincing.

Is a trace of revenge discernible in the general economy of desire?
Is a diffuse spirit of vengeance burned into the general etiology of desire itself, one that might become inflamed in particular constituencies, times, and places and dispersed in others? If the magnetism of
models of desire derives in part from a fullness of being they falsely
appear to possess,[23] then the disappointment accompanying failure
to attain this fictive fullness might regularly sow a seed of resentment. And under stressful conditions of social existence this seed can
grow into a subterranean will to revenge, a drive aimed at any constituency whose way of being calls the naturalness or superiority of
your identity into question. The forms identity assumes vary significantly across time and place (and the language of "identity" fits
some cultures far better than others). And the cultural tendency to
inflate or deflate the call to revenge varies significantly too. But a
flexible predisposition to revenge might traverse these variations,
helping to account for discernible tendencies in every culture to dogmatize its own way of being. Any such speculation should be advanced with caution, as should those that assert otherwise. (A theory
of infinite cultural variation is just as universal in *its* basic projection
as one identifying diffuse tendencies flowing across those variations.)

So, for instance, the twin drives in modern America—to present
the paradigmatic individual as a free, responsible, rational agent and
to celebrate America as the paradigmatic place where such individualism thrives—might derive from the conjunction of particular accidents of American culture, a quest to present the identities sanctioned by it as full and embedded in nature, and a subterranean
reservoir of resentment against conduct that counts presumptively
against the universality, superiority, and wholeness of this cultural
paradigm. The intense cultural insistence today that everyone convicted of crime is either a responsible agent deserving punishment or
an unstable being may contain such an element of revenge in it. Perhaps many resent the accidents through which they have acquired
form. Or insist upon taking full credit themselves for the apparent

correspondence between what they are and the norms of the order. Or both.

The dominant model of responsible agency has never been proven to correspond intrinsically to those human beings constituted and judged through it. It receives its most powerful contemporary redemption, rather, through cultural *insistence* that everyone must correspond to one or another of the categorical pair reiterated endlessly in canonical texts, court decisions, everyday gossip, cop and robber programs, trial films, talk shows, and newspaper reports. And it receives supplementary support from a fallback position advanced by many in the cultural elite, namely: *these categories must be assumed to be true even if we lack the ability to prove them so.*[24] This supplement is particularly revealing. It balances admission of the hypothetical status of bedrock categories against the insistence that preservation of civilization itself demands refusal to cast these hypotheticals into doubt. The price of disturbing this hypothetical imperative now becomes the loss of "our common humanity" itself. Such a fallback defense implicitly concedes that, when the pressure is on, the intrinsic justice of operational categories of responsibility and punishment is not the most fundamental issue. The formula politely conveys a general cultural disposition to sacrifice socially defined others to protect the appearance of integrity and cleanliness in the messy cultural categories of agency and responsibility. Save the categories; waste those whose conduct or subject positions disturb them.

This identification of a subterranean current of sacrifice running through contemporary life parallels the charge Girard issues against "traditional" cultures of overt sacrifice. In the contemporary case, cultural policing of categorical lines between the responsible agent, the irresponsible offender, and the unresponsible delinquent conceals a subterranean pattern of desire flowing across these boundaries. A lot of cops resemble a lot of criminals who resemble a considerable number of politicians who resemble a fair number of judges; and many among us who do not kill on the streets, beat up losers on the beat, rape prison inmates, celebrate state terrorism, or demand prison sentences without parole reflect a subtle and durable refusal to examine the role of revenge in established codes of desire and responsibility. We remain resolutely silent about legal violence, about the sacrifice of entire constituencies to stabilize uncertain cultural practices through which we receive protection, dignity, and transcendence.

Does this reading of uncertainty, duplicity, and revenge in the order of desire drive its own thesis into a corner from which there is no escape? Must it not, for instance, presuppose the very model of responsibility it interrogates if there is any hope to respond to the conditions delineated? Or does the analysis project so much into the structure of desire that it undermines any chance to modify it? Or does it forfeit contact with any political constituency powerful enough to respond to the condition it delineates? It runs all these risks and others besides, including the most familiar one in academic life in which a critical interrogation of cultural categories is translated into airtight traps by others to restore the appearance of necessity and stability to the practices interrogated. But such ambiguities, binds, and risks are built into the culture from which this account proceeds. In the current setting, any analysis that refuses such risks should be treated with suspicion: it almost certainly conceals the dirt and sacrifice built into the culture it celebrates. Attempts to loosen, stretch, and modify these cultural binds invariably risk becoming captured by them. In what follows I try to identify one or two ways to loosen these binds.

THE MICROPOLITICS OF DESIRE

The reading of desire presented here asserts that we are not sovereign agents who will the codes of desire that circulates through us, even though we do possess variable abilities to move or modify particular patterns of desire by tactical means. Such an acknowledgment constitutes a major virtue of this perspective. Its major delinquency, in turn, is that it thereby sacrifices the cultural appearance of clean and coherent categories through which to judge, convict, sentence, and detain those who rob, rape, kill, and terrorize others. The perspective acknowledges a need to take protective action without pretending to secure equivalence between the case for protection from violence and the desert of those you are protected from. It suspects that every attempt to secure equivalence in this domain conceals a secondary element of injustice in its formula of justice. This critical perspective, then, sacrifices the appearance of equivalence to work on the call to revenge within the desire to punish.

Moreover, while the critical perspective endorses political action to remedy large, institutional sources of crime—at a minimum, to overcome poverty in a culture where affluence is celebrated while poverty is racialized and urbanized, to generate decent jobs for those stuck at the bottom of the political economy of work, to offer reasonable education to all classes—it is unable to promise that crimes of violence would disappear even if these goals were accomplished. The etiology of desire is too uncertain, too delicate, and, particularly, too far beyond the crude capacities of general state or corporate action for such a promise to carry credibility. This approach to crime and punishment breaks with two different types of utopian promise often projected into the retributive and utilitarian models of punishment respectively. The first implies that punishment would become perfectly just under ideal practices of self-responsibility; the second that crime would disappear if a sufficient set of social reforms were enacted. The way in which these two contending promises wash clean the hands of those who advance them goes some distance toward explaining why the academic debate about crime oscillates between these two perspectives. Such promises cannot be issued here. Even if a reasonable ideal of critical pluralism were actualized, there would still be violent crime; and the practices through which people were protected against crime would still retain elements of injustice in them.[25] The hope is that these practices would be less unjust than those in operation now and more resistant to the flow of revenge into criminal judgment and prisoner confinement.

Let us bypass here two traditional questions, "What might be done to rehabilitate violent criminals, given the etiology of criminal desire?" and "How might the social conditions from which crime emanates be transformed?" in order to open up a neglected question implicit in both: "What might be done, first through micropolitics, to both honor desire and to resist the flow of revenge into judgments of criminality by a significant number of people defined to be normal, responsible, uncriminal, and decent, that is, judges, juries, politicians, and citizens?"[26] Responding to this third question is a preliminary to redefinition of the first two. For, as I have urged, the call to revenge is not only discernible in violent criminality it is also discernible in culturally congealed identities through which normality is defined, responsible agency is constituted, and criminality is punished.

To proceed on this front, consider another example of cultural change, now precariously installed in a few sectors of contemporary life. Consider recent changes in cultural responses to "homosexuality." The two situations are different, first because heterodox sexuality is not involved in crimes of violence; second because a gay/lesbian movement now advances its case with skillful organization, political fervor, and tactical intelligence, while there is no comparable movement in the domain of criminality; and third because the politics of sexuality crosses the fault lines of race, gender, and class while the theatrical politics of crime and punishment conforms more closely to them. But the two are also comparable along some dimensions, in that "sodomy" is criminalized in many states; in that gays have remained under powerful cultural imperatives either to stay in the closet or to face penalties in housing, employment, and education for stepping out; in that recognition of contingency in homosexual desire immediately opens up the question of contingency in heterosexual desire; and in that punitive responses by many straights to gay demands for parity of sexual freedom express a spirit of revenge against heterodox sexualities that disturb the experience of naturalness or normality in straight desire.

How, in the context of the gay/lesbian movement, is the spirit of revenge sometimes drained from the structure of straight desire? Several factors seem to converge here. There are historical genealogies of desire and agency that call into question the certainty, naturalness, and normality of dominant codes of sexual desire, supporting the case that both gay and straight desire are contingently en-gendered. Such genealogies place gays and straights on the same plane of desire, even as they may find themselves projecting different objects of desire. This division in the object of desire begins to feel less fundamental as a whole series of other contingent differences that flow across this line are identified: differences in intensities of desire, in the relation of sensuality to affection, in the role of imagination in sexual stimulation, in the degrees to which these variable objects, intensities, relations, and imaginations are entrenched in specific codes of desire, and so on, and on, endlessly.

Genealogies of sexual desire scramble and compromise hierarchical divisions previously taken to be fundamental and cumulative. These effects can thaw out the frozen codes of those who engage them. These micropolitical effects operate in tandem with political movements that initiate reforms in marriage, family, housing, military, legal, and occupational practices.

Through such engagements a variety of straight constituencies may respond favorably to the claim for parity, while others, encountering internal resistance to these claims, may identify fragments of critical subjectivity in themselves to deploy in working upon entrenched presumptions and blockages in this domain. Perhaps an ambivalent ally loves a son who is gay, another respects gay friends who demand the right to a sexuality untainted by the medicalization of "homosexuality," another feels tremors of gender ambiguity in himself or herself, and so on. While the catalyzing power of the gay/lesbian movement is crucial, the cultivation of responsiveness among others is also pertinent to the shape and efficacy of that movement.

Once the desire to modify an entrenched code becomes operative, further responsiveness to claims of the other can be cultivated by a variety of tactics: by watching films in which ambiguous figures uncover latent ambiguities in sensual desire; by "little deviant acts," to quote Nietzsche, involving participation in gay rights marches or wearing gay/lesbian insignia at strategic events; by breaking the code of straight silence in this domain through speech and writings; and by experimental enactment of new, uncertain understandings until they become more effectively articulated and more solidly entrenched in the feelings.

The possibilities here are numerous. By such experimental tactics, you reengage some of the performances through which your established code was engendered. But now you do so in a different key and to a different end. You thereby become, as Judith Butler has shown, more alert to the performative element always already operative in identity and desire, enhancing your ability to experiment further with the effectivity of performance in the cultivation of feeling and desire.[27]

Such microgovernment of the self through experimental performance contributes to change in cultural codes of identity and desire, even though its reach is variable and its effects never certain.[28] This micropolitics of action on the self is always already operative anyway below the threshold of self-attentiveness, if the etiology of desire presented in this essay and, particularly, the Foucauldian emphasis on the intersection between symbolic practices and corporeal disciplines, is on the right track—only in the first set of instances the self is the object of institutional/symbolic systems working upon it.

When the self makes itself an explicit site of micropolitics, it becomes a domain to be worked on cautiously and experimentally *by* the self, in response to the identifications and performances through which it has acquired its current shape. By working patiently on specific contingencies in oneself, one may become more appreciative of the crucial role of contingency in identity and desire. And this in turn opens up new possibilities of ethical responsiveness to difference.[29]

One might, by these means, begin to subdue subterranean resentment of the absence of wholeness in what one is, treating the absence as a source of possibility for experimental enactment. One might, thereby, drain off some of the ressentiment that so readily inhabits desire, rendering one more responsive to differences through which one's own desires congeal. One might come to appreciate creative possibilities that the contingency of being opens up, even while refusing to replace one's previous presumption of *intrinsic* identity with another asserting one's consummate ability to *choose* what one is. For these two models of the intrinsic self and the self-chosen self form two disparate paths through which punitive practices of desire, agency, and responsibility have historically been legitimized.[30]

The Nietzschean/Foucauldian conception of the self as a contingent formation modestly open to further strategies of craftmanship authorizes the practice of self as "work of art." Here the mature self works experimentally and cautiously upon itself and the relationships through which it is constituted. It patiently applies tactics to itself to modify itself, prying open thereby some creative distance between itself and the institutional disciplines of normalization. Some of these tactics are explicit and conscious. When they do their work they may render the self more available for additional work that exceeds the reach of the intentional technology. Your dreams change. Your feelings acquire new valences. Your sensibility becomes modified in unexpected ways. You then reappraise what is happening from the vantage point of the aspirations that launched the effort, and you reconsider those aspirations from the vantage point of these shifts in sensibility.

Eventually, it may become possible to work through these arts of the self (these "real practices" applied by the self to itself) to recover a modified conception of the responsible self, a self that draws upon fragments of its contingent subjectivity to work patiently and cautiously upon those elements in its code of identity, desire, and judgment that are ugly, vengeful, or otherwise less admirable than they might be. A self that works on itself to develop critical responsiveness to that which it is not, to cultivate critical responsiveness to those identities whose very mode of formation may tap into differences within it regulates to be what it is. The ideal of self as work of art is not a recipe of narcissistic individualism; it is a formula of self-ethicization through a mode of individualization that works against vengeful, narcissistic demands to atomize or transcendentalize what you have become relationally and contingently. And this work upon the self can also become translated into work upon larger constituencies through interventions into television talk shows, programming of cop shows, everyday gossip, letters to the editor, and computer networks.

This preliminary focus on cultivating responsiveness to culturally heterodox sexualities enables us to turn to the issue of responsiveness in the domain of criminal punishment. For here, responsiveness is the key: there is today no legitimate constituency of convicts and parolees able to spearhead a positive political movement in this domain.

Do you find brutal acts by violent criminals to be senseless and horrendous? Surely the latter judgment is sound, even while the former is highly questionable. But to say such acts are horrendous is neither to vindicate the attribution of sovereign agency to violent criminals nor to show that they conform to the delinquent double of the responsible agent. For this framing of options invests the category of responsible agency with a coherence that has only been vindicated through cultural concealment of a variety of incoherences circulating through it. Perhaps another route is possible when we consult an etiology of desire crossing and scrambling this duality. In the light of this etiology, it may be possible to move through the everyday experience of paltry, imperious desires in oneself to recognition of their more dramatic embodiment in violent criminality.

Surely, even within a privileged subject position, you experience recurrently a burning desire to stare at passing figures who reflect your current ideal of sensuality, or to exhibit yourself to strangers, or to conform meekly to arbitrary authority, or to rage against authority figures of the opposite sex, or to insist upon the last word in each argument, or to steal trinkets for the sheer thrill of it, or to translate your most intense interests into transcendental principles you purport to obey. Or, perhaps, all of the above. Surely, paltry little sovereignties in your particular code of desire reveal a link between its relatively fortunate etiology and more violent sensualities in some others located in both similar and different subject positions. The refusal to walk across this bridge may reflect an implacable desire for revenge against the violent other. *And that latter desire itself might eventually come to be received as evidence that your contingent code does indeed contain imperious desires within it.* Sometimes such an imperious desire attains sovereignty over the self, remaining unamenable to micropolitics. At others, it falls within the reach of such tactics. In *these* two respects, then, does your code of desire not parallel a corollary set of variabilities in the etiology of criminal violence?

To the degree the etiology of desire outlined here speaks to the potential imperiousness of violent desire, it also speaks to the violent inflation of responsibility in the contemporary identification and punishment of crime. And as it draws attention to this inflation, it supports efforts to disperse the call to revenge installed in established practices of legal justice. Endorsement of this etiology of desire (or some cousin of it) supports the case for the conventional, legitimate self to work both on its own code in this domain and on the codes of those constituencies to whom it is closely bound by ties of identification and interest. Such a micropolitics of desire forms an essential element in any attempt to politicize more actively and generally the role of revenge in the domain of punishment. We are already working modestly on this register when we explore the elements of social structure, chance, opacity, and tragic possibility in the etiology of desire. Such work, ironically perhaps, calls upon us to subdue the desire to theorize desire too deeply, totally, or completely.

Dontay Carter's crime astonished me. It inspired fear and a guttural will to vengeance in me when his case hit the media. Part of me became implacable. It wanted the streets of Baltimore cleared of monsters. It wanted *security* for citizens like me to drive, park, and move as we please. And it wanted cultural categories of agency and responsibility to *vindicate* these desires. It wanted, that is, its drive to revenge to feel clean, righteous, and unencumbered. Another part of my subjectivity (for the self is a complex social structure) sought to combat the perspective engendered by this nexus of astonishment, fear, righteousness, and implacable judgment. This part encouraged me to ponder how easy it is to disencumber the self by closing up a problematical set of cultural categories and judgments. That re-

sponse in turn prompted me to consider the effects vengeful codes of
desire exert upon culturally sanctioned categories of agency, responsibility, and punishment.

I continue to prize my security and mobility. But now a larger
part of me thinks and (sometimes more precariously) *feels* that
Carter should be imprisoned only to protect others from the fate suffered by his victims, and only as long as the probability is high that
he will repeat such acts in the future. I am once again appalled by the
regime of prison life that awaits offenders like Carter and ashamed
of my implication in a culture that endorses or tolerates such practices. Though the victims suffered an outrageous fate they did not
deserve, and though others deserve to be protected from any intractable drive to revenge that continues to inhabit Carter, he by no
means deserves the layer upon layer of revenge visited upon him by
contemporary juridical/penal practices. And he certainly deserves
new opportunities to translate into alternative channels a desire to
take revenge against a fate he did not deserve. Perhaps Dontay
Carter, given a chance or two, might become a leader of prison reform or urban renewal in the country that engendered, defined, and
confined him. His statement to the court in his self-defense showed
promise in this respect.

There is no cosmic guarantee that a just feeling of outrage can
be brought into intrinsic correspondence with a just amount of
punishment. The implicit demand that "there must be" such correspondence secretly projects a call to revenge into the desire to punish and the desire to punish into culturally selected judgments of responsible agency. This demand for "correspondence" may even
contain traces of resentment against the world for failure to provide equivalence between an authentic intensity of feeling and an
intrinsic order of desert. And though it is difficult to punish the
world, it is easy to locate classes of human beings as substitutes.
The pattern of substitution follows familiar cultural paths once
racial/class channels, dug partly by the history of just such feelings,
have become entrenched.

Such considerations might grip your feelings as you move *from*
the experience of paltry, imperious desires in your (say, white, male,
"middle"-class) self, *through* reflection upon the contingent installation of imperious desires in agents of violence marked by differences
of class and race, *to* work upon the covert element of violent revenge

in your normal response to criminal violence, *toward* reconsiderations of established models of responsibility and social causality through which racial violence is conventionally engaged. As such practices proceed, it becomes more possible to reconsider the confidence of judicial judgments; the length of prison sentences; the provision of opportunities for inmates to experience love, sex, education, work, and income during detention; the introduction of reasonable possibilities for release; and reconfiguration of the appropriate levels of risk to be accepted by those with relatively lucky subject positions or etiologies of desire or both.

These considerations, in turn, prepare the way for more active macropoliticizations of criminal punishment and class/race relations. For it is abundantly clear that reforms in established practices of criminal judgment, sentencing, and punishment cannot advance far unless whites and blacks stuck at lower levels of the race/class system outside prison gates are provided greater opportunities in education and employment. As long as life for many outside the gate is too close for comfort to life inside it, right-wing mobilizers of cultural revenge through the state can refer to the condition of the white working class to inflame resentment against urban blacks and to the ideology of middle-class agency to forestall improvements in the condition of the white working class. In other words, they can invoke twice the same fantastic model of responsible agency to divide constituencies that would have to coalesce if class/race inequality and legal punishment were to be reconstituted together.

These two imperatives—to reconfigure the cultural desire to punish and to improve opportunities outside prison gates for a reasonable life—presuppose each other. But today productive work on each imperative is blocked by the same code of desire. That is to say, today the micropolitics of desire in the domain of criminal violence has become a *condition* for a macropolitics that reconfigures existing relations between class, race, crime, and punishment. It is too late in the day to say that work on the first front must await success on the second. For while the left waits for the pivotal macropolitical moment to arrive, the right (now too large to be called a "wing") retains its hold over the most influential media of micropolitics.

Exploration of the opaque etiology of desire in the domains of class, race, and crime opens up interrogation of the desire to punish. Mysteries and opacities in the cultural etiology of desire ensure that we will never grasp fully the desire of the other. Nor, to make the same point another way, fully come to terms with the place of the other in our own desires. This result increases, rather than relieves, the claims of difference upon the self. For desire, a most beautiful thing, would stop dead in its tracks if the element of difference in it disappeared. The question persists: How do so many whites remain so aggressively righteous about juridical practices of legal violence against a growing warehouse of young, racialized convicts disenfranchised from speaking on their own behalf?

3

Democracy, Equality, Normality

MODELS OF DEMOCRACY

C. B. Macpherson, a Marxist political theorist, was a democrat and a visionary, with each of these terms conditioning the other. His contributions to democratic theory, written mostly between 1966 and 1977, provide an opportunity for self-reflection and critical renewal for those who were his students and colleagues. In reviewing Macpherson's writings, I also gain the opportunity to reconsider my own thinking during the decade of the New Left. I was fortunate enough to participate in a six-week colloquium in Irvine, California, in 1969 where Brough Macpherson and Arnold Kaufman—the author of *The Radical Liberal*[1]—presented seminars on democratic theory, often arguing against George Will and Joseph Tussman, who also were active in these seminars.

I was aligned with Macpherson and Kaufman during the Irvine conference. I confess (if that is the right word) that the three of us met a few times to chart out strategy for the next day's debates, with Tussman and Will providing our favorite debating partners. We took pleasure in these exchanges, partly because these guys were squirming under the pressure of life during the late sixties and partly because we were confident that the track of the democratic left was preferable to the utopian realism they peddled. I wouldn't mind seeing Tussman and Will—or their functional equivalents—squirm again: Tussman in defense of his insistence that a conservative community is the necessary condition of democratic politics, and Will in defense of his insistence upon linking unfettered market competition to a restrictive vision of cultural diversity. That little surge of anticipatory revenge, however unlikely it is to be realized, reminds me how indebted my thinking remains to the critical spirit of Kaufman (who died in a plane crash two years later) and Macpherson, even though I now disagree in some ways with the *form* the idealism of each assumes.

Macpherson's explorations of the democratic ideal occurred in the context of several debates that have now been displaced. The pluralist-elitist debate, the role of apathy in supporting or undermining democracy, the idea of power as the intentional exercise of constraint over others or the structural production of limitations, the clash between participatory and representationist ideals of democracy, the relation between economic equality and democratic citizenship, the comparative superiority of capitalism or socialism, the world role of the United States as either imperial power or defender of the free world, the relation of "facts" to "values" in political inquiry, the comparative value of behavioralism and interpretation in political inquiry, the relationship between Marxist and liberal theory—these issues crossed and crisscrossed, so that a political theorist concerned with one eventually would be compelled to engage most of the others.

The pluralist-elitist debate became translated into the liberal-communitarian debate in the late seventies, and the latter then moved from a debate within political theory to one that infiltrated empirical programs of research. Broadly associated with this shift is a transition to questions about the primacy of justice (or rights) over the good, the relation of hermeneutics to models of rationality, the extent to which genealogy exposes hidden affinities between interpretation/hermeneutics and universal codes of rationality, the decline of the American empire, the deflation of socialist idealism, the attenuation of democratic idealism, the role of post-Nietzschean thought in political theory, the danger of nihilism, and the insufficiency of the sovereignty problematic to the late-modern condition.

It is easy to discern continuities flowing through these discontinuities. More significantly, perhaps, it is possible to discern losses submerged within these shifts in the terms of political discourse. For Macpherson, whose thought is defined within the first set of issues, linked his democratic concerns about apathy, participation, freedom, and self-realization to questions about the structure and performance of a capitalist political economy. More specifically, he persistently pursued the essential connection between political democracy and economic equality. This latter issue has not disappeared in the new debates, but it has receded markedly, as debates between communitarians and liberals over the ideals of individual rights and collective allegiance surpass the ability of either to specify the mode of political economy that best protects and nourishes its vision of the good life. The recent decline of socialist idealism in the West, though, may ironically engender a corollary return to criticism of capitalist idealism. Certainly the latter is needed in the aftermath of Reaganism and Thatcherism. And Macpherson would help to identify the pertinent issues, were he writing today.

These shifts in the dominant terms of academic discourse correlate with a certain displacement of "democracy" itself from the center of theoretical controversy. There are many democrats in theory but fewer theorists who organize their thinking around a vision of democracy appropriate to late-modern states at the end of the twentieth century. We need Macpherson today.

Macpherson's critical analysis of four "models" of democracy places class relations at the center of attention. For each of the first three models, presented roughly in order of their chronological appearance in the modern West, is defined by the problematic relation it bears to class inequality in capitalism. "Protective democracy," formulated by Jeremy Bentham and James Mill, presupposed the hegemony of a market economy; it sought regular elections to advance market interests and to protect against the tyranny of the state within this setting. Its problem was to "produce governments which would establish . . . a free market society and protect citizens from rapacious governments."[2] It thereby sought to regulate and restrain interests already established in civil society rather than to become a "morally transforming force."[3] Its acceptance of class inequality inclined it toward a series of exclusions from effective citizenship and restrictions in the rights of those granted citizenship, but its commitment to democracy required it to equivocate with respect to these restrictions. Macpherson quotes James Mill to illustrate this "seesaw": "the business of government is properly the business of the rich. [We have finally enacted that ideal in the United States.] . . . If they obtain it by bad means, the government is bad. If they obtain it by good means, the government is sure to be good. The only good means of obtaining it are the free suffrage of the people."[4]

"Developmental democracy" represents a notable advance in democratic idealism; its best representatives were John Stuart Mill and T. H. Green. The key problem was to elevate working-class men into "rational beings" because they "can no longer be governed or treated like children."[5] In the Millian conception, the "model of man" as a possessive individualist (that is, as "conflicting, self-interested consumer and appropriator") is compromised by the conception of "man" as "a being capable of developing his powers or capacities."[6] And now democratic participation becomes the central route to the development of responsible citizens and fulfilled selves. Mill was confounded, in Macpherson's reading, by the deep incompatability between "the claims of equal human development and the existing class inequalities of power."[7] He did not develop an effective strategy for coping with this "problem," treating it as a temporary residue from the past rather than a necessary effect of capitalist organization:

> Mill had seen the contradiction between his developmental ideal and the class-divided and exploitive society of his own time. [But] he did not see that it was a contradiction between capitalist relations of production as such and the developmental ideal.[8]

Those following Mill in this tradition, including John Dewey, Robert MacIver, and John Findlay, saw the structural contradiction less clearly than Mill did. Moreover, unlike him, they thought the perfection of democratic education could reduce the contradiction to workable terms.

"Equilibrium democracy," otherwise known as pluralist democracy, was enunciated by Joseph Schumpeter in 1942 and elaborated by a constellation of American political scientists, mostly from Yale University, in the 1950s and early 1960s. It enhances the "realism" of democratic theory by resubmerging its developmental dimension. That is, it reifies the political effects of capitalist economic life by representing them as the universal order of life. Such a realism, situated ambiguously between a description of actual arrangements and the idealization of settled modes of democratic representation as the best form of governance available to modern life, depreciates the value of participation and celebrates the functional importance of "apathy." Apathy among the majority of citizens now becomes functional to democracy. For intensive participation is inefficient to rational individuals. It also activates antidemocratic authoritarianism in the masses. And it overloads the political system with demands it cannot meet. The equilibrium model, according to Macpherson, sinks participation under three waves: first, by treating democracy as the institutional means to register "the desires of people as they are" rather than a process that contributes "to what they might be or wish to be";[9] second, by condensing the desires and interests of citizens into the vocabulary of possessive individualism; third, by legitimizing elitist barriers against popular pressures and demands that exceed the capacity of the state to respond to them.

Democracy now becomes a vehicle for rationalizing and legitimizing the limited capacity of the state to represent citizens within the existing class structure. Realism conceals these historically specific restraints through a language that universalizes them. Macpherson, chiming in with other critics of pluralist theory in his choice of a contemporary exemplar of the equilibrium model, quotes Robert Dahl to seal his case:

> If the democratic system depended solely on the qualifications of the individual voter, then it seems remarkable that democracy has survived through the centuries. . . . But when one considers the data in a broader perspective—how huge sections of the society adapt to political conditions affecting them or how the political system adjusts itself to changing conditions over long periods of time—he cannot fail to be impressed. . . . Where the rational citizen seems to abdicate, nevertheless angels seem to tread.[10]

These angels tread heavily on democratic ideals of equality and development, according to Macpherson: "the equilibrium it produces is an equilibrium in inequality; the consumer sovereignty it claims is to a large extent an illusion."[11] Social inequality engenders political apathy; it is an apathy of resignation and hostility among excluded members rather than one reflecting a rational allocation of time among contented participants. The equilibrium model protects against tyranny, but it provides little support for developmental democracy.

Macpherson then endorses "participatory democracy," though

neither with the unfettered enthusiasm displayed by many of its supporters during the sixties nor with great confidence that it can be installed in Western capitalist states. The problem is that structural
changes in the political economy are needed to transcend class inequality, and the transcendence of class inequality is required to enable participatory democracy. Macpherson inscribes his own version
of Rousseau's paradox of politics into the center of modern democracy when he says:

> We cannot achieve more democratic participation without a prior
> change in social inequality and in consciousness but we cannot
> achieve the changes in social inequality and consciousness without a
> prior increase in democratic participation.[12]

Macpherson finds it difficult to envisage an institutionalization of
participation that reaches the level of issues fundamentally relevant
to the welfare of an entire modern state. He thus reluctantly endorses representative institutions, holding out some hope that they
may wither under the weight of participatory practices in the future.

I hope this brief summary brings out connections between the development of deliberative capacities and the conquest of class inequality in Macpherson's delineation of "models of democracy." I
want now to think further about these two standards.

DEMOCRACY AND EQUALITY

A significant reduction in economic inequality is surely crucial to a
robust democracy. But such a project must be pursued in ways that
do not undermine either existing cultural pluralism or future possibilities of democratic pluralization: equality must be viewed not simply as an end in itself but also as a condition of democratic pluralization. If these conditions are granted, it is probably neither necessary
nor feasible to remain as attached to command economies as
Macpherson tended to be. If managed markets are included as
means of organizing capital, determining production and organizing
work, a compromise in the pursuit of economic equality may also be
unavoidable. It seems to me that the standard of equality demanded
by democracy now becomes both a little less stringent than that intimated by Macpherson and significantly more demanding than that
acknowledged by most contemporary liberal, realist, and communitarian theories of democracy.

If the appropriate standard is one in which every citizen receives sufficient opportunity for work, income, education, and security to enable effective participation in the cultural economy, then the goal of economic equality becomes the still difficult objective of lifting the floor below which no citizens are allowed to fall. If one adds, as I would, the even more controversial condition that no class receive so much income that it automatically manufactures collectively destructive private escapes from public failures in ecology, personal security, public transportation, civil peace, and public education, then the objective becomes more difficult yet to approach. But, properly conceived, it is still not so demanding that its pursuit requires sacrifice of the essential virtues of openness, cultural variety, and future pluralization.

Two goals, then: first, to establish a floor below which no one is compelled to fall, because such a floor enables anyone and everyone to participate in the common life *if* he or she is inclined to do so; second, to establish a glass ceiling that is difficult to break through. Such a ceiling would impede economically privileged minorities from constructing costly private escapes from the general conditions of education, crime, military service, and the environment, and it would encourage formation of political coalitions to forge affirmative public responses to the collective damage and suffering engendered by the history of private escapes. For when private escapes to pressing collective issues are too readily available to privileged minorities, they build up structures of compensatory consumption that intensify the collective losses from which they escape, and they set up powerful political barriers to attempts to respond publicly to these issues in the future. This can be discerned today, in the United States and elsewhere, in the domains of transportation, education, military service, medical care, the environment, and suburbanization. In each of these instances a large portion of tax dollars provides infrastructural support for services that effectively exclude large constellations of people from using them; and this use impairs public support for more inclusive systems of education, health care, military service, housing, personal security, and transportation. People who have struggled to finance (often eventually futile) private escapes from collective problems are extremely wary of paying higher taxes to respond to the collective issues they have (temporarily) left behind.

A democratic politics is one in which the terms of public representation respond to fundamental issues impinging upon the common life as such, and in which contemporary responses to such issues sustain the prerequisites of democratic citizenship into the future. So Macpherson is not the only one who faces a version of Rousseau's paradox. My translation of it into the relation between economic life and political representation is this: economic equalization is a prerequisite to effective democracy, but effective democracy is also a prerequisite to equalization. Each must be fostered for the other to occur; but, as things stand, neither provides an adequate condition for the other.

How could a late-modern democracy institutionalize equalization, *after* many of its members translated the realist's ahistorical representation of fixed institutional constraints into the language of historically specific institutional binds? It seems to me that the best prospect would be to combine a steep progressive tax, including luxury taxes for those commodities whose use imposes heavy collective costs, with active state support for modes of consumption that are inclusive rather than exclusionary in form.[13] It would probably be necessary to move on both of these fronts if either were to advance very far. The institutionalization of inclusive modes of consumption could increase support for a more progressive tax system, for this dividend would now be recognized by more constituencies to be spent on programs that support their interests.

An exclusionary item of consumption is one whose generalization (a) decreases the private value of the good to those who already have it, (b) increases the private costs of its use as it is extended, (c) accentuates the adverse social effects (and costs) of its use, (d) increases (directly or indirectly) the costs borne by the state in subsidizing this good or rectifying the adverse effects of its use.

Few staples of consumption fit all these criteria perfectly, though many come close: a transportation system built around public highways and private cars, a housing system centered around single-family suburban units, a high-technology medical system built around doctors' private fees and a private health insurance system. When the social infrastructure of consumption (for example, enabling laws, tax subsidies, governmental grants, architectural design, materials of construction, governmental highway programs, the organization of medical research) is built around the generalization of exclusionary goods, it becomes increasingly difficult for even middle-class households to make ends meet while participating in the socially available forms of transportation, housing, insurance, education, medical care, and security. Such a system of production and consumption presses the state either to increase subsidies for those at the lower end of the income scale while alienating middle-class taxpayers already squeezed by the imperatives of consumption facing them *or* to expand punitive policies against constituencies already marginalized by the regular operation of the economy. The American political culture has opted for the second priority in recent decades.

The American political economy is built around the illusory promise of universalizing exclusionary goods. As it becomes increasingly clear to a variety of constituencies that they are losing ground in this elusive quest, they either drop out of institutional politics or vent their anger on the most vulnerable scapegoats available. An economy built around the elusive promise to generalize exclusionary goods eventually turns against the promise of pluralism, as many caught in the binds it creates respond by identifying with restrictive visions of family life, sexual practice, gender authority, race relations, consumption practices, and norms of self-sufficiency rooted in rosy memories of the past.

An inclusive good reverses these pressures. It is susceptible to generalization because its private value increases as it is extended; because its unit social costs are reduced through extension; because state supports for its development and extension reduce the per capita public costs of meeting consumption needs in its domain; and because it curtails *economic* sources of the politics of revenge against vulnerable constituencies.

A couple of examples must suffice here. If the sizable state subsidies for health care in the United States were shifted from private insurance programs to enabling legislation and subsidies for the universalization of health maintenance organizations, the inflationary and exclusionary effects of the present medical system could be curtailed. As successful experiments with such programs showed (before they were crunched in the States during the Reagan years), the system of salaries for physicians, preventive health care, enhanced patient involvement in prevention and self-care, reduced rates of surgery, and incentives within health care units to reduce high-technology expenditures while protecting patients from serious and expensive diseases fosters general health care, cost reduction, local control, and client self-reliance.[14] Similarly, if public funds were poured into development of rapid transit systems within and between high-density urban areas, these investments would both help to forestall the decline of urban areas and enable poor and lower-income residents clustered in those centers to participate in the transportation system. The combination of the automobile, the highway system, high per-unit energy costs, high auto insurance rates, and public subsidies for all four currently close many out of participation in this crucial dimension of social life. These examples could be multiplied in many areas of consumption. If changes were instituted by a combination of state mandates, infrastructural supports, and subsidies, they would affect the forms and materials of production as well as the dominant modes of consumption. They would not necessitate a reduction of diversity in ethnicity, religion, irreligion, gender practices, sexuality, and so on. This pattern of economic equalization fosters a culture of pluralism and pluralization. Changes in state policies to foster more inclusive patterns of consumption would thus mitigate the objection that has plagued egalitarian democrats in the past: that every egalitarian program necessarily fosters social uniformity.

One additional effect might also be noted. The goal of perpetual economic growth in pursuit of private affluence has become one of the overriding objectives of late-modern capitalist political economies. But this economic objective increasingly runs into conflict with the practice of constitutional democracy to which it has been joined historically. New forms of discipline, regulation, and surveillance are introduced to promote economic growth under difficult conditions of realization and to control or neutralize those populations excluded from its benefits. These interventions threaten to erode both democratic citizenship and cultural variety. If the end of growth has now become a structural imperative of the civilization of productivity while the generalization of private affluence has receded as a credible promise for many, democratic programs to reconstitute the infrastructure of consumption could help to reconstitute the growth imperative itself, translating it into state policies to generalize *inclusive* goods.

On this reading, then, it is possible both to foster economic growth and to catch a large number of households in economic binds. But such a combination is deadly for the prospects of a pluralizing democracy. It is deadly because it closes out whole classes of people from effective participation in the general economic life, because it propels some in these latter positions to violence, and because virulent responses to these latter threats by vulnerable members of the middle class threaten to convert the democratic state into a mechanism for punishment and internment of its most disaffected elements. The recent emergence of "gated communities" in Los Angeles and other urban areas, the proposal in the rich town of Palo Alto, California, to build a wall separating it from its poor, ethnic neighbor, East Palo Alto, and the readiness of a majority of white middle-class Americans to increase state expenditures for prisons while curtailing them for welfare and education are three examples of how such a negative dialectic advances.

I believe this perspective on the economic conditions of democratic politics has something in common with the spirit of Macpherson, even though there are significant differences between us over how that spirit is to be expressed, balanced, and activated. I also concur that the perspective advanced here merely initiates the task of rethinking the relation between economic reform and cultural diversity in contemporary life.

DEMOCRACY AND NORMALIZATION

Things become more complicated in considering the linkage Macpherson identifies between democracy and the realization of human powers or capacities. Macpherson distinguishes between extractive power and developmental power. Extractive power involves the ability to command benefits for oneself from the labor or actions of others, usually by controlling resources they need. Developmental power is the ability to realize and "exercise human capacities." The former divides people, while the latter generally unites them, once each accepts the principle that the development of one person must not occur at the expense or exploitation of another. Let Macpherson speak in his own voice about developmental power:

> But this leaves open the question, what are these human capacities? . . . [They] include the capacity for rational understanding, for moral judgment and action, for aesthetic creation or contemplation, for the emotional activities of friendship and love, and, sometimes, for religious experience.[15]

How are these capacities to relate to one another within each self and between a variety of constituencies in a democratic society?:

> The further assumption which is at first sight a staggering one, is that the exercise of his human capacities by each member of a society does not prevent other members exercising theirs: that the essentially human capacities must all be used and developed without hindering the use and development of all the rest. . . .
>
> Now to describe as essential human characteristics only those ones which are not *destructively contentious* is of course to take a fundamentally optimistic view. That view has been at the root of the democratic vision, and indeed of the liberal vision. . . . That men if *freed from scarcity* and from *intellectual error* (i.e., the ideologies inherited from the ages of scarcity) would live together *harmoniously* enough, that their remaining contention would only be creative tension, cannot be proved or disproved except by trial. But such a proposition is basic to any demand for or justification of democratic society. . . . The case for a democratic *society* fails without the assumption of *potential substantial harmony*. . . . In any case the postulate of non-opposition of essentially human capacities cannot be said to be contradicted from experience, for it is asserted of the capacities that would be held to be human in a society as yet nowhere realized.[16]

A few points deserve notice here. First, Macpherson not only introduces economic equality as an essential condition of democracy, he further postulates that once equality is introduced and contrived scarcity overcome, it will be possible for all to realize their capacities in harmony with everyone else and for the entire democratic ethos to exude a consensual harmony that eliminates destructive contention. Class inequality is not only an impediment to democracy. It also comes close, for Macpherson, to constituting the problem of evil and the key to its solution. Second, Macpherson treats this fundamental conviction as a *postulate* to be acted upon experimentally rather than something he knows to be true. And, third, the level of generality achieved by the formulation is so high that it is difficult to say just how warm, harmonious, consensual, unalienated, and communitarian a realized democracy is projected to be. The young Marx haunts these passages.

I agree with Macpherson that every political theory, whether realistic or idealistic, individualistic or communitarian, unitarian or pluralistic, egalitarian or inegalitarian, democratic or authoritarian, contains somewhere in its structure deeply contestable postulates or projections about the relation between the actual and the possible. I concur, too, that many of the most fundamental differences between contending theories have not yet been settled by the play of historical experience, scientific evidence, or reason. Macpherson is exemplary in striving simultaneously to articulate the key postulates in his perspective and to flag their persistent contestability. The democratic theorists he reviews are often less reflective on both of these scores, particularly and ironically those who pride themselves so much on their realism about "human nature" as it always has been and must be.

I do not agree, however, that one set of postulates (say, Macpherson's as opposed to those governing the equilibrium model) is automatically more "optimistic" than its competitors. Standards of what counts as an instance of optimism and of pessimism are already entangled in a set of prior convictions concerning the character of the good life and the range of possibilities within which it can be sought. For example, the realist or equilibrium theory of democracy is optimistic about the degree to which Western capitalist states can approximate the ideal of democracy as they conceive it. Macpherson is pessimistic on this score when he is judged from their perspective. And these examples can be proliferated. These are intratheoretical judgments sometimes presented as neutral criteria of assessment between theories.

Macpherson qualifies his postulates temporally, suggesting that the right set of social "trials" may allow us to reach definitive judgments in the future about the most fundamental ones. But he exaggerates here. It is probably wiser to treat such "postulates" as both unavoidable and contestable projections. They are unavoidable because no theory or operative practice can dispense with some such set. They are contestable because, while they are subject to a variety of historical and speculative tests, some of the most fundamental postulates in each perspective are unlikely to be susceptible to definitive settlement.

I find Macpherson's postulates, indeed, to be dangerous in some ways. From my perspective, they are inattentive to profound dangers in the pursuit of unity, coherence, and harmony; and they are unalert to the indispensable, ventilating effects of political disturbance and the enactment of new identities, even in the most developed or "realized" democracy.

Balanced against this judgment, though, is the sense that the very generality of Macpherson's formulations may well render them compatible with some postulates and ends of a pluralizing democracy. So, instead of trying to pin his generalities down, I will elaborate a few elements in the vision I endorse.

Macpherson theorizes democracy within a three-tiered problematic: alienation/repression/collective realization. People are alienated from a harmonious identity; this alienation is fostered by institutions that both repress the self and disable the collectivity from forming a higher, unifying consensus; and the highest institutional arrangements would enable individuals to flourish within a harmonious whole. Since it would be unfair to reduce Macpherson to a cultural stereotype without doing so to myself, my counterproblematic contains three corollary components: normalization/depoliticization/pluralization. Pressures to normalization are deeply inscribed in the contemporary order; these pressures depoliticize consensual conventions that injure many; a pluralizing political society would foster cultural diversity while relieving many of these injuries. Enunciating these two problematics in such a codified way may exaggerate the distance between them, ignoring elements on the margin of each that touch core considerations in the other. The two caricatures, however, do bring out salient differences.

Those who find alienation to be the most fundamental defect in contemporary society tend to divide between those who contend that things are falling apart into relativism, nihilism, anarchism, fragmentation, and/or narcissism and those who think that things are held too tightly together by repressive institutions that thwart alternative possibilities for harmonious community. These two alienation perspectives both resist realist, pluralist, equilibrium, and individualist ideals of democracy.

But the perspective advanced here resists both versions of alienation theory while conforming to none of the alternatives Macpherson recognizes and criticizes.

To say that late-modern societies are, among many other things, normalizing societies is not simply to say that they bestow institutional privilege on a restrictive set of identities and apply intensive institutional pressures to secure those identities as norms against which a variety of modes of otherness are defined and excluded. It is also to say that those who endorse these norms tout them as natural or intrinsically true standards. They claim that the self, the group, the nation, and/or the world would endorse these standards once they acquired the experience of their intrinsic truth. To translate such a naturalization of norms into the critical language of normalization is not to gesture toward an order in which no norms exist. For the ethic I endorse, as we have already seen, accepts the importance of disciplines applied to the self and the group. Such disciplines, though, encourage the self and the culture to come to terms more affirmatively with contingent, relational elements in established cultural identities and to cultivate a more generous ethics of engagement between contending constituencies.

A normalizing society treats the small set of identities it endorses as if they were intrinsically true; this puts it under tremendous pressure to treat everything that differs from those intrinsic truths to be fundamental threats, deviations, or failures in need of correction, reform, punishment, silencing, or liquidation. To challenge such a perspective is to presume that every social identity is a constructed, relational formation *that engenders human differences, resistances, remainders, and surpluses through the very politics of its consolidation.* It is, therefore, to resist the drive to translate all of those remainders into modes of otherness in the futile pursuit of final redemption or completion. Contemporary social life requires identity (at various levels) to be, but the dogmatization and universalization of dominant identities translates some of the very intrasubjective and intersubjective differences through which they are organized and regulated into modes of otherness to be assimilated, punished, or liquidated.

Such a critical perspective does not deny the necessity of limitations and exclusions. Those who resist the pressures of a normalizing society, indeed, must explore what can be done to restrict dogmatic constituencies who strive to repress the very differences upon which they depend for their organization. This poses difficult and dicey issues. But even as those issues are being addressed, it is necessary to find political means by which to expose the dependence of dogmatic identities upon the differences they vilify. For a dogmatic identity translates the differences upon which it depends into modes of otherness to be opposed and condemned, *doing so to a degree far surpassing the requirements of living together when the presumptions of intrinsic identity are reciprocally resisted by the parties involved.* Such a politicization of dogmatic identities forms an essential prelude to the effort to devise creative ways through which a wider variety of identities can negotiate less violent terms of coexistence.

Everyone does not become the same in a normalizing society. The opposite is more likely to occur. Nor is a normalizing society automatically mobilized against "the individual." It might, for instance, embody a general conception of the normal individual against which every difference is appraised. A normalizing society resists the proliferation of affirmative individualities and positive associational styles. It does so not by making everyone the same, but by translating the cultural diversity that exists and struggles to exist into *perversified diversities*. It identifies multiple deviations from the norms it endorses and then translates them into an impressive variety of intrinsic perversities. There is thus plenty of *variety* in a normalizing society. The numerous groups and individuals who deviate are shuffled into multifarious categories of abnormality, perversity, incapacity, irrationality, sickness, irresponsibility, personal defect, and so on. These abnormalities vary across domains (e.g., medical practice and sexual customs), severity (e.g., eccentricity, a sick sense of humor, madness), and perceived degree of threat to the identity of an entire civilization (e.g., welfare freeloaders, sexual deviants, atheists, nihilists). A normalizing society, then, proliferates abnormalities, treating the broad array of types that threaten its claim to correspond to the natural or divine order of things to be *in themselves* in need of help, love, self-correction, improvement, or punishment. Its consummate irony is that it fosters the world of antagonism, violence, and fragmentation to which it purports to be the corrective.

All societies elaborate boundaries, restrictions, standards, and limits; every order devises penalties for the infractions it recognizes. A normalizing society proliferates detailed norms of identity; it establishes them more through the abnormalities it proliferates than through affirmative proofs of those standards; it interprets deviations as psychological defects among its members; and it devises finely meshed strategies of therapy, self-confession, and self-policing to situate its intrinsic standards of normality deeply in the identity of the self, the group, and the nation. It treats, say, gender duality as a complex constellation of norms inscribed in nature itself, manufacturing thereby an abnormal constellation of "homosexuals," "hermaphrodites," "bisexuals," "the sexually impotent," and "perverts" in need of surgery, therapy, silencing, or marginalization. To the extent that it succeeds in installing these standards within the psyches of the abnormalized it succeeds in getting them to treat themselves as a key source of their own difficulties. Its most fervent proponents debate among themselves whether a particular abnormality flows from the perverse *choice* of the abnormals or from a *disorder* within them for which they are not responsible; they seldom explore how the very institutionalization of the normalizing imagination spawns so many abnormalities.

Normalizing societies subjugate and deploy otherness without eliminating difference. They are not always or necessarily orderly societies. Individualist and communalist doctrines of normalization diverge in where they locate the site of normalization—in the body of the normal individual or in the character of the realized community. But they often pursue complementary strategies once these contending sites have been identified. Each does so by treating one set of identities as if it were intrinsically true and by defining ulterior dispositions operating below this threshold as intrinsically abnormal. Either in idealizations of a possible future for the normal individual and the realized community or in descriptions of the present, too many norms are treated as if they harmonized with the intrinsic character of those constituted and judged through them. In political theory such judgments are not typically presented through explicit argumentation, but through the persistent failure to contest or problematize operational practices of normalization and abnormalization. You can often recognize an intellectual's place in the politics of normalization by ascertaining where he or she stands on the strategies of deconstruction and genealogy. For these critical strategies through which to expose and contest the cultural politics of normalization are often overwhelmed by the complementary ideals of the normal individual, the unified nation, and the realized community.

A normalizing society politicizes difference by converting it into neediness or otherness; it then demoralizes and depoliticizes those constituted as abnormal and those who would call this conversion process itself into question.

The perspective advanced here is wary of postulates about true identity and harmonious community, particularly when contestable assumptions within operational codes of the individual, harmony, identity, realization, capacity, commonality, fulfillment, and civic virtue are not flagged by the proponents of these ideals. The objection is not to the projection of any ideal against which actuality is appraised; for to honor the ethos of pluralism and the ethos of pluralization is surely to pursue an ideal. The objection is to tendencies within some forms of idealism, first, to obscure the definitions of difference upon which they depend and, second, to treat their own vision of unity as something beyond the need of self-problematization and ambiguation. You might problematize your ideal, for instance, by treating it as an inherently contestable projection to which you are devoted, while admitting the call to maintain room for other ideals to compete for public attention and space in the same world. The highest form such a stance could assume, in my ideal world, would not conform to the mode of *tolerance,* where one perspective exercising hegemony over the culture allows others to exist as enclaves within it. It would incline closer to a culture of *selective collaboration* and *agonistic respect* in relations between a variety of *intersecting and interdependent constituencies,* none of which sets the unquestioned matrix within which the others are placed. Other modes of self-problematization are pertinent too. You might adopt a stance in which your very assertions are compromised by gestures that call them into question, even for yourself. Or pursue genealogical investigations of the social and historical processes by which the ideal you prize has come into being. To put the point briefly, to resist practices of normalization is to *politicize* socially established unities implicitly taken by many to reflect a natural harmony within the self, between the self and the group, between a people and its god(s), and between the group and the dictates of a nation. It is also to pose and repose a general question deferred by devotees of intrinsic models of identity: What are the most admirable ethical relations to cultivate between carriers of contending ideals inhabiting the same territorial and cultural space when none holds a lock on the truth?

Macpherson shares something with realist and equilibrium theories of democracy here. While he tends to think that the true identity requires realization of a new institutional framework, they assume that the established institutional framework already enables the intrinsic self as a self-interested agent. The realists ignore the extent to which the self-interested self is a highly organized social formation; he ignores the extent to which his ideal of the virtuous self complements the realist model he opposes.[17] Macpherson and realist democrats vary in their theories of identity, but not in the hegemony they give to the problematic of intrinsic identity. In response, I do not say that no preference can be defended between one standard or another. Nor that modern life can be lived outside the medium of a cluster of interdependent identities providing its members with preliminary dispositions and bearings.[18] Far from it. Rather, I insist that a democratic ethos, at its best, *introduces an active tension between cultural drives to identity and the persistent ethical need to contest the dogmatization of hegemonic, relational identities.* And I do suggest that the pluralist sensibility most compatible with generosity and forbearance between interdependent and contending identities is not anchored in the fictive ground of a transcendental command or universal reason. It flows, as we shall see later, from care for the protean diversity of life and from critical responsiveness to new drives to pluralization.

MAJORITY ASSEMBLAGES AND ECONOMIC EQUALITY

But wait a minute. Is there not a palpable contradiction between the two pillars of democracy presented here? A democracy requires a consensus on economic equalization; but a pluralizing democracy must contest, loosen, and disperse any unified cultural identity that might make such a consensus possible. Doesn't such a perspective both require and defeat the politics of consensus? No. There is a tension here, but it does not assume this form. The form it does assume is much more susceptible to negotiation.

Consider, first, the perspectives from which this charge of self-contradiction is most likely to issue. Theorists of community and the normal individual often *concur* in presuming that general action through the state rests upon a fundamental unity around which concerted action is organized. A significant difference between them is that communalists prize the capacity for collective action while individualists suspect it. Arboreal pluralists pretty much concur with both on this crucial point. Arboreal pluralists, such as Tocqueville and Hegel and many Anglo-American pluralists, appreciate diversity as limbs branching out from a common trunk, fed by a taproot. The trunk might be Christianity or Kantian morality or the history of a unified nation or secular reason.

From these three perspectives it does seem contradictory to pursue a general politics in support of economic egalitarianism and then to loosen up the center from which such a politics must proceed. But consider the rhizome as a counterpoint to the arboreal imaginary:

> A rhizome as subterranean stem is absolutely different from roots and radicles. Bulbs and tubers are rhizomes. . . . *A rhizome ceaselessly establishes connections between semiotic chains, organizations of power and circumstances relative to the arts, sciences and social struggles.* A semiotic chain is like a tuber agglomerating very diverse acts, not only linguistic but also perceptive, mimetic, gestural and cognitive. . . . To be rhizomatic is to produce stems and filaments that seem to be roots, or better yet connect with them by penetrating the trunk, but put them to strange new uses. . . . We're tired of trees. *They've made us suffer too much.* . . . Every rhizome contains lines of segmentarity according to which it is territorialized.[19]

A rhizome might be varieties of plant life without deep roots, connected by multiple nodes. Or it might be a variety of human constituencies, each touched in what it is by the dense, multifarious networks, human and nonhuman, in which it participates. The rhizome confounds the individualist/communitarian pair. It is not that a rhizome is simply nonviolent while trees are violent. For a rhizome, too, can become violent, unless it is inhabited by a general ethos of generosity and forbearance among its elements. A rhizomatic *pluralism* would generate such an ethos from multiple sources rather than from a single, exclusionary taproot. In rhizomatic pluralism the possibilities of collaboration around a particular issue increase as each constituency enhances the experience of contingency and social implication in its own formation. Rhizomatic pluralism is most likely to decline into warring fragments when some of its constituencies insist upon sinking deep, exclusionary roots, disabling possibilities for the formation of democratic assemblages. It is when powerful constituencies become hitched to the arboreal ideal, in one of its forms, that the twin risks of social fragmentation and tyranny are the greatest.

Let us defer exploration of how a general ethos drawn from multiple sources might come to inhabit a rhizomatic culture of pluralism. The idea now is to suggest how general action on behalf of economic equalization could be generated from such a cultural multiplicity. For a culture of economic equality, appropriately maintained, is compatible with a cultural world crossed by multifarious lines of ethnicity, religion, irreligion, sexuality, "race," gender performance, household organization, and so on. Indeed, cultural generalization of the experience of contingency and interdependence in what you are, while it need not become the universal understanding through which all identities are lived, forms a superior cultural basis for the formation of majority assemblages in pursuit of economic equality. Fundamentalists in the sphere of identity often foment fervent opposition to public programs that would draw a broad range of constituencies into the general economic life, for such programs would reward constituencies fundamentalists seek to punish. Watch daily presentations on the upper-numbered channels of cable television in the United States if you doubt this. A universal health care program? It rewards too many freeloaders, sexual deviants, AIDS carriers, promiscuous women, and proabortionists. Increase public expenditures for urban transportation? It subsidizes lazy minorities clustered in the cities. And so on.

When many constituencies enhance their appreciation of the relational, constructed character of identity, and when they exercise generosity in their relations with the differences they depend upon to be, two crucial conditions for the formation of majority assemblages in support of economic equality have been fostered. Such an assemblage would not take the form of a general consensus, in which each constituency supports the programs in question for the same reasons as the others. Nor would it reflect the will of a nation, organized around a unified language, ethnicity, race, or religion. Nor would it amount to a simple coalition of interests. Rather, a majority assemblage is a mobile constellation in which some support the programs in question out of dire economic need, some out of particular self-interest, some because they are implicated with others who need these programs, some because they endorse such programs in exchange for assemblage support for others ethically or materially crucial to them, some because they believe that the negative effects of steep inequality will eventually undermine the good life they now participate in, some because they seek to meet responsibilities flowing from this or that creed, and most out of some mixture of these diverse considerations. Moreover, some participating in the assemblage will find its dominant aims and priorities to resonate deeply with their own identities, while others will connect to it in more attenuated ways.

A majority assemblage is closer to food at a potluck supper than to courses at a formal dinner; closer to a diverse set of grasses and bushes spreading over a hillside than to the limbs of an oak tree branching out from a single trunk.

In a democratic ethos of generalized respect for multifarious ways of being, many will have a preliminary stake in supporting the economic conditions of that ethos. For example, employment practices organized around expanding inclusive modes of consumption would both ease those demands on the working-class budget that now press its members to resist new governmental programs for the underclass *and* draw a larger segment of the underclass into the general life of the economy. Two constituencies that became divided in the United States during the seventies and eighties might thereby be drawn closer together. The trick is less how to sustain such an assemblage once it is established (though that is tricky enough) and more how to generate such an assemblage when neither the needed cultural economy nor the needed economic culture are in place. For each of these effects is a preliminary condition of the other; and neither is likely to proceed far unless it is preceded by the other. Such a temporal tension is not unique to the conception of democracy endorsed here, however; it is endemic to every democratic ideal with at least two key, interdependent conditions of existence still coming into being. This is a tension to be negotiated, stretched, and loosened rather than a closed paradox that defeats the comparative viability of the vision of cultural multiplicity in which it is set.

The most fundamental advantage of the politics of collective assemblages is that they enable action in concert through the locality, the regional assembly, and the state without intensifying monistic pressures for the perversification of diversity built into the pursuit of the normal individual, the realized community, or the unified nation. Collective assemblages relax those pressures.

A politics of collective assemblage through the state can support the economic conditions of a multifarious, pluralist ethos. Such a politics, of course, requires its own exclusions and limitations, several of which we will discuss in the last chapter. But it does not require the degree of cultural homogeneity that nationalists, collectivists, and communitarians invoke whenever they encounter the Deleuzian language of multiplicity and difference or the Lefortian language of the democratic dissolution of final markers.[20] There is no guarantee, certainly, that the contingent politics of assemblages will proceed in the desired way. There never are guarantees of this sort.

Perhaps the contemporary enchantment with arborealism, in its several forms, is governed by the wish to secure ethical and practical guarantees in a realm where they are never available. But many are now growing tired of the theorists's romance with trees. This romance has made too many suffer too much.

An assemblage *might* assume the form of a constellation in support of cultural monism. Or several contending assemblages might induce a politics of stalemate in which no dominant assemblage emerges. But it is important to call attention to the affirmative *possibility* of assemblages that foster cultural variety and economic equality together, doing so to trim the sails of unitarian idealists—those unconscious carriers of fragmentation and nihilism—who pretend that democratic action through the state is impossible unless it is undergirded by singularity. Indeed, the politics of stalemate, while possible under the cultural conditions specified here, is most likely to arise in a state where contending fundamentalisms engage in implacable struggle, with each committed to universalize itself through cultural wars against the others.

THE CONSTITUTIVE AMBIGUITY OF DEMOCRACY

With this background we are in a position to delineate the constitutive ambiguity of a democratic ethos oriented simultaneously to economic equalization, the uncertain element of contingency in identity, and the politics of pluralization. A pluralizing democracy is the site of tension or ambi-valence between politics as general action to sustain the economic and cultural conditions of existing plurality and the dissonant politics of pluralization. When this constitutive tension is maintained, a democratic culture thrives. Better, a democratic ethos is one in which this productive tension is always coming into being through the energization of that side of the equation that has most recently fallen into neglect.

Such a perspective on democracy expects that every constellation of identity\difference relations, because it is established upon human beings not predesigned to coalesce entirely with any particular mode of being, will itself engender surpluses, resistances, intransigencies, and protean energies of diversification. It is from these persistent remainders that political energies to subvert the dogmatism of identity are generated. And it is through a cultural ethos of critical responsiveness to such infusions from nowhere that new possibilities of cultural coexistence are created. It is not, as critics of "Foucauldianism" used to charge, that for them every order subjugates difference to the same degree, making it impossible to choose between alternative orders. For a democratic culture that disrupts dogmatic identities opens up possibilities for a politics of pluralization: it increases the number of positive identities and changes the tone of contention and collaboration between constituencies. Such an ethos constitutes a significant improvement over other alternatives.

Within this ethicopolitical problematic, then, the politics of governance must share honor with those social movements that disrupt the sense of completeness, closure, and moral innocence in dominant formations. This counterbalances prevalent cultural drives either to *presuppose* the existing constellation of identities to be natural or normal (realist democratic theory) or to set up the promise of a future harmony against which the tensions and contingencies of the present are measured (Macpherson's democratic idealism). In the countervision of democracy pursued here, disturbance and pluralization both acquire a positive valence, in the present and in the future honored by the regulative ideal of *ambi-valent democracy*.

It is impossible to become detached entirely from identities coursing through us; for we float, swim, and sink in the pool of normality and abnormality in which they are set. But partial distantiation is both possible and ethically laudable. Many of us, for instance, participate in modes of identification currently defined to be suspect or marginal by dominant constituencies. This provides an initial foothold. A genealogical sensibility is needed to make further progress on this front, to foster defamiliarization of internalized standards of cultural normality, and to open up thereby the question of how much violence and cruelty to difference is being imposed to sustain these standards. Democratic contestation can also unsettle such naturalized settlements, disturbing conventional judgments of abnormality and exposing something of the contingent and power-laden character of these settlements. Of course, the politics of disturbance can backfire, inducing that identity panic upon which the politics of fundamentalism feeds. So while disturbance of naturalized identities is one key to ambivalent democracy, the scope and intensity of disturbance must be measured against the historical context in which it is set.

Such a perspective on democracy gives a certain priority to life over identity, treating identity not as the deepest truth of the self or the community, but as a specific formation drawn from energies of life (di*f*erence) never exhausted by any particular organization. Identity\difference\diference. It would be a travesty to reduce this triad to two, or to (re)locate "difference" on one side of a division between "the universal" and "the particular" or "the community" and "the individual." For every identity becomes fixed by engendering and organizing a set of differences; it dogmatizes itself to the extent that it simply converts difference into negativity and ignores the fugitive claims of diference. Diference (pronounced *difference*) points to the noise, energies, and remainders that circulate through every cultural configuration and are not captured by their self-identifications. Diference (*différance* translated into English) simultaneously confounds attempts by any interpretation or cultural identity to consolidate itself fully, tempts idolaters of intrinsic identity to violence in their futile pursuit of completion, opens up possibilities for the enactment of new identities out of obscurity, and provides a fugitive source from which an ethos of respect for the protean diversity of being might grow. Diference is never exhausted by the claims of identity or difference: *this* article of faith provides both a basis upon which contestation of dogmatic identities is grounded and a source from which an ethos of generosity and forbearance in social relations can be cultivated.

If restrained political engagement between alternative constituencies can enhance the experience of contingency, heighten awareness of the relational character of identity, and fold agonistic respect into conflicts between contending identities, these possibilities become more probable when a large number of constituencies have already registered the effects upon themselves of previous movements to pluralization. The contemporary world, then, where time moves faster and multicultural intersections have multiplied, forms a condition of possibility for emergence of a more generous pluralism.[21] That is, the cultural conditions of *possibility* for a generous pluralist ethos are set by the contemporary acceleration of speed and the multiplication of multicultural intersections. Another condition will have been achieved when several constituencies rebel against the suffering imposed by recurrent cultural wars between dogmatic identities.

Still, these conditions of possibility do not carry logical certification or dialectical compulsion with them. A generous pluralism is not simply *implicit* in the shared understandings or overlapping consensus of American culture. The defeat of such possibilities would not, thereby, signal a refusal to accept dictates implied by the culture itself. The American identity is itself the site of numerous conflicts, and their political negotiation or resolution does not point in any necessary direction. You might state one of the general terms of conflict this way: cultural affirmation of a generous pluralism and the fundamentalization of disturbed constituencies form two contending responses to the same contemporary conditions; each possibility is rooted in the same cultural circumstances, and there is no dialectical logic that places one much closer to the "implicit" cultural identity than the other. The acceleration of speed and the multiplication of border crossings in late-modern life create distinctive possibilities and dangers simultaneously. It is unlikely that we will soon reach a time when these alternatives between pluralization and fundamentalization are replaced by a "return" to the politics of liberal neutrality, or the privatization of public conflicts, or a restrictive pluralism rooted in a simple consensus.

I have suggested that the acceleration of speed in so many domains of contemporary life sets one condition of possibility for a more generous pluralism. Let us consider how democratic institutions sometimes mobilize these possibilities. We shift attention, then, from democracy as a medium for the organization of collective assemblages of action to the role democratic institutions can play in mobilizing citizens as critical agents in multiple cultural arenas.

Representative democracy, by constituting its members as citizens who vote, thereby defines them as more than role bearers with a set of social assignments. It constitutes them as political agents who can question, interrogate, doubt, dissent, protest, organize, resist, disturb, prod, and disrupt fixed priorities, as well as mandate and obey general laws. This capacity of the self as a citizen/dissident informs and energizes its other roles within bureaucratic institutions, career planning, erotic engagements, family life, gender performances, class relations, and cross-national social movements. This disruptive, denaturalizing dimension of democratic citizenship is to be prized. It is essential to the effective contestation of those pressures for normalization lodged in the psychic needs of self-reassurance, the inertia of settled vocabularies, the force of habituation, the institutional consolidation of abnormalities, and state pressures for collective coordination. While democratic idealists often celebrate the citizen as the consummate agent through which legitimacy, freedom, and a common will are realized, and while democratic realists often reduce the citizen to a self-interested calculator voting in periodic elections, this conception prizes the citizen partly because it participates in defining new laws of the state and partly because *its corollary role as critic of previous patterns of state authority* supports and energizes its critical political capacities in numerous arenas. Democratic citizenship is idealized here *because* citizenship itself is the site of a constitutive ambiguity: it is at once the means through which general programs are crystallized and enacted through governing assemblages and a medium through which previous settlements sedimented into institutional practice are interrogated and unsettled. These two contending dimensions of politics can be embodied in the same political subject: the citizen as participant in the representational politics of the state and as activist in social movements that interrogate previous patterns of settlement in the state and other social institutions. Maintenance of productive tension between these interdependent dimensions of citizenship constitutes the perfection of democratic politics.

In a series of interviews conducted by Charles Taylor, Paul Rabinow, Martin Jay, Richard Rorty, and Leo Lowenthal in April 1983, Michel Foucault was asked—it is not be too difficult to guess by whom—about his orientation to the pursuit of consensus:

> There is a vision of politics associated in America with Hannah Arendt, and now Jürgen Habermas, which sees the possibility of power as acting in concert, acting together, *rather than* power as a relation of domination. The ideal that power can be a consensus, a realm of intersubjectivity, common action is one that your work seems to undermine. It is hard to find a vision in it of alternative politics. Perhaps, in this sense, you can be read as anti-political.

> FOUCAULT: . . . The idea of a consensual politics may indeed at a given moment serve either as regulatory principle, or better yet as a critical principle with respect to other political forms; but I do not believe that liquidates the problem of the power relation. . . .

> INTERVIEWER(S): If one can perhaps assume that the consensus model is a fictional possibility, people might nonetheless act according to that fiction in such a way that the results might be superior to the action that would ensue from the rather bleaker view of politics as es-

sentially domination and repression. . . . It might in some sense be better, healthier, freer, whatever positive value one uses, if we assume that the consensus is a goal still to be sought rather than one we simply throw away and say it's impossible to achieve.

FOUCAULT: Yes, I think that is, let us say, a critical principle. . . .

INTERVIEWER(S): As a regulatory principle?

FOUCAULT: I perhaps wouldn't say regulatory principle, that's going too far, because starting from the point where you say regulatory principle, you grant that it is indeed under its governance that the phenomenon has to be organized, within limits that may be defined by experience or the context. I would say, rather, that it is perhaps a critical idea to maintain at all times: to ask oneself what proportion of nonconsensuality is necessary or not, and then one may question every power relation to that extent. The farthest I would go is to say that perhaps one must not be for consensuality, but one must be against nonconsensuality.[22]

It seems to me that Macpherson might have been an interlocutor of Foucault in this exchange. I pretty much concur with Foucault in the distributive nuance and emphasis of his response with respect to the politics of social movements. But I wish to qualify his orientation to the politics of action in concert through the state.

Consider first the politics of social movements. Foucault's point can be placed positively on the register of democratic theory, I think, by repeating that a democratic politics is one in which tension is maintained between ruling and governance, on the one hand, and disturbing the naturalization of the results of action in concert on the other. And unlike the suggestions advanced by the questioner(s) about the unidimensionality of Foucault's conception of power, I do not find his response to be at odds with the range of concerns available to him prior to that interview. It is possible to construct a democratic theory appropriate to late-modern states that combines a critique of consent and consensus when they are *absent* with critical engagement with them when they are *present*. For the absence of consent suggests that overt injuries need to be addressed while its presence suggests that there may be subterranean injuries in need of attention. These points are reenforced when we recall how such a complex condition as consent or consensus is never fully "present" and how likely it is that the consent we give to a practice at some levels is qualified by dissent and resistances at others.

But Foucault, while making strides in his later years toward identifying elements in the liberal, democratic problematic converging with his concerns about normalization, never really overcame his wariness of political action through the state. He downplayed state political action out of fear that such an emphasis would support the formation of a suffocating consensus.[23] I want to say, in opposition to this, that state action through the construction of majority assemblages is crucial to the contestation of normalization Foucault so admirably pursues. The risk of the state becoming a nation-state is always there, as we shall see in a later chapter. But these risks must be run and resisted by those committed to a pluralizing democracy; we must include the state as *one* key site of political action among others. The Foucauldian theme of the ubiquity of politics is undermined if Foucauldians shy away from the state as a political site. The appreciation of democracy as an ambiguous medium through which the absence of consensus is interrogated and the presence of consensus is read as a sign of danger is indispensable then; and this appreciation must be applied to several sites of political action, including the state.

But what if democracy itself, in the ambivalent way I thematize it, were to form the consensual background of late-modern life? Is this, finally, a consensus to treat unambiguously? Is it time, at last, to be reasonable? Probably. And yet so many conditions of life push in the direction of consensualizing hegemonic identities—including the inertia of shared vocabularies, the pressures to make the self more "calculable," and persistent tendencies toward transcendental narcissism in which constituencies strive to translate what they are into the intrinsic order of being—that I am tempted to worry about this limit-condition only if and when its time comes. For democracy is the cultural practice that enables participation in collective decisions while enabling contestation of sedimented settlements from the past. To achieve an operative consensus on the ambivalence of democracy would be to consent together to a world in which criticism of the politics of nonconsensuality is enabled while the deceptive comforts of stable consensuality are attenuated. These tensions constitute my ideal of democratic equilibrium, or, if you prefer, of democratic politics as an ambiguous medium of enactment and disturbance.

This portrait of a democratic ethos is pluralistic not merely in the diversities it engages, but also in the types of ground for identity and ethics incorporated into democratic debates. (I'm tired of trees.) It appreciates contestation between those who support the model of the normal individual, those who seek the comforts of an intrinsic community, those who ground morality in the commands of an opaque god or a transcendental subject, and those who revere the protean excess of being over identity. These are contests internal to a pluralizing culture itself, particularly when representatives of *each* perspective acknowledge the shakiness of the ground upon which they themselves stand. So, if a pluralizing ethos presupposes a "consensus," it is mobilized above all around reciprocal appreciation of the contestability of contending presumptions about the fundamental character of being. It is an ironic consensus.

My thinking denies a fundamental purpose, harmony, law, or plasticity of the world. Diference is fundamental. That projection, in turn, is problematized *within that thinking* by treating it as contestable and by calling attention to the role it plays in guiding my political interpretations. It is to be problematized *in relations between theories* by pursuing relations of selective collaboration and agonistic respect with perspectives that, explicitly or implicitly, project alternative fundaments into their interpretations. This restrained pathos of distance and engagement between alternative theoretical perspectives enacts in theoretical discourse the ambivalent ideal it projects onto the democratic culture.

The ambivalent *demos* needs both Macpherson and Foucault, then. Such a reworking of the pluralist imagination draws from Mac-pherson in its respect for the construction of political ideals, its appreciation of economic equality as a critical principle, its emphasis upon the indispensable role of projection (or "postulates") in political reflection, its delineation of the state as a pivotal site of political action, its appreciation of persistent, uncertain intersections between academic discourse and political practice, and its attention to possible uses and misuses of its thought in future contexts. It draws from Foucault in its contestation of the alienation model through which the deceptive comforts of the normal individual and the future community are pursued, its appreciation of constitutive tensions between identity and difference, its pursuit of a pluralizing ethos drawing sustenance from the abundance of life over identity, and its cultivation of agonistic respect for contending interpretations of the fundaments of being.

4

Fundamentalism in America

FUNDAMENTALISM

Fundamentalism, as conventionally understood in the country where
the term was introduced, is a general imperative to assert an absolute,
singular ground of authority; to ground your own identity and allegiances in this unquestionable source; to define political issues in a
vocabulary of God, morality, or nature that invokes such a certain,
authoritative source; and to condemn tolerance, abortion, pluralism,
radicalism, homosexuality, secular humanism, welfarism, and internationalism (among other things) by imputing moral weakness, relativism, selfishness, or corruption to them. A fundamentalist is an
American dogmatist who is proud of it. This combination is what
renders fundamentalism so tenacious politically, so capable of converting each objection against it into new energies for its expansion.

It is also the quality that leads most of us to recognize fundamentalism only in "the other." So, it may be productive to stretch the
range of the word somewhat, to open the possibility of touching
those (liberals, secularists, modernists, rationalists, scientists, moder-
ates) who habitually perceive fundamentalism only in the other. Let
me try this: while every doctrine, culture, faith, identity, theory, and
perspective rests upon fundamentals more or less protected from internal interrogation, fundamental*ism* is a set of political strategies to
protect these fundaments by defining every carrier of critique or
destabilization as an enemy marked by exactly those defects, weak-

nesses, corruptions, and naïvetés you are under an absolute imperative to eliminate. Fundamentalism, then, is a political formula of
self-aggrandizement through the translation of stresses and disturbances in your doctrine or identity into resources for its stabilization
and aggrandizement. It converts stresses and strains in itself into evidence of deviation and immorality in the other; and it conceals the
political dynamic of this strategy of self-protection by enclosing it in
a vocabulary of God, nature, reason, nation, or normality elevated
above the possibility of critical reflection. It is marked by the strin-
gency of its exclusionary form and its insistence upon treating the
putative sources of exclusion into certain, unquestionable dogmas.

All of us have strains of fundamentalism flowing through us. And
no component of cultural life automatically escapes colonization by
fundamentalist impulses. Indeed, every doctrine has some such impulses. But there are important differences of degree along both of
the two major dimensions. Take individualism, the pride of those
who define America through the vocabulary of "exceptionalism."
Individualism contains multiple possibilities. It might be the celebra-
tion of individual*ity,* that is, the appreciation of variety in styles of
living, sensualities, modes of participation in public life, and so on.
Such an individualist celebrates diversity because of the diverse, uncertain, and contingent forces that enter into the constitution of
every self, and because the individualist has little confidence in our
collective ability to vindicate a conception of reason, nature, or normality stringent and certain enough to fix a narrow range of conduct
as the single authoritative standard. Or individualism might congeal
into a doctrine of the normal individual, a conception of normality
constituted through the conversion of differences into diverse abnormalities to be disciplined, reformed, and corrected. In the latter instance individualism becomes a species of fundamentalism. Or take
the political left. It might spawn a critical radicalism that pursues
economic equalization while extending cultural space for a variety of
cultural self-definitions. Or it might become governed by a stingy set
of demands for "political correctness."

Indeed, the strains of fundamentalism can be heard today in a variety of political tunes: the aggressive nationalism of many white
male secular blue- and white-collar workers, the unquestioned faith
of laissez-faire conservatives in the automatic beneficence of the
market, the doctrine of "original intent" in constitutional judg-

ments, the homophobia of many straights and the heterophobia of some gays, the selection of Supreme Court justices by reference to one or two litmus tests, the demand for cultural uniformity in public subsidy of the arts, the tendency to view every issue in foreign affairs through the lens of national security, the aggressive nationalism of leaders who believe that the United States is predestined to provide the moral center of a new world order, and the cultural tendency to blame internal and external scapegoats for every lack, failure, or weakness in the American political economy. What each of these stances embodies is an overweening drive to assert: "What I am (believe, demand, pray, do) is what morality (God, nature, reason, science) itself requires; and anything (person, creed, nation, movement) deviating from these exclusive imperatives is an other to be converted or conquered or both." George Bush crystallized this spirit at the level of the nation when he announced to Americans and Iraqis just before launching the Gulf War, "What we say, goes."[1]

Fundamentalism can become consolidated in rural, evangelist counties of the southeastern United States and in suburban, private universities of the northeast. In contemporary America, it is when doctrines housed in the latter sites establish resonances with the former that the politics of fundamentalism becomes particularly dangerous. Consider an example of how such an intersection is formed.

In a statement entitled "Morality and Homosexuality" printed in the *Wall Street Journal* in February 1994, the Ramsey Colloquium of Christian and Jewish Scholars asserts the sinfulness of homosexuality and links it to a series of other practices created by the "sexual revolution":

> It is important to recognize the linkages among the components of the sexual revolution. Permissive abortion, widespread adultery, easy divorce, radical feminism, and the gay and lesbian movement have not by accident appeared at the same historical moment. They have in common a declared desire for liberation from constraint. . . . They also have in common the presupposition that the body is little more than an instrument for the fulfillment of desire. . . . Finally, they all rest on a doctrine of the autonomous self.[2]

The authors display no appreciation of the contestability of the conceptions of divinity, nature, and sin that propel them. Hence, their judgments are categorical. "In a fallen creation, many quite common attitudes and behaviors must be straightforwardly designated as sin." "Sin occurs in the joining of the will, freely and knowingly, to an act or way of life that is contrary to God's purpose." But has the fuzzy problematic of "the will" been established as the undeniable foundation of action and judgment? Does a consensus by one subset of Jews, Catholics, and Protestants suffice to ratify the theological doctrine of sin for an entire culture? And then to warrant supreme confidence that homosexuality, abortion, adultery, "easy" divorce, and "radical" feminism fall under its rubric? The refusal by the signatories to express any uncertainty on these points slides into the description of those who refuse them as selfish and self-indulgent. And the attribution of self-indulgence to the adversary quickly becomes a call to impose social discipline on those who cannot or will not discipline themselves. Everything that might be read as a sign of variety in the world is translated into the vocabulary of permissiveness, casual lifestyles, instrumentalism, willfulness, sinfulness, irresponsibility, predatory behavior, contrariness, and unnaturalness because it deviates from the conceptions of a god and nature governing the manifesto. These absolute designations of the other define the self-identities the authors profess as the unquestioned standard from which all identities, conducts, judgments, and punishments are to be judged. The only indulgence that remains exempt from interrogation in this manifesto is the one that equates the identities of the authors with the universal character of the good. That omission may explain why the authors are so attracted to the vocabulary of self-indulgence—and so eager to apply it to the other.

These anxious authoritarians would tickle me pink, if it were not for the social context of their pronouncements. Their quest to embody unquestioned social authority in a highly questionable world is transparent. They present themselves as somber *servants* of God and Nature in order to become *tyrants* over everything and everybody deviating from the straitjackets of identity they profess. The most ominous sentence in the Ramsey Manifesto would thus be laughable in its pretentiousness if it were detached from the contemporary political context of its appearance: "We expect that this success [of self-indulgent homosexuality and other sexualities] will encounter certain limits and that what is truly natural will reassert itself." But what does that statement mean? Do these moral agents of social punishment suggest that nature is already reasserting itself by taking vengeance against gays through the spread of AIDS? What, then, do earthquakes in Southern California mean? Or devastating floods in the very heartland of America? More likely, do they "expect" that natural law will reassert itself through the political action of righteous moralists who recognize and enforce it? For if nature has not *yet* reasserted itself sufficiently all by itself, it seems unlikely to do so without political assistance in the future. Fortunately, as the authors must know, there is a pool of rural, poor, white, high-school-educated activists, resentful over the social treatment they have received, poised to act against gays, feminists, atheists, and liberals and the universities in which many of them are housed. The Ramsey prophecy that "what is truly natural will reassert itself" invites ordinary fundamentalists to act belligerently on behalf of the natural and godly, while it provides elite fundamentalists with a thin veneer of deniability if that action becomes too coarse or repressive. For they have proposed no overt programs to force gays back into the closet or to punish divorcées.

If all goes well, nature might reassert itself in the university too. The conservative academic elite will then return to its natural place of unquestioned authority. What a marvelous dream! It tickles me *pink*. If only God and Nature play the parts written for them. The academic fundamentalist elite lubricates the social machine of fundamentalist politics in America. It is the machinery itself that requires further attention.

PARADIGMS OF FUNDAMENTALISM

According to Harold Bloom's fascinating study entitled *The American Religion,*[3] the Southern Baptist movement broke with its partner in the north in 1845, partly to protest against its opposition to slavery. The Southern Convention pressed two theological themes. The first emphasized the "soul competency" of all individuals to commune with God in their own terms. The second emphasized the absolute and singular authority of Scripture or the Christian Bible. These two conflicting themes articulate in theological terms the conflict in American culture noted earlier between individuality and normal individualism. Perhaps they even provide important cultural sources of that debate. Most immediately pertinent here, each theme is compatible with a certain resistance in the church to theological and secular doctrines of modernity. A modern, liberal secularist, for instance, is likely to dismiss both perspectives, the first because it seems to link each human to a divine spirit, the second because it overwhelms objections against the very possibility of a literal reading of Scripture. Secularists who makes these critical points are also unlikely to locate any corollary points in their own faith through which to think sympathetically with and against the faith of the Baptist.

Anyway, by the latter part of the nineteenth century the members of the Southern Convention felt betrayed by the defeat of the South in the Civil War, by the demise of slavery, by the rise of commercial liberalism, and by the dismissive way northern liberalism treated its key components of faith. The Southern Baptist church was consolidated through a common feeling of betrayal and resentment. This combination of military defeat, deep resentment against the victorious forces, and aggressive moralization to overturn those forces forms the recurrent basis of fundamentalism in America.

By the late 1970s the durable conflict between these two points of doctrine in the Southern Baptist Convention was resolved officially in favor of the primacy of scriptural dogmatism over a plurality of routes to divinity. The resolution occurred against a background of resentment against the American defeat in Vietnam and the emergence of a "counterculture" within American life. It was propelled through intense resentment by a majority within the Convention over the Supreme Court's 1973 decision to treat abortion as a woman's right. This event sufficed both to overturn the church's traditional hesitation against direct involvement in politics and to give primacy to literalism in Scripture as its consummate moral weapon.

It may be that the power of *Roe v. Wade* to trigger the politicization and fundamentalization of the Convention flowed from an implicit item of faith in the church, namely, that each individual, once conceived, participates in a spark of divinity that precedes creation itself. I am not certain about this, since the refinements of Baptist doctrine exceed my pagan sensibilities. But the catalyst provided by this event was extremely potent. When Jimmy Swaggart, a Pentecostalist, cries out against "abortion, atheism, evolution, communism, liberalism, infanticide, euthanasia, ERA, homosexuality, lesbianism and perversion,"[4] he also articulates the sentiments and fervor of the victorious wing of the Southern Baptists.

By 1979 the victorious side of the church had officially grounded its political fundamentalism in the Bible. The Hebraic/Christian

Bible, with all its murky metaphors, disparate sources, conflicting stories, and centuries of disparate translations across several languages, was converted into an icon of clarity, authority, and literalness. It serves as the absolute basis of authority whenever an issue involving abortion, the role of women, racial policy, sexual diversity, art, pornography, or national honor came up for review. As Resolution No. 5, "The Priesthood of the Believer," asserted in 1988, the Convention formally reaffirmed its "doctrine of the Priesthood of the Believer," but it also nullified the anarchistic effects of soul competency through other provisos:

> Be it further Resolved, That we affirm that this doctrine in no way gives license to misinterpret, explain away, demythologize, or to extrapolate out elements of the supernatural from the Bible; and
> Be it further Resolved, That the doctrine of the Priesthood of the Believer in no way contradicts the biblical understanding of the role, responsibility, and authority of the pastor which is seen in the command to the local church in Hebrews 13:17, 'Obey your leaders, and submit to them; for they keep watch over your souls, as those who will give an account.'⁵

The political fundamentalism of the Southern Baptist Convention might have been a modest, minor event if it had not touched, and sometimes sparked, a series of corollary developments in other domains of American political culture between the late 1960s and the present. Consider northern, male, white, blue-collar workers and white-collar workers of modest means. Although many members of this constituency are secular, a large section defines itself religiously, and some brought Southern Baptist energies with them in their migration from the South after World War II in search of better jobs in the frost belt. This point of resonance between these two constituencies could easily grow if each became convinced that the enemies of the other were also its own enemies.

A defining element in the identity of white, male, married factory workers with children in the middle sixties was an "ideology of sacrifice." Their dignity was primarily defined by their role as "head of household," their freedom by a willingness to sacrifice personal pleasures now to insulate their spouses from the rigors of the workplace and to improve future prospects for their children. This masculine, working-class identity doubtless contained considerable self-delusion and self-aggrandizement within it, and the opportunities it provided for others were ambiguous. Blue-collar wives, for instance, did not always see the protection provided them in such glowing terms, since it often implicated them in a network of male authoritarianism. And successful offspring were liable to move away geographically and culturally, casting uncertainty on the future respect and recognition actually received by the fathers. Nonetheless, sacrifice through work was pivotal to the identity of this constituency and to the political loyalties it cultivated to welfare-state liberalism.[6] This identity of secular sacrifice later provided these men with channels through which to link up politically to the theology of sacrifice nurtured by their kissing cousins in the South.

By the early seventies, the civil rights movement, the American defeat in Vietnam, the growth of middle-class feminism, the conversion of the welfare state into programs of the Great Society, the rise of middle-class environmentalism, and the conversion of many industrial jobs into service jobs had thrown a series of body punches to this constituency. If a man's identity revolves around menial work, freedom through voluntary sacrifice, the protection of family, and projection of a better future for his children through sacrifice, then social movements, political rhetoric, public programs, and changing job markets that jeopardize these relations between dignity, sacrifice, and freedom will be experienced as attacks on the very fundaments of his being. Thus, if school busing programs lift the educational opportunities of urban "blacks" (as African-Americans were called during this period), then they also reduce the sense of self-control over educational opportunities among "whites" (the other term in this bipolar constitution of identity through color) who cannot afford to move to the suburbs; if welfare programs appear to be extended to minorities on the grounds that they are not responsible for their dependencies, then white blue-collar workers are implicitly deprived of recognition for the jobs they have secured; if women and minorities are promised affirmative action in employment because they have been discriminated against historically while upper-class male professionals are assumed to merit the positions they hold, then white male blue-collar workers are implicitly told that they are the only ones in the country who deserve to be stuck in menial jobs; if environmental programs sacrifice luxuries of consumption most available to the working class, then they threaten one of the compensatory outlets available to it; if a war fought mostly by poor and working-class blacks and whites is defined to be a national mistake and disgrace, then the nationalism of these constituencies is betrayed by the country that propagates it and calls upon them to fight; if tax increases are proposed to finance growth of the welfare state, then its old beneficiaries hear themselves being told to sacrifice again to pay for the sacrifice of the identity of sacrifice that sustains them; and if the connection between a high school education and a decent job is broken while the costs of higher education escalate, then new members of the working class are held accountable for their failure to land good jobs and their children are denied the future promise that once vindicated the ideology of sacrifice.

Don't get me wrong. In each of these instances, there were (and are) crucial issues to be addressed. But it was equally crucial for the welfare state to address them, programmatically and symbolically, in ways that did not deeply alienate one of its most significant constituencies of political support. The way the issues of ecology, racism, feminism, education, job discrimination, and taxes were defined set up this core constituency of the welfare state for a hostile takeover by the American right. The rhetoric accompanying the new initiatives accentuated threats to the self-identity of white workers even when the initiatives themselves failed to make impressive inroads into the real injustices they identified. Equally important, large sections of the working class living close to the margin faced hardships not incorporated into the agenda of national debate: a decline in the number of good jobs available to blue-collar workers, no national health care plan, poor retirement prospects, and no effective programs to subsidize higher education for their sons and daughters. The politics of welfare liberalism from the late sixties onward betrayed the white working class, driving a section of it toward a fundamentalism of gender, self, race, and nation. This is not merely a retrospective view of the situation; some of us within the democratic left articulated it during the period in question.[7]

The contemporary subject position of the white male blue-collar worker, then, is well designed to foster a culture of social revenge and hypermasculinity. If boys in this class are inducted into a traditional code of masculine authority and gender responsibility, if they then find it increasingly difficult to get jobs that embody that ideal, if liberal rhetoric addresses this vulnerable condition in ways that assault that masculinity without opening up viable alternatives to it, then one predictable effect is the emergence of hypermasculine urban cowboys who drive pickup trucks and listen to Rush Limbaugh. Using the terms in their traditional valences (in the valences through which many in this subject position receive them), we might say that this constituency is first inducted into a masculine ideal, then feminized through the structure and insecurity of the work available to it, then assaulted in its masculinity by representatives of the gender it is supposed to govern and protect, and finally courted by right-wing elites who idealize the very model of masculine assertion that has been promised and denied.[8] The effect, of course, is formation of a masculine fundamentalism in which many white working-class males belligerently assert primordial rights against women, gays, intellectuals, and African-Americans. The apparent increase in male working-class violence against lovers and spouses may reflect this development. So might the upsurge of public support to build new prisons to house minority populations, while every other expenditure of the welfare state is to be curtailed.

The fundamentalism of the white working class remains a minority drive within it. But it is almost surprising that it does. Its code is grounded in the assertion of hypermasculinity in nationalism, work life, gender, and race. Everything and everybody posing a threat to this fragile set of identities is to be sacrificed, to render payment for unrecognized sacrifices already imposed on the code of masculine sacrifice, and to cover up a sense of fragility and uncertainty within that very identity that must not be publicly acknowledged.

The first public manifestation of this shift was the attraction of northern white workers in the late sixties to the strident rhetoric of a white southern racist and fundamentalist, George Wallace. This working-class revolt against liberalism was later consolidated through support for tax cutbacks, movements to roll back school busing, demands to curtail welfarism, opposition to affirmative action in education and employment, increased support for "literal" readings of the Constitution, and the emergence of aggressive nationalism in state security and economic policy. This constituency now becomes ripe for a political alliance with Southern Baptists; for both feel that their current sacrifices are undervalued while the dominant rhetoric of public discourse calls upon them to sacrifice the very identities that sustain them.

If the Southern Baptist Convention and the white working class provide happy hunting grounds for fundamentalism, they certainly do not exhaust its forms. Consider one more version, well designed to speak to resentments festering within these constituencies. Here I focus on a movement, emanating from the academy, to reinvigorate the United States as a nation. It is fueled by those who identify the contemporary university as a hotbed of multiculturalism, political correctness, relativism, and postmodern literary theory. The implication of these negative characterizations is that a unified, vital culture, tolerance for reasonable diversity, and the authority of universal rationality would all be *restored* to their rightful preeminence if it were not for these wild excesses pouring out of the university. One version of this story is particularly pertinent here.

In "The Post-Modern State," published in *The National Interest*, James Kurth asserts that only a few peoples have consolidated themselves into a nation; fewer yet have had the good fortune to become viable nation-*states*.[9] Many states are not nations, and many protonations lack a state. By the beginning of the twentieth century there were only

> five exemplary nation-states—Britain, France, Germany, Italy and Japan. Each operated in the cultural, security, and economic dimensions of social life and was supported by the three great pillars of literacy, bureaucracy, and industry. These, in turn, were institutionalized in the school, the army and the factory, which [were] engaged in mass education, mass conscription, and mass production. . . . The nation-state had brought into being an ensemble of mass organizations, which in turn made the nation-state even more of a macro-organization, the organization of organizations, than it had been before.[10]

While many of Kurth's allies remain content to criticize postmodernism as a nihilistic social movement centered in the academy, urban centers of gay life, and MTV, Kurth now defines the United States itself as the paradigmatic "postmodern state" and "multicultural society." As a postmodern state it has depleted the energies it developed between 1890 and 1960 to become a nation-state. This, indeed, is Kurth's definition of American exceptionalism. Most fundamentally, the United States, under the influence of internal movements of pluralization and the internationalization of national corporations, has evolved from a relatively well centered culture to a multicultural regime, from a melting pot to a salad bowl, from mass education to mass entertainment, and from an industrial economy to a service/finance economy:

> It is the proto-typical post-modern society, post-literate culture, post conscription military and post industrial economy. The United States is no longer a nation-state. Perhaps it never really was one completely. . . . In any event, since the 1960's, it has steadily become less a nation and more a multicultural society.[11]

Kurth does not detail what racial, gender, and religious exclusions were maintained during these six decades of American nationhood; nor what subordinations his five paradigmatic states had to impose on internal and external populations to achieve nationhood; nor the extent to which his presentation of them as nation-states may exaggerate; nor why the absence of a nation *must* render a state's educational and economic institutions weak. For instance, a case could be made that the most severe damage to American education and industry occurred during the 1970s and 1980s when the theme of America as a nation was pressed the hardest by three Republican presidents. And many of the new constituencies of the multicultural American state would support programs for universal education and new manufacturing jobs if only some political party would present them. Only someone who presumes that effective governance requires a national consensus over the sources of values would rule out in advance the possibility of constructing majority political assemblages in support of effective education out of diverse cultural groupings. Kurth, however, makes things appear clean and simple, to prepare us for the *necessity* of cultural war.

Kurth's reading of the nation-state and the multicultural regime respectively resonates with the traditional code of the masculine and the feminine we have discerned to be operative in the contemporary working class. This makes many in that constituency predisposed to receive the message he sends. Thus, one line of Kurthian equivalences consists of postmodernism, a multicultural regime, deconstruction, poor education, a service economy, high illiteracy, economic weakness, mass entertainment, the loss of capable leaders, and military insecurity; each item of this list is enlisted as a cause and effect of the others. The contrasting, positive set consists of modernity, nationhood, reconstruction, literacy, an industrial economy, high culture, a unified pool of leaders, and a large military establishment. To be for any item on either list is to become implicated in the others. Take your choice, man! And select your weapons. But don't forget that nation-states are the "makers" of history, while multicultural states are its "takers."

A concerted drive to "restore" nationhood would be deadly given the postmodern condition Kurth himself specifies. We inhabit a state where new diversities of immigration patterns, ethnicity, race, religion, irreligion, sexuality, gender performance, and household organization surround, modify, and stretch the old (putative) culture of Anglo-Americanism, Christian monotheism (with "Judeo" recently and precariously appended to it), nuclear families, and heterosexuality. The drive to restore the United States as a nation-state would require massive policing of American borders, repression of a whole series of emergent cultural formations, and frightening political control over a set of institutions such as the university, print media, television shows, film production, and popular music. In a postmodern regime, the drive to (re)nationalize becomes the fundamentalization of the nation: the attempt to (re)instate the nation-state as the "organization of organizations" must assume the form of a culture war between the forces of nationalism and multifarious ways of being that deviate from this dream, with the warriors for nationhood engaging in a relentless struggle with the opponents already discernible in the grim prose of their academic anticipators. Listen to Kurth's appraisal of this "titanic struggle," to what he says, what he intimates, and what he refuses to say:

> Can there be a reversal of this deconstruction, a new reconstruction, of the American nation-state? It would seem that for this to happen there would have to be a return to the central purposes of the classical nation-state with respect to culture, security and the economy. . . . The role that the United States plays in this titanic struggle [between the archetype organizations of two types of state regime] will depend on the outcome of another. For early post-modern history will involve a parallel struggle, a civil war within the United States between multicultural enterprises and mass entertainment on the one side, and national culture and mass education on the other. For now, it appears the post-modern camp will prevail. If so the United States, in the traditional sense of the American people and the U.S. government, will

not be the actors, but rather the audience . . . of the post-modern world. They will become takers rather than makers of history.[12]

Multiculturalism and mass culture, modern and postmodern, makers and takers, a titanic struggle, a civil war. The drive to restore the American state to the nationhood it never quite achieved provides the most general, pervasive, and dangerous rallying call of fundamentalism in America today. You can easily slide "man" in front of "hood" as well when you consider the unities required and the means to them, doubling the pleasure of the dream. *We* will assert collective masculinity by feminizing assertive foreign lands and unruly domestic constituencies. This drive to collective mastery both expresses and veils the personal disempowerment felt by many of those who are drawn to it. "I must obey the boss. And things are tough with the wife and kids at home. But what *we* say goes, baby!" This call to renationalize by aggressive means is well designed to feed upon the collective fears, gender anxieties, and fervent hopes of conservative Christians and dislocated males in the white working class.

THE FUNDAMENTALIST POLITICAL FORMULA

We need now to pick up subterranean developments that also contribute to the resurgence of fundamentalism in American politics. The first is a growing sense that the civilization of productivity—the civilization of investment, work, sacrifice, freedom, and security built upon the promise of a higher standard of living for each successive generation—no longer includes large numbers of young Americans, particularly in the working and middle classes. While young black men in the inner city are systematically closed out of the future that is generally promised, and while young, white, middle-class women may hold some hope for a better future, young white male blue- and white-collar workers often feel that they are now being closed out of the future once promised to them. Their prospects have become uncertain while their sense of entitlement has become more certain. Such a combination has profound effects upon the character of class politics, particularly upon the selection of targets to blame for the injuries you suffer.

The second development is a growing feeling that the American state, as the highest institution of democratic accountability, now participates in a global economy that limits and confines the terms of its domestic accountability. This disruption of the link between democratic accountability and the sovereignty of the state threatens to compromise the traditional commitment to democratic politics, for now the state is more than ever open to the charge that it is not really accountable to the electorate. And in these new world conditions attempts to reestablish old appearances of state self-sufficiency and accountability would almost certainly take the shape of aggressive foreign and military policies. In the meantime a whole set of issues and concerns stretches beyond the scope of state control. The state receives these global pressures and translates them into disciplines and sacrifices imposed upon those with the weakest market and political positions.

If you recall that fundamentalism and postmodernism are two responses to the same general conditions of existence, the two developments noted here can be colonized by fundamentalist sentiments by treating "postmodernism" as their source. Consider: one effect of the implicit loss of confidence in the future of the civilization of productivity is to draw people closer to those things that seem to be subject to their own immediate control rather than to general identifications that depend upon faith in the efficacy of the state and the economy to build a brighter collective future. This shift in national mood might draw some toward the salvational promise of fundamentalist religion, others to a self-protective careerism, others to a drug culture, and yet others to hedonistic withdrawal from the common life. Each of these distinct responses, of course, has its own particular class, age, cultural, and regional preconditions, and none of them is sufficiently explained by these global shifts in national mood. Indeed, in the political culture of contemporary America they are generally thought to be radically disparate developments. But they also involve disparate responses by distinct constituencies to the same general condition. Each reaction has something in common with the others: all deflate a politics of the general, generosity to the other, and faith in the future; all inflate a politics of the self, the particular, and the immediate. But some of these effects are treated by fundamentalists as the cause of the general problem while others are treated as the basis upon which a national remedy might build. Hence the fundamental political formula we have already discerned in Kurth and in the Ramsey Colloquium.

This effect is complicated but not reversed by the changed international context in which the American state operates. For while the erosion of democratic sovereignty works in one direction to increase disaffection from internal state politics, it works in another to intensify chauvinist nationalism with respect both to competing states (Japan, the former Soviet Union) and to foreign developments that signify the decline of American sovereignty (e.g., Latin American revolts, Middle East oil politics, terrorism, international corporations, the role of the United Nations, worldwide environmental issues).

Indeed, the implicit decline of faith in the American future and the decline of confidence in democratic sovereignty today often combine to intensify political sentiments on behalf of "restoring" the nation. They encourage one president, for example, to base an entire campaign on the theme that it is "morning in America." The political consolidation of such sentiments externalizes responsibility for internal weaknesses in the American state and mobilizes a domestic politics that resists responsive adjustments to new world conditions. For, at the deepest level, the fundamentalisms of self-identity, religious faith, ethnic identification, and the nation replicate each other. They are parallel, mutually reinforcing responses to the same developments. Each externalizes threats to fixed identities threatened by new evidence of their contingency and lack of self-sufficiency; each deflects pressures to renegotiate relations with differences with which they are implicated. The fundamentalism of the self and religion asserts itself in relation to the other within domestic politics; the fundamentalism of the nation asserts itself in relation to the foreign inside and outside the state. Those others often overlap, as Jimmy Swaggart's list reveals. If egoistic fundamentalism is treating one's own premises of action as unquestionable imperatives for others, if associational fundamentalism is treating the premises of our faith as unquestionable imperatives for all associations, the fundamentalism of the nation-state extends these imperatives to the largest territorial unit of political identification. These responses, at different levels of identification, register the same general disposition: My identity is the intrinsic standard for others in my state; our identity is the intrinsic standard for those outside it. What *I* say goes, baby. What *we* say goes, fellah.

We are now in a position to summarize the political deployment of fundamentalist sentiments in contemporary American life. If we recall that fundamentalism is from the outset a political formula—

one in which the identity of the self, the association, and the nation are secured by converting differences that jeopardize their self-certainties into abnormalities and dangers that must be chastised, punished, or corrected—then it is not too difficult to see how these complementary fundamentalisms became ripe candidates for organization through a more general political formula.

The political formula of contemporary fundamentalism in America was crystallized by George Wallace, adjusted by Richard Nixon, consolidated by Ronald Reagan, and given a kinder, gentler polish by George Bush. The most important constituencies it seeks to mobilize are Southern Baptists and northern workers already made ripe for defection from the Democratic Party by the defeat in Vietnam, cultural movements of the sixties, affirmative action in race and gender, the pluralization of sexual and gender identities, the decline of factory work, and the changing role of the American state in the world. But a variety of other constituencies also show some susceptibility to these themes.

The single most important refinement of the fundamentalist formula was the displacement of the racist rhetoric of Wallace. Racist rhetoric was translated into such slogans as "welfare cheats," "the responsible poor," "the liberal welfare state," "governmental inefficiency," "liberal tax and spend," "the work ethic," "the silent majority," "the moral majority," "law and order," "family values," and the Republican Party as the party of "normal Americans." Indeed, the struggles of race, class, sexuality, and gender were condensed into a code of white masculinism that enabled a degree of deniability on the subject of race while still sustaining viable outlets for racial hostilities. Reagan's version was the most effective. It succeeded in drawing disparate constituencies together not only by mobilizing latent opposition to urban African-Americans, feminism, gays, and liberals, but also by binding these sentiments to a masculine campaign of anticommunism. The anticommunist campaign cast a second pall over the ameliorative programs of the welfare state while allowing the president to mobilize support for a series of little nation-building wars against alleged communist proxies. These little wars mobilize a nationalist sentiment waiting to be tapped without entangling the United States in a long, unwinnable conflict. The dissolution of the communist threat accompanying the dismantling of the Soviet state thus constitutes a serious challenge to the politics of fundamentalism. But as long as the political formula speaks to the resentments of many, new external threats will be constructed to complement and support wars against the foreign within.

The political formula of Republican and conservative fundamentalism has worked something like this: You cut taxes, reduce welfare programs, and deregulate the corporate economy in the name of efficiency, the failure of liberalism, and faith in the market. You concentrate electoral attention on those issues of abortion, communism, the welfare state, homosexuality, and family values that attract to your old political base new constituencies plagued by a diffuse sense of betrayal and resentment. You shift new responsibilities to state governments mostly governed by Democrats while you decrease the tax resources available to them. You then blame new signs of weakness in employment, the economy, the family, the welfare state, or foreign relations upon the same set of forces: Congress, liberalism, welfare freeloaders, feminism, gay and lesbian movements, terrorism, postmodernism, secularism, unfair competition by foreign states, and so on. In the rhetoric of Oliver North, "the enemies of America from within" must be opposed more fervently once the Soviet Union has been dismantled. You thus install a circulation of symbols and affects that conceals your own contribution to the decline you decry and projects their causes onto programs and groups that already threaten the identities of your key constituencies. George Bush's Willie Horton ad, the demonization of Bush's former ally Saddam Hussein (not such a hard thing to do), the conversion of the Anita Hill/Clarence Thomas issue into an attack on Congress, the reiteration of family values amidst policies that weaken the family's institutional basis of support, the Kurth portrayal of the multicultural regime, the Manifesto of the Ramsey Colloquium—all provide timely examples of this general formula in operation.

LIBERALISM AND FUNDAMENTALISM

The Reaganite formula of fundamentalism is not, of course, the only arrow in its electoral quiver. It also deploys strategies (which I bypass here) that attract financial and electoral support from its traditional constituencies in small business, certain professions, and the corporate world. What I would like to attend to, however, is a related question: Why does American liberalism today present itself as such a vulnerable target for the politics of fundamentalism?

The most controversial element in my answer resides in the judgment that while fundamentalists grossly exaggerate the certainty, objectivity, and intrinsic character of their faiths and identities, they are nonetheless onto something in their belligerent characterizations of American liberalism. For American liberalism too often takes the form of a doctrine that conceals its own strain of fundamentalism from itself. By doing so it helps to manufacture some of the very resentments it fights against. Southern Baptists, displaced white workers, angry academics, and the Reaganite political formula together expose a dimension of liberalism that its own leading representatives fail to acknowledge. This failure contributes to the efficacy of the political formula deployed against liberalism.

There are several variants of liberalism. Some are far less problematical in this respect than others. But those liberalisms founded upon the idea that (1) secularism provides a neutral matrix in which American politics is practiced, (2) the state can be neutral with respect to divergent conceptions of the good life, (3) when people pretend to judge behind a "veil of ignorance" they will almost always recapitulate the basic ingredients of the liberal welfare state, or (4) "the individual" provides the unquestionable basis of fundamental rights all convert a series of deeply contestable faiths into the pretense of a neutral or necessary foundation of common judgment. When George Wallace screams at "pointy-headed intellectuals," when Jerry Falwell charges that the media are governed by a "secular liberal bias," when Patrick Buchanan rages about "taking our culture back," when George Bush (the son of American aristocrats, a graduate of Yale) accuses Michael Dukakis of being too cozy with Harvard intellectuals, when Oliver North campaigns for money by inviting his supporters to "picture the look on the faces of those left-wing Senators who tormented me . . . during the Iran-Contra hearings as I walk onto the floor of the Senate,"[13] the cultural resentment each taps into reflects a pervasive sense by nonliberals that the root assumptions of liberal dogma are anything but neutral, necessary, or incontestable. These articulations reflect and mobilize resentment of attempts to impose a liberal creed upon others in the name of a universal reason, a natural subject of rights, a neutral state, or a fictive contract conveniently skewed in favor of liberal presumptions and priorities. As one who is much closer to liberal presumptions than to those considered so far, I nevertheless want to suggest that the resentment against liberalism energizing the Reaganite political formula is augmented by the deafness among liberals to the strains of fundamentalism circulating through their own public doctrines. The fundamentalist strain in liberal dogma helps to spawn the redneck fundamentalism it opposes. And liberal strategies against fundamentalism too often track too closely the fundamentalist formula they condemn.[14]

Perhaps an example will crystallize the unconscious strain of fundamentalism inhabiting this cluster of views. Ronald Dworkin, in an influential effort to devise a liberal way to reduce the divisive effects of fundamental religious and doctrinal conflicts, once argued that a liberal society is one in which differences with respect to the true order of being and the good life are left out of public, political discourse. We must inhabit a procedural republic together, following neutral procedures of debate and decision while leaving our fundamental differences about the good life in the private realm. Liberalism, he said, "supposes that political decisions must be, so far as possible, independent of any particular conception of the good life, or what gives value to life. Since the citizens of a society differ in their conceptions, the government does not treat them as equals if it prefers one conception to another."[15]

Dworkin's recommendation is admirable in its attempt to respect diversity in religious and doctrinal perspectives while enabling these same constituencies to combine together to govern in the public sphere. But the solution he proposes misrecognizes the partisanship upon which it rests. Its presumptions about procedure, reason, and neutrality are highly congenial to secular liberals who endorse individual rights and who believe there is a universal matrix of procedural reason drawing together people who diverge at other levels in their conceptions of the good life. But evangelical Christians, Orthodox Jews, secular communitarians, rhizomatic pluralists, Amerindian peoples, Marxists, and postmodernists in various ways contest several of these liberal postulates. And they find some of their key convictions consigned to the "private realm" by secular liberal neutrality. They are told to leave their bags of faith at the door when they enter the public realm, while Dworkin and his buddies are allowed to bring several suitcases in with them.

When Christian fundamentalists hurl the charge of "secular liberal bias," they are recognizing, exposing, and resisting the very mis-

recognition that sustains the claim to the neutrality and incontesta-
bility of basic liberal themes. And when liberals remain deaf to
charges of bias and hypocrisy leveled against them, they deepen and
extend this rage. This is precisely how some versions of liberalism
help to exacerbate the fundamentalist temper they set themselves
against: they project fundamentalism solely onto the other and fail
to recognize its strains in themselves.

Let us now place this same issue on a related field and explore the
fundamentalist strain in the liberal constitution of "postmodernism." I will define this cultural movement a little differently here,
calling it postfundamentalism to underline the lines of dispute it
opens up with both conservative and liberal fundamentalisms. Liberalism too often stands to postfundamentalism today as "redneck"
fundamentalism stands to liberalism. And liberal responses to postfundamentalism further disclose the strain of fundamentalism circulating through it; these very responses, again, reveal the element of
veracity in the accusations "redneck" fundamentalists make against
liberals.

Liberal *post*fundamentalism, as I construe its contemporary man-
ifestations, strives, first, to expose unconscious and problematic fundaments in alternative doctrines while deploying strategies such as
genealogy and deconstruction to display comparatively the content
and contestability of its own operational fundaments; second, to cultivate a critical responsiveness to new drives to pluralization so that
"they" have a chance to define themselves and "we" can work on
ourselves to negotiate new terms of coexistence between old identities and new movements; and, third, to open up reflection on how
the "we" and the "they" in these formulations shift in unexpected
ways as issues change. Such a liberalism is postfundamentalist, then,
not in rejecting the modern or in gesturing toward a new world that
is simply unmodern, but in challenging the presumptions to universality, inherent rationality, historical necessity, intrinsic identity,
common sense, and so on that are installed in several liberal defenses
of the modern, the secular, the rational, and the moral, doing so to
explore possible elements of immorality in established codes of
morality and justice.

It is exactly this feature of postfundamentalism that brings out
the red in the necks of some liberals. They too often label postfundamentalists nihilistic, anarchistic, amoral, relativistic, and irrational

without exploring explicitly how their own pretense to provide the neutral, uncontestable matrix of politics, reason, and morality is challenged by these postfundamentalist positions. Numerous examples of this tendency can be found in such journals as the *New Republic,* the *New York Review of Books,* and the *Nation,* where opponents often define postfundamentalism, but proponents are rarely offered space to define themselves. Can you recall the *New York Review of Books* inviting Foucault, Derrida, Irigaray, Deleuze, Butler, Fish, or Herrnstein-Smith to write an essay in that forum, though several have been defined negatively numerous times in it?

Here is one example of how the liberal production of postfundamentalism proceeds. In a 1993 issue of *Political Theory,* David Johnston chastises a political theorist for bringing Foucauldian assumptions to the exploration of John Locke's conception of rights and individuality. Uday Mehta is charged with identifying injuries and closures in Locke's theory of freedom without himself offering a formula for discriminating between "an excessively truncated or confined" individuality and constraints required for living together in society. Johnston concedes vaguely that Locke "was less willing to accommodate difference than many of us today would like him to have been" without indicating either where he stands with respect to this "us" or whether "we" might have learned from numerous social movements since Locke that *yet another new formula is precisely the wrong thing to offer here.* For every such eternal formula offered in the past to establish the line between the acceptable and the intolerable has had to be changed later in response to new social movements whose successful redefinitions of themselves change the location of the line. Johnston concludes not by pondering this issue, but by generalizing the charge of failure he levels against Mehta:

> This last problem is emblematic of a more general difficulty with the Foucaultian style of criticism of which Mehta's book is an example. The general strategy that defines the style is to expose the socially constructed character of our understandings of everything. A clear grasp of that character enables us to consider how we might change those understandings. But Foucaultian criticism offers no means of distinguishing between changes in our understandings that might help us to improve our social lives and changes that would only make matters worse. From a Foucaultian point of view, social criticism is a night in which all cows are black.[16]

Johnston, who generally thinks a text should be read sympathetically in its larger context, suspends this demand when it comes to
"Foucauldians." As I read both Foucault and Derrida, however, neither denies the importance of drawing lines in specific settings between what is allowable and what is not. But each interrogates the
sufficiency of a morality reduced to a general code through which
such discriminations are made. Foucault's genealogies expose the social construction of exclusionary norms; he then cultivates critical responsiveness to constituencies who have been degraded unnecessar-
ily by the *very codifications of normality and justice currently in
vogue*. The Foucauldian ethic of cultivation through genealogical
critique, as any reader of *The Use of Pleasure* quickly learns, both
overtly endorses the need for a code and pursues the reformation of
existing codes.[17] Most crucially, it refines our appreciation of how
operational codes of justice, indispensable as Foucault says they are,
draw upon a more fundamental, *uncodifiable ethos that exceeds
their reach*. The ethical point is to struggle against the temptation to
allow an existing code of authority or justice to dominate the field of
ethics entirely; the ethical idea is to maintain critical tension between
a congealed code of authority and justice and a more porous fund of
critical responsiveness that might be drawn upon to modify it in the
light of the contemporary injuries it engenders and positive possibilities it ignores.

Johnston ignores these complexities. He asserts authoritatively
how morality as such must function and then condemns "Foucauldians" for not living up to the model he invokes. He thereby
translates a potential debate over the purity or ambiguity of ethics
into a charge of failure by the opponents of his position, thereby in-
sulating his brand of liberal morality from the critical exchange his
competitors strive to open. Luckily, there are liberals such as Bernard
Williams, Donald Moon, Richard Flathman, Nancy Rosenblum, and
George Kateb whose reflections on morality rise above this game.

This is the strain of fundamentalism circulating through a popular version of liberalism. It holds postfundamentalists responsible for
not providing the kind of moral formula liberalism itself remains unable to secure; then it protects this contestable agenda from critical
scrutiny by pretending that postfundamentalists eschew the ethical
project altogether or reduce it to aesthetics. It pursues this course by
focusing on the disruptive effects of genealogy and deconstruction

and by ignoring the cultivation of critical responsiveness to differ-ence pursued within both traditions.

A postfundamentalist liberalism would strive to expose and ac-knowledge the contestability of the fundaments governing *it,* includ-ing its governing conception of morality. It would struggle to intro-duce a new generosity into rivalries between alternative perspectives based upon recognition of their reciprocal contestability.[18] Such a postfundamentalist liberalism may be a beam of light glimmering on the horizon of the contemporary political landscape. If it were to shine more brightly it might open up positive possibilities of negotia-tion between conventional fundamentalism and liberalism.

RENEGOTIATING FUNDAMENTALISMS?

On my reading, then, it is not possible to participate in an identity, doctrine, theory, movement, or culture without projecting funda-ments that exceed your current ability to articulate and redeem them. But it is possible to challenge those fundamentalisms that cele-brate and exacerbate this cultural condition. It is also ethically and politically important to do so if one of your (contestable) funda-ments is the conviction that unnecessary violences and exclusions are fostered by the insulation of a privileged set of fundaments from challenge and disturbance—and if one of your concerns is to figure out how to drain support from the academic, media, and govern-mental warriors who are building political capital for a campaign to fundamentalize America.[19]

American liberalism is well positioned, by its place in the geogra-phy of American politics and by its traditional commitments to plu-rality and tolerance, to contribute to such a development. But it is poorly positioned, I have argued, to capitalize on these possibilities because of the ways it defines conservative fundamentalism and postfundamentalism. What, then, are some promising moves to make in this regard? I will list a few possibilities briefly and pro-grammatically. Since there is no neutral place to stand, my list itself reflects a partisanship in search of new coalitional possibilities. It will articulate a few openings to be pursued in the domain of "cul-tural politics" on the grounds that it has spoken to the economic conditions of defundamentalization in chapter 3.

(1) The defection of large sections of the white male working class from the old liberal/welfare state coalition is not adequately

represented through statistics of party affiliation, since both of the parties have changed significantly in response to this constituency movement. The defection reflected a sense of being sold out to new constituencies and priorities introduced into the New Deal coalition. But this defection could have been mitigated to a considerable degree, and might possibly be rectified now, even while supporting diversification in the domains of gender, race, religion, and sexuality. Affirmative action in education and employment could, for instance, more explicitly incorporate a class or income dimension. This in itself would go a long way toward easing the sense of insult and discrimination among Reagan Democrats, for their children would have a better chance to respond to the twin pressures of fewer good blue-collar jobs and escalating costs of higher education, and they would no longer be singled out as the only constituency that deserves to be stuck in the crumby jobs now available to it. Such a shift in affirmative action might eventually encourage a relaxation of the hypermasculinism upon which fundamentalism feeds. Moreover, universal programs in the areas of family allowances, health care, and transportation (discussed in chapter 3) would go further in this direction, promoting ends crucial to the new constituencies of the tattered welfare state while recognizing those in the white working class who have felt frozen out. These reforms, of course, must be connected to programs to increase the number of decent jobs in the country for those without advanced educational degrees. Modest success on these fronts could have impressive political effects: they would give those members of the white working class who are already drawn to concerns of racial and gender justice more reasons to pull away from the working-class politics of masculine fundamentalism.

(2) The moderate wing of the Southern Baptist movement might become more open to dialogue with proponents of liberal secular humanism if more of the latter groups showed agonistic appreciation of the doctrine of soul competency. Indeed, those who prize individuality and diversity in styles of living might appreciate the subterranean role the dogma of soul competency has played in fostering the spirit of secular humanism, secular individuality, and secular pluralism in the American setting. The "literal" readings of the Bible with respect to abortion, feminism, and diverse sexualities are harder nuts to crack, but even here divergences between us might be

phrased differently. It is not, for instance, that every woman has an inviolate right to choice grounded in reason or the primordial character of the individual. Rather, both this presumption and the opposing contention that a divine spark resides in life from the moment of conception reflect contestable dogmas of faith. Since neither can be proven, since, surely, the state is incapable of doing so, abortion cannot be proven to be murder. Soul competency and respect for a diversity of faiths both suggest, then, that the particular faith of each adult should be determinative in exactly this territory. Such a stance, while many will fervently oppose it, might be met with a certain agonistic respect—that is, *respect* for the way the position one opposes is articulated, *underscored* by public enunciation of the contestability of corollary presumptions in one's own faith, *matched* by the way opposition to the alternative stance itself is expressed—by others. That would be a considerable advance.

(3) Now that religion has overtly and actively entered the political sphere, new lines concerning the "separation" of church and state must be negotiated. When any constituency insists upon imposing the implications of its faith upon others through politics, it becomes legitimate for others to explore critically and publicly the terms of that faith. In an age of religious politicization, piety can no longer serve as a cover exempting any faith from critical examination, for that would amount to guarding the premises of one or two public doctrines from critical public scrutiny while opening the rest up to it. Piety can function as an exemption from public scrutiny when the pious make a credible claim either to remain outside the political fray or to leave their faith behind when they enter it. The first claim has pretty much fallen by the wayside today, and the second has always been exaggerated as an operational practice in American politics, mostly through the pieties of liberal "neutralism" and neo-Kantian universalism. It hardly applies anymore to a whole host of issues in contemporary politics. Such a renegotiation of public/private boundaries will not merely affect religious fundamentalism; as I have already suggested, it will touch the self-protected pieties of liberalism as well. For most of the fundamentalist critics of liberalism are well aware that it brings a private and contestable secular faith into the public sphere while refusing to sanction the same privilege to nonsecular faiths. A postfundamentalist liberalism may hold more promise in opening negotiations

across political divides. Over the long term, such an adjustment in the self-presentation of liberalism could make a real difference.

(4) More critical attention might be paid to the discrepancy between the moral appeals of elite fundamentalists in and around the academy and the effects of the economic programs they support on the lower-income constituencies to whom they are often addressed. The white male working-class section of this constituency may be open to efforts to drive a wedge between it and elite fundamentalists, particularly if the rhetoric and social policies of a modified liberalism speak to the issues of race, gender, and sexuality in ways that honor the constituency's claim to dignity and self-respect. And particularly if a reconstituted liberalism comes out of the closet with respect to the contestability of the dogmas to which it is most deeply committed.

(5) In an age of globalization of economic relations, communications, ecological effects, nuclear danger, gender issues, race issues, and so on, it is imperative to the ethos of democracy to generate cross-national, nonstatist modes of political action that exceed the political boundaries of any state. For under the conditions of late modernity the democratic state, just because it is the highest forum of formal accountability to citizens through elections, threatens to become the consummate medium for the intensification of nationalism. The unconscious logic of this equation in state politics is this: "If the state is our highest unit of political agency and democratic accountability, *we* can see ourselves as free to the degree we pretend it is a self-sufficient actor." Such a pretense could be sustained by a few states in the past, but the attempt by any state to maintain it today requires it to suppress from "domestic politics" its own implication in some of the most pervasive global dangers. To protect its pretense of sovereignty, the state deflects, ignores, demonizes, or otherwise fundamentalizes a whole series of issues that would otherwise expose the huge gap between the terms of its electoral accountability and the scope of its efficacy. This fundamentalism of the state constitutes the most dangerous fundamentalism of our time. The problem is that the contemporary means available to resist it may increase the fundamentalism of the state over the short term, while the refusal to resist it will have the same effect. I opt for the first set of risks.

Three characteristics of our time are crucial in this regard. First, we are (almost) all ruled by states. Second, none of us is exhausted ethically or politically by the state that rules us. Third, each of us is capable of recognizing dangerous ways in which states that rule us filter and "domesticate" global issues affecting the life prospects of future generations. These three timely points of affinity among citizens residing in different states establish new possibilities for political movements exceeding the boundaries of any particular state.

The effects of economic globalization today set new conditions of possibility for nonstate, cross-national political movements to exert external and internal pressures upon the established priorities of states. The possibilities here are already evident in Greenpeace, Amnesty International, the international divestment movement opposing apartheid in South Africa, the nuclear freeze movement, the internationalization of the feminist movement, and so on. They could become salient, too, in labor movements that, say, link workers in northern Mexico to workers in the States and link employees of Japanese firms in the States to those in Japan. As such movements extend and consolidate across states, they may exert salutary effects upon state priorities with respect to currently underpublicized and underrepresented issues. For example, it is not impossible to imagine automobile workers in Japan and the United States entering into negotiations to curtail the worker vulnerabilities created by collusion and competition between producers in the two states. What was once a promising internationalism among workers has declined today, even as corporations and states globalize the economy. Its renewal today might reduce the appeal of state fundamentalism to workers while improving their negotiating leverage with capital.

Such cross-national, nonstatist interventions might eventually subvert the sense that the state presents the highest point of political obligation and loyalty for every citizen. Over the longer term a new pluralization of political identifications could thus provide a significant counterpoint to statist pressures toward intensive nationalism. The pluralization of democratic movements across state lines might allow a democratic ethos to close up some of the distance between its contemporary confinement to states and the globalization of capital, markets, communications, travel, tourism, criminal rings, and dangerous contingencies.

Such a series of shifts and modifications could alter the trajectory of fundamentalist politics in modest ways. To the extent that they cracked the ice of fundamentalism, they might open up prospects for change in two crucial domains: reduction of the class inequality that creates a huge reservoir of diffuse social resentment upon which the fundamentalism of race, gender, sexuality, religion, and nation feeds, and reworking of the nineteenth-century American pluralist imagination that today authorizes some of the cultural presumptions from which contemporary fundamentalism proceeds. We (merely) began to address the first issue in chapter 3; we will turn to the latter in chapter 6.

5

Democracy and Territoriality

THEORY AND NOSTALGIA

In late modernity, the nostalgic idealism of territorial democracy fosters the nostalgic realism of international relations. And vice versa. The nostalgia is for a time in the past when the politics of place could be imagined as a coherent possibility for the future.

Today, nostalgic realism and nostalgic idealism coexist within the compass of the state. While political movements, economic transactions, environmental dangers, security risks, cultural communications, tourist travel, and disease transmission increasingly acquire global dimensions, the state retains a tight grip over public definitions of danger, security, collective identification, and democratic accountability. Even when a fragment within the state seeks to break this monopoly it usually does so by imagining itself as a state. And even while international capital flows through and over the state, the state sets itself up as the center around which citizen identifications are organized. The more global capital becomes, the more aggressive the state is with respect to citizen allegiances and actions. The democratic, territorial state sets itself up to be the sovereign protector of its people, the highest site of their allegiance, and the organizational basis of their nationhood.

What role does democratic theory play in overcoding the contemporary state? Nostalgic realism and nostalgic idealism converge upon democratic theory to maintain a rough set of correspondences among the following elements of the political imagination:

(1) the grounding of "internal" politics upon a contiguous territory;

(2) the recognition of a people (or nation) on that territory, bound together by a set of shared understandings, identities, debates, and traditions that, it is said, makes possible a common moral life and provides the basis upon which citizen/alien and member/stranger are differentiated;

(3) the organization of institutions of electoral accountability and constitutional restraint that enable the territorialized people with shared understandings to rule themselves while protecting fundamental interests and freedoms;

(4) the maintenance of a high degree of economic self-control and self-security to enable the territorial state to shape its fate according to its own deliberations and decisions;

(5) the elaboration of internal differentiations that enable a plurality of styles of life to coexist within the frame of the national territorial state; and

(6) the recognition, as sovereign and legitimate, of other states that cross the pertinent thresholds with respect to the preceding five elements, making it possible for the internal politics of state rule to be ratified through its recognition by other sovereign states.

This familiar political imaginary fosters the experience of connection between the life of the members and the common meanings that draw them together, between the desire to shape the common fate through democratic politics and the construction of territorial structures of public accountability, and between the territorialization of democratic politics and the production of the national security state.

This territorial imaginary conditions the realism and idealism of democratic politics in the modern epoch. It is probably impossible even to imagine a form of democratic politics today that breaks entirely with this model. And yet few states, if any, actually maintain close alignment between this image of the sovereign, territorial, national, democratic security state and their actual practices.

One familiar response in political theory (but not there alone) to this asymmetry between the expectation of alignment and the recurrent experience of disalignment is to define the gaps and breaks as deficits in political actuality falling below the essential threshold of democratic unity. The gaps are figured as sources of estrangement, alienation, exile, or the decline of "the political." This sense of loss is then monumentalized through appeals to previous times when the politics of place is said to have been intact, as in the Greek polis or in a few nineteenth-century nation-states, or in the local politics of some sections of early-nineteenth-century America. You might call this variant of nostalgia the politics of homesickness. It laments the loss of place by comparing this experience to a fulsome past that probably never was; and it demands the return of that past through the vocabulary of community, nation, or people.

But the nostalgia of theory does not always express itself directly as homesickness. The mournful stance can be concealed artfully through the introduction of stopgap concepts that treat the politics of place as if it were pretty much intact. On such a reading, it is only necessary to bring a few stray constituencies, understandings, and institutions into line to express a unity that is already there implicitly. Whenever these stopgap concepts become installed in cultural self-understandings they conceal a series of cruelties, dangers, and violences in the present that need to be addressed. I expose and criticize such stopgap concepts in this essay. The upshot is not to demand the deterritorialization of modern life. It is to support a more cosmopolitan, multidimensional imagination of democracy that distributes democratic energies and identifications across multiple sites, treating the state as one site of identification, allegiance, and action among others.

This alternative imaginary itself expresses a yearning in which the present is appraised from the vantage point of a fictive future that could never *be* in any finished form, but could, perhaps, *become* more active below, through, and above the state. By challenging the sufficiency of territorial democracy with a more multiplicitous spatialization of democratic energies, covert complementarities between nostalgic realism and nostalgic idealism can be addressed. Perhaps we can contest the yearning for a single, settled politics of place by disrupting the experience of sovereignty in both its "internal" and "external" dimensions.

THE PARADOX OF SOVEREIGNTY

Rousseau understood the founding of a general will to be paradoxical. He located the paradox in time (perhaps to imagine another time when it could be resolved):

In order for an emerging people to appreciate the healthy maxims of politics and follow the fundamental rules of statecraft, the effect would have to become cause; the social spirit, which should be the result of the institution, would have to preside over the founding of the institution itself; and men would have to be prior to the laws what they ought to become by means of laws.[1]

For a general will to be brought into being, effect (social spirit) would have to become cause, and cause (good laws) would have to become effect. The problem is how to establish either condition without the previous attainment of the other upon which it depends. This is the paradox of political founding.

But Rousseau then conceals the legacy of this paradox in the operation of the general will after it has been founded by the creative intervention of a wise legislator. If the free, unconditioned political will is to function as the regulative ideal of politics as such, the violences upon which its perpetual pursuit rests must be artfully concealed. To note merely one instance of concealment: Rousseau's artful efforts to legitimize the subordination of women can be seen, first, to express the necessity of subordination (of either men or women) within the family so that the will of a unified family can contribute a single will to the public quest for a general will, and, second, to conceal the violence lodged within the practices of male authority in the family by treating subordination as suitable for women as such. The appearance of a pure general will (which must be common and singular) requires the concealment of impurities. Such a strategy succeeds if violence in the founding is treated by the hegemonic political identity to have no continuing effects. Acting as if, for instance, the subordination of women is both essential to the general will and natural to them, or as if, on another plane, the systematic violence against indigenous inhabitants in the founding of the United States carries no continuing effects into the present. The paradox of sovereignty dissolves into the politics of forgetting.

So Rousseau both exposes the paradox in the founding of the general will and coneals it in his presentations of that will once it has been founded. His double relation to the paradox of sovereignty is not unique. It is built into every theory of sovereignty as a self-sufficient practice.

Paul Ricoeur explicitly delineates this paradox. He reads it as a paradox of politics as such. A political act is legitimate if it reflects the previous consent (or will, or decision, or tacit agreement, or rational consensus, etc.) of a sovereign authority (a people, an elected assembly, a ruler following a constitution, etc). But, Ricoeur persuasively argues, no political *act* ever conforms perfectly to such a standard. If it did it would not be a *political* act, but one of administration or execution; because it does not, a political act always lacks full legitimacy at the moment of its enactment. It always invokes in its retrospective justification of the act, presumptions, standards, and judgments incompletely thematized and consented to at its inception. Sovereignty always occurs after the moment it claims to occupy. The paradox of politics/sovereignty resides in this temporal gap between act and the consent that enables it. And the temporal gap contains an element of arbitrariness that cannot be eliminated from political life. Ricoeur states the indispensability and corrigibility of political acts through the language of consent:

> It is of the nature of political consent, which gives rise to the unity of the human community organized and oriented by the state, to be able to be recovered only in an act which has not taken place, in a contract which has not been contracted, in an implicit and tacit pact which appears as such only in political awareness, in retrospection, and in reflection.[2]

If Ricoeur is right, the very structure of sovereignty compromises the integrity and coherence idealists of democratic sovereignty demand. Its logic corresponds to Alice's realization in Wonderland that there is always "jam yesterday and jam tomorrow, but *never* jam today." And it recalls, too, the experience of a "divided will" in Christian conceptions of sin, where the sinning agent is responsible because the will is one's own, but the will is never completely one's own because it always divided against itself. If I read Ricoeur correctly, it is not primarily that the practice of sovereignty/politics reveals the human truth of the Christian concept of divided will but that the early Christian conception of will contains a dark premonition of the "labyrinth of politics."[3]

How does one prove (or disprove) the "paradox of sovereignty"? Such an issue is likely never to be settled definitively. Perhaps the best way to make the case for its significance and persistence is to examine paradigmatic studies that presuppose its absence and then run into predictable difficulties because they do so.

(SCHUMPETERIAN) REALISM AND (WALZERIAN) IDEALISM

Joseph Schumpeter has widely been treated as a "father" of American realist theories of democracy. Criticisms of his theory that were elaborated in the United States during the 1960s concentrated on its reduction of democracy to a method for electing officials, its demolition of the common good, and its devaluation of direct participation as a means to educate citizens to the common good.[4] Schumpeter does criticize theories of the common good and the general will, but he does not quite reduce democracy to a method.

The "general will" cannot express the will of the people, says Schumpeter. Rather, it is the effect of strategic and rhetorical devices such as "affective reasoning," "reiterated assertion," "evasions," "principles of association," the "psycho-technics" of exalting "certain propositions into axioms" and putting "others out of court." In manufacturing a general will, leaders deploy "pleasant associations . . . of a sexual nature"; they associate their objectives with "pretty girls"; they draw upon "ideology," "sentimentality," and "fits of vindictiveness"—to create a common will or at least to "manufacture" the majority sentiment they then purport to follow. This is all "realistic," since it is simultaneously impossible to discover a general will as the "classic theorists of democracy" imagined it and impossible in modern life to retain a legitimate state for long without subjecting potential leaders to competitive elections.

Still, this demolition of the general will as the magic source of democratic legitimacy does not reduce Schumpeterian democracy to a mere method for electing officials. The electoral method must still be legitimated. Schumpeter legitimates it by calling it a rational mode of governance, by condemning conceptions of democracy that involve popular activism and agitation as irrational, and by supporting the sober, cool, detached governance of leaders accountable to citizens only on election day. Throughout his textualization of the irrational production of the general will flows a subtext of contrast to rational democratic governance. While the general will is conditioned by that which undermines its pretext to unconditionality, rational governance rests upon the integrity of reason itself. Thus, in the manufacture of a general will, "there is indeed nearly always some appeal to reason. But mere assertion, often repeated, counts more than rational argument and so does the direct attack upon the subconscious, which takes the form of . . . pleasant associations of an entirely extra-rational character."[5]

Schumpeter invokes a universal code of rationality to vindicate a realist democratic method. The method contains a variety of rules such as the imperative of periodic elections, the necessity of slogans in electoral competition, the insulation of governors from the vicissitudes of public opinion between elections so that they can promote the "long term interest," a split between foreign and domestic policy that insulates foreign policy initiatives even further from the electorate, the cultivation of an independent civil service, the education of citizens into the wisdom of patience and reticence between elections, and so on. Just to take one example: "The voters . . . must respect the division of labor between themselves and the politicians they elect. They must not withdraw confidence too easily between elections and they must understand that, once they have elected an individual, political action is his business and not theirs."[6] These are the musts of political rationality, and deviation from them is irrational. Now that a code of rationality has replaced the general will as the deepest source of democratic legitimacy, how is this code redeemed?

The text does not first iterate a conception of rationality and then show how its application places one set of conclusions on the upper side of a divide between rational and irrational government. Rather, it places rationality, bosses, experts, "words as bullets," maturity, efficiency, periodic elections, the insulation of elites, and the national interest along one line of positive correspondences and domestic politics, vote trading, sexual associations, reiteration, sentimentality, fits of vindictiveness, the general will, manipulation, indulgence, voters, evasion of reality, "the nursery," repetition, and "degeneration of foreign policy into domestic politics" along another, negative set.

How is each item associated with the others on its line and each line differentiated from the other? By the same ("extra-rational") tactics Schumpeter detected in the production of the general will. Items on the first list are coordinated by a traditional code of masculinity (bosses, bullets, maturity, efficiency, etc.) that is never named but always insinuated, while those on the second are united by a corollary code of femininity (pretty girls, vote trading, reiteration, sentimentality, fits of vindictiveness, indulgence, evasion, etc.). The text is sprinkled with formulations of the following sort: a "rational treatment" of crime "requires that legislation . . . should be protected from both the fits of vindictiveness and the fits of sentimentality in which the laymen in the government and in the parliament are alternatingly prone to indulge."[7]

Capitalism, Socialism and Democracy exalts a realist model of rationality by enclosing it within a traditional cultural code of masculinity, and it exalts political realism by associating it with this masculinist economy of rationality. It then contrasts this network of associations with a feminine set equilibrated through inversion of the same tactics. This intertextualization of political rationality and masculinity follows the same logic Schumpeter identified in the irrational production of the general will: it "attempts to evoke and crystallize pleasant associations of an entirely extra-rational, very frequently sexual nature." Here, too, "we find the same evasions and reticences and the same trick of producing opinion by reiterated assertion that is successful precisely to the extent it avoids rational argument."[8] The text deploys feminine strategems to produce the superiority of masculine equivalences, inadvertently revealing the dependence of masculine/realist/rationalist equivalences on a feminine practice of equilibration said to be alien to them. Schumpeter is a cross-dresser with a deep voice. He is a realist.

The realist textualization of democracy forgets the paradox of politics by slipping the silver bullet of political rationality into the opening just vacated by the general will. To reiterate (yes): democratic realism instantiates masculine rationality through feminine strategems while simultaneously denying the indispensability of these tactics through masculinist imperatives. It conceals the paradox (the gaps) it opens by covert recourse to the tactics it ridicules.

Michael Walzer's *Spheres of Justice* opposes this valorization of universal reason. It evinces suspicion of any cold drive to universalization, whether Schumpeterian, Kantian, or Rawlsian in character. It unfolds through the warm words of plurality, diversity, spheres, complex equality, membership, belonging, shared understandings, and connected intellectuals, contrasting these spherical shelters to an icy world of abstract reason, external standards, simple equality, strangers, and disconnected intellectuals who would insert standards "from nowhere." If Walzer forgets or evades the paradox of politics, it cannot be in the name of Schumpeterian standards. For Schumpeter imposes, while Walzer belongs.

Walzer views the democratic state through the optics of a plurality of "spheres" such as the market, the family, education, religion, medical care, and citizenship, each with internal understandings of justice in its sphere that can be brought to bear whenever (a) an injustice is discovered within it or (b) its internal principles illicitly leak into other spheres. Thus selling consumer goods is fine, but selling votes or sex exceeds the bounds of justice; the home is a place of privacy, but its confines must not become an excuse to exclude children from education; intellectuals are judged by reasonable standards of scholarship but not by standards of faith and heresy appropriate to a religion. These delineations, richly developed and exemplified, might play a role in any theory that evinces respect for diversity and individuality in contemporary life.

The book, however, is replete with general qualifications that are not applied to particular cases and with particular criticisms and concessions that are not allowed to accumulate to disperse its central theme. No detailed accounting can be presented here, but a series of fundamental divisions—between having a job and pursuing a career, between having a high school education or less and having a college education or more, between being identified as a normal adult and as abnormal in some way, between being a black male in the inner city and a white male in the suburbs, between being a criminal and a law-abiding member of the community, between being an illegal immigrant and a citizen—disrupt the Walzerian spheres both as descriptions of actuality and as norms capable of integrating outcasts, abnormals, marginal workers, and aliens. Constituencies who bring a couple of these liabilities to a particular sphere encounter expectations, resentments, demands, and cruelties that demean, confine, and depoliticize them systemically.[9] Explorations of these divisions might preserve the idea that different standards of justice come into play in different domains of life, but it would also disperse the warm vocabulary of membership, spheres, belonging, and shared understandings through which the Walzerian textualization of contemporary life proceeds. The world of spheres is cracked.

Two themes in this book do the most to conceal paradox and to confine the scope of democratic energies. They revolve, first, around the presentation of "shared understandings" and, second, around the delineation of the master line dividing the world inside the state from the outside.

Shared understandings do for Walzer what political rationality did for Schumpeter. They reinstate sufficient standards of judgment jeopardized by the Walzerian devaluation of abstract rationality; they provide the glue that holds each sphere together; and they contain this spherized diversity within the boundaries of the territorial state. Belonging not only protects you from a cold world, it provides you with bearings through which to be a moral agent inside the warm world of the state.

Walzer must locate enough coherence in the understandings of each sphere to provide "us" with sufficient leverage to identify "violations" and "deviations" when they occur and (though this is not emphasized) this coherence must then be compelling enough ethically so that "we" do not feel compelled to resist or rework the shared understandings themselves.

This delicate distribution of emphasis is discernible in a summary statement advanced by Walzer in *Political Theory* shortly after publication of the book in 1983:

> We can say that a (modern, complex, differentiated) society enjoys both freedom and equality when success in one institutional setting isn't convertible into success in another, that is, when the separations hold, when political power doesn't shape the church or religious zeal the state, and so on. There are, of course, constraints and inequalities within each institutional setting, but we will have little reason to worry about them if they reflect the internal logic of institutions and practices (or as we have already argued in *Spheres of Justice,* if social goods like grace, knowledge, wealth, and office are distributed in accordance with shared understandings of what they are and what they are for). But all too often the separations don't hold.[10]

So the internal logic of an institution provides the standard against which violations in it are measured. But how is this internal logic distilled from a practice that must exceed it if that logic is to be wheeled out to detect *violations*? *Spheres of Justice* does not confront this issue directly. Rather, it resolves the issue through the strategic presentation of internal logics. Consider an example in the domain of crime, punishment, and imprisonment:

Similarly, our understanding of the purpose of a prison (and the meaning of punishment and social roles of judges, wardens, and prison guards) sets limits to the exercise of power within its walls. I am sure those limits are often violated.[11]

A statement about prison walls itself divided by a grammatical wall. "Our," "purpose," "understanding," and "limits" are placed on one side; "I," "am sure," "violated," and "often" on the other. The dominant theme locates laudatory standards in shared understandings; the subtheme communicates a subtext of realism in Walzer's understanding. The subtheme is communicated under his breath, so to speak, to the very constituency ("us") who putatively share the first set of understandings. The grammatical wall stems the flow of understandings to knowledge, of norm to violation, and of our to us; but it also allows them to seep surreptitiously through this barrier to the other side. The Walzerian wall is a membrane. This porous wall, created by a period and a one-eighth-inch gap on the printed page, gives Walzer the kind of deniability/implication with respect to our shared understandings that wardens and police chiefs practice with respect to prison and police violence. For *everyone* "is sure" these "understandings" are "often violated." They are broken so regularly and systematically that the logic of violations forms part of the understandings. We, like Walzer, live on both sides of the Walzerian wall between understandings/knowledge, I/we, practices/violations; our understandings, like his, contain a series of walls/membranes within them.

There are, for instance, nationally televised programs in which juvenile offenders are graphically informed by hardened prisoners exactly what will happen to them inside those walls if they are sent to prison. "We" view these programs, ambivalently rooting for the youths to get the message and for the prospective agents of revenge to teach them a lesson if they fail to do so. This folk wisdom—this shared understanding—of prison life forms part of the state's strategy of criminal deterrence; it functions, too, to construct walls of identification dividing those outside prison walls from those inside.

An alternative formulation might read thus: Our understanding of the purpose of a prison simultaneously sets limits to the exercise of power within it and sanctions deniable violence behind its walls.

The walls perform a triple function for us: they protect us from offenders; they organize our ambivalences about crime and punishment into a psychically tolerable structure; and they offer us deniability during those rare moments when prison violence becomes too visible to ignore.

The revised formulation—breaking down walls the Walzerian grammar constructs—intensifies pressure to respond in new ways to old ambivalences. It carries Foucauldian resonances. It might press some of us to pull further away from the old "we" in our interpretations and proposals; this reconstituted we might listen more closely to muffled sounds behind prison walls, partly so we can better hear ambivalences outside them too. We might engage more actively the powerful role revenge and resentment play in practices of crime, responsibility, punishment, and imprisonment; and we might ponder more closely how prevailing spheres of understanding mobilize and channel these powerful forces.[12]

What one could no longer do is assert easily that shared understandings suffice to characterize prison violence as a "violation," a violation that would be removed once a preestablished we is informed of it and lives up to its understanding. These walls—and thus those gaps—exist within the understanding. They are not exterior to it. "We" must change ourselves to reconfigure the walls, and vice versa. With that recognition we find ourselves contesting some dimensions of prison practice/understanding.[13] As we do so, our operational conception of politics becomes more complex, less colonizable by the discourse of belonging, sharing, connectedness, and spheres. We remain implicated in practices we endorse or contest, but not in a way that is reducible to belonging and sharing. Shared understandings no longer cover political life with a blanket; the gaps, porosities, and ambivalences they contain become sources of political disturbance and innovation. So do the textual strategies by which they are consolidated and concealed.

Walzerian "shared understandings" and "internal logics" protect the legitimacy of his normative vision by attributing it to us; its attribution to us vindicates it as a rough and ready description of our collective condition; and this description proceeds through a series of divisions and excisions that conceal/forget the paradox of politics.[14]

But Walzerian understandings are not bound by time alone. They are also bounded in space. The spheres portray horizontal divisions within the state, while the spatial division establishes the most basic separation between the inside and the outside of the state. Here are formulations that construct this wall of walls:

> The primary good that we distribute to one another is membership in some human community. And what we do with regard to membership structures all our other distributive choices: it determines with whom we make those choices, from whom we require obedience and collect taxes, to whom we allocate goods and services.

> Statelessness is a condition of infinite danger.

> We who are already members do the choosing, in accordance with our own understanding of what membership means in our community and of what sort of community we want to have. What precisely [strangers] owe to one another is by no means clear, but we commonly say that positive assistance is required if (1) it is needed or urgently needed by one of the parties; and (2) if the risks and costs of giving it are relatively low for the other party. . . . This is our morality; conceivably his too.

> Here I only want to point to mutual aid as a (possible) external principle for the distribution of membership. . . . The force of the principle is uncertain, in part because of its own vagueness, in part because it comes up against the internal force of social meanings. And these meanings can be specified . . . through the decision-making processes of the political community.[15]

The text explores fruitfully a variety of difficulties that arise when a state debates its terms of membership. But the line of demarcations it constructs between us/them, inside/outside, protection/danger, community/stranger, and our morality/conceivably his is not confined to this issue. Inside the wall of walls there is the rich, warm world of we, community, primary goods, membership, internal understandings, our morality, meanings, distributive mechanisms, mechanisms of state security, democratic accountability, obligations, and obediences. On the other side there are alternative worlds of strangers, danger, external principles, uncertain obligations of mutual aid, and conceivable moralities. Many of these others live in other states (with, conceivably, their own warm meanings that are only tepid to us), while others of these others exist in the infinite coldness of statelessness. But not very much connects either set to us politically, morally, temporally. That's just the way it is, baby. The very thought of democratic currents flowing over state lines draws the Walzerian mind back to the (hopeless) issue of *timeless* principles.

This fusion of shared understandings with the territorial state as the fundamental unit of political membership constitutes the Walzerian space for democratic action. Beyond this boundary there are interstate and state/stateless relations, but not democratic politics.[16] Since the overtly conceived hypothetical alternatives to this division are the anarchy of a universal market without states or the oppression of a world state, the reader (in a rich, powerful, democratic state) settles back into the comforting rhetoric of democratic politics inside a territorial state governed by shared understandings and common principles of membership. The threat of anarchy and coldness outside intensifies the pressure, first, to treat "shared understandings" as sufficient standards of political judgment within the state and, second, to treat the territorial state as the highest unit of political loyalty, identification, and democratic participation.

This representation of a wall guarding the warm inside from the cold outside occludes ways in which the outside forms part of the inside in many contemporary states. In the United States, for example, there is a Third World circulating inside every large city (the "inner city") that approximates the Third World outside the state. And the policies the state applies to this Third World of impoverished minorities, drug addicts, criminals, welfare clients, and homeless wanderers within too often approximate those it applies to the Third World outside.[17] There is also a discernible affiliation between "shared understandings" applied by dominant constituencies to outsiders both inside and outside the borders of the state. The earlier reflection on prison life exemplifies this. But such a proliferation of inside/outside divisions does not mesh smoothly with the presumption of alignment between belonging, territory, state, sovereignty, and shared understandings.

We are now in a position to gather these bits and pieces together by asking, How do Rousseau, Schumpeter, and Walzer stand with respect to Ricoeur's paradox? Ricoeur poses powerful objections to the sufficiency of a general will, political rationality, and shared understandings in these respective presentations of democracy and sovereignty. These constructions function to conceal the paradox of politics; they depoliticize life just where more active politicization is needed.

But, when it comes to the wall dividing democratic politics inside the state from the outside, Ricoeur joins Rousseau, Schumpeter, and Walzer in overcoding the boundary of the territorial state (numerous others could be named on this list—including my former self—but who's counting?) Walzer, indeed, is almost the only one among contemporary political theorists who explicitly tries to justify the boundary.

None of the theorists on this list considers the possibility of disaggregating elements in the democratic imaginary so that democratic energies already exceeding the boundaries of the state might be mobilized and legitimized more actively. All, moreover, give too much priority within the state to practices of democratic rule; none gives sufficient attention to the positive role played by a *democratic politics of disturbance* in projecting new challenges to old relations of identity and difference, disrupting the dogmatism of settled understandings, and exposing arbitrary violences and exclusions in fixed arrangements of democratic rule. The "internal" pluralism of each—admirable to the extent it is elaborated, with Rousseau at one end and Ricoeur/Walzer at the other—is too closed in its internal articulation and too dichotomous in its definition of externality.

THE DEMOCRATIZATION OF TERRITORIAL SECURITY

If political theory is the academic field where questions of individuality, loyalty, community, rights, belonging, democracy, justice, and freedom inside the contours of the state are debated, international relations is the field where diplomacy, subversion, order through anarchy, war, low-intensity conflict, economic interdependence, diplomacy, and national security are observed through the optics of interstate relations. It is not just the differences between them but also how these two fields produce one another that now requires attention.

John Herz provides an illuminating example here because he wrote a book focusing on the declining role of territoriality in the politics of security and then a later essay taking much of the first study back. These two studies, when they are juxtaposed to the three theories of territorial democracy just reviewed, expose the tenacity of state territorialization in contemporary politics. They may also inadvertently expose a need to pluralize the spatializations of democratic politics.

The first Herzian analysis seeks to maintain coherence between epistemic realism and political realism[18] while calling the strategic/political primacy of territoriality into question:

> What is it, ultimately, that accounted for the peculiar unity, coherence, or compactness of the modern nation-state, setting it off from other nation-states as a separate unit and permitting us to characterize it as an "independent," "sovereign," "power"? It would seem that this underlying something is to be found neither in the sphere of law, nor even in that of politics, but rather in the ultimate, and lowest, substratum where the state unit confronts us, in, as it were, its physical corporeal capacity: as an expanse of territory, encircled for its identification and defense by tangible, military expressions of statehood, life fortifications and fortresses.[19]

The epistemic realism of this passage is contained within the terms "underlying," "ultimate," "lowest," substratum," "physical corporeal capacity," and "tangible." These contrast to surface, secondary, ideational, incorporeal, and intangible dimensions lodged, apparently, in such practices as law, sovereignty, democracy, and ideology.[20] The key to the consolidation of the territorial state between the sixteenth century and the middle of the twentieth resided in its growing capacity to protect populations inside these borders from external enemies. The state became "the ultimate unit of protection" because in the long run people "will recognize that authority, any authority, which possesses this power of protection."[21]

The state became a sovereign unit because it was able to create a relatively "impermeable shell" around its territory; other virtues of the state, including its provision of possible space for democratic institutions, flow from this: "everything . . . reflects the internal pacification of the new territorial state and its external defensibility."[22]

But by 1959 the old link between territory and security had broken. The old world system depended upon vast "open"(!) areas outside the European theater of sovereign states, areas that were open to exploration, exploitation, and colonization by dominant states.[23] Also, in the old days (within "the family" of states) states were often defeated but seldom "wiped out as such." After World War II, though, a state can be wiped out as a result of advances in military hardware; and the motive to destroy it expands with the depletion of virgin areas for colonization. The emergence of new ideologies that stretch across territorial lines makes states more vulnerable to unrest fomented from outside, and international media of communication ("radio broadcasting") exacerbate this process. The introduction of "air war" is pivotal: "With it . . . the roof blew off the territorial state."[24] And, finally, the possibility of nuclear devastation has upset the whole logic of state security through territorial impermeability: "Now that power can destroy power from center to center everything is different."[25] In general, the postwar state cannot establish its economic self-sufficiency, national security, or ideological unity with the same confidence it did in the past.

These tendencies toward state interdependence and boundary permeability have intensified radically since 1959. Nonetheless, by 1968 Herz had withdrawn most of the political implications he had detected in these patterns. Against his expectation, the old territoriality failed to dissolve into new forms of collective security and international organization. Rather, a "new territoriality" has inscribed itself rapidly upon the old and extended itself into new areas; everywhere the "territorial urge and the urge to maintain (or establish or regain) one's 'sovereignty' and 'independence'" (re)assert themselves.[26]

The new territoriality is not grounded in the substratum Herz initially excavated. Forces previously construed as effects have now become causes, and the epistemic realism upon which the Herzian analysis previously rested has now been quietly subverted. Herz, for example, now treats "world opinion" as a potent restraint on nation-states, because the new interdependencies and permeabilities of states make the military option less available and render it prudent to respond to this opinion in advancing state interests.

Here is the new Herzian analysis of territorialization in a nutshell: a "nation" is at home with itself only if it governs itself; nation-states need internal legitimacy to promote stability, external security, and economic efficiency; the most legitimate mode of self-governance today is democracy; and modern democracy must be organized within a bounded territory if it is to be. Thus the new territoriality has become an effect of causes it apparently used to produce. Here are a few formulations expressing these linkages:

> In a positive way, nations, in order to be effective actors in international relations, must prove to be 'legitimate' units, that is, entities which . . . can be . . . considered as basic and 'natural' for the fulfill-

ment of essential purposes, such as protection and welfare of the people.

What, then, renders a nation-state legitimate? Legitimacy originates from feelings and attitudes of the people within as well as neighbors and others abroad in regard to the unit, its identity and coherence, its political and general 'way of life'.

Being compelled to fight for or defend one's territory generates true nationhood.

Internal legitimacy (without which . . . the unit as such can provide little solidity) in our day is closely related to democracy in the broad sense of people having the conviction that they control their destinies and that government operates for their welfare.[27]

And so you have it. Herz and Walzer. Schumpeter and Herz. Sovereignty and democracy. Legitimacy and security. Nationality and shared understandings. Nostalgic realism and nostalgic idealism. The democratization of territorial security. The statification of democratic identity. All grounded in the mystique of territorial democracy. The pull of the democratic imaginary holds the territory together despite those (un)real forces that threaten to blow off its roof. Herz, Walzer, and Schumpeter together produce correspondences between state, territoriality, nationality, sovereignty, democracy, belonging, and legitimacy. Do they conceal/forget gaps, cruelties, exclusions, and dislocations within this set of correspondences?

Today the territorial/security state forms the space of democratic liberation and imprisonment. It liberates because it organizes democratic accountability through electoral institutions. It imprisons because it confines and conceals democratic energies flowing over and through its dikes. The confinement of democracy to the territorial state—to a (paradoxical) sovereign place where (ambiguous) understandings (dis)organize the common life—consolidates and exacerbates pressures to exclusive nationality. Every protean nation demands a state, and every state strives to become a nation—often in the name of territorial democracy. If competing demands for nationhood do not fit well together on the same territory—they often don't, as the examples of Ireland, Israel, South Africa, Spain (the Basques), Maine, Canada, the former Yugoslavia, Iraq/Turkey/Syria (the Kurds) and the former Soviet Union testify—a crisis is fomented or a set of suppressions is transcribed into the background noise of territorial politics. And in more settled territorial democracies, when the reach of issues affecting people exceeds its bounds, the stomach of the state digests the excess into strategic interests, diplomatic issues, or political excrement. The territorial state too often stifles democratic energies or translates them into national chauvinist sentiments.

THE DISAGGREGATION OF DEMOCRACY

What these theorizations of territorial democracy by Rousseau, Ricoeur, Schumpeter, Walzer, and Herz share is the demand that all the elements of the democratic imaginary fit together on the same space. This is the imperative that imprisons democracy through state territorialization. But if the practice of modern democracy involves shared understandings, formal institutions of electoral accountability, and the capacity to act in concert within a sovereign state, does it not therefore require state territorialization to be?

Yes and no. Yes, institutions of electoral accountability do form a key condition of democracy, and the territorial state is the modern site upon which this institutionalization is built; but, no, institutions of electoral accountability, while they are necessary, do not exhaust the affirmative possibilities built into a democratic ethos. Democracy does not require so many shared understandings in the strongest sense of that phrase, but—as I have already suggested—it needs public spaces and points of reference through which issues can be defined and pressures for action can be organized. Democracy, indeed, is a form of *rule* or *governance,* but it is much more than that as well: it is an egalitarian constitution of cultural life that encourages people to participate in defining their own troubles and possibilities, regardless of where these troubles originate and how narrow or broad they are in scope; it is, moreover, an ethos through which newly emerging constellations might reconstitute identities previously impressed upon them, thereby disturbing the established priorities of identity\difference through which social relations are organized; it is, therefore, a social process through which fixed identities and naturalized conventions are pressed periodically to come to terms with their constructed characters, as newly emergent social identities disturb settled conventions and denaturalize social networks of identity and difference; it is, thereby, a distinctive culture in which many constituencies respond politically and affirmatively to modern pressures to problematize those final markers (God, natural law, the divine right of kings, the natural basis of traditional identities, a fictive contract) that might have governed their foremothers and forefathers, a political culture in which a variety of constituencies responds affirmatively to uncertainties, diversities, heterogeneities, and paradoxes of late-modern life by participating in the construction and reconstruction of their own identities.

Democracy is, among other things, an affirmative cultural/ political response to the problematization of final markers that helps to define the late-modern condition. It contests authoritarian and totalitarian modes of response to this same condition because they draw upon contemporary instruments of surveillance, repression, and social mobilization to reinstate coercively old markers that have become destabilized.[28] It treats the contestation of final markers as a contribution to freedom, self-formation, and self-governance among constituencies no longer required to believe that how they have been constituted historically is what nature requires them to be. And it cultivates a politics of agonistic respect among multiple constituencies who respond differentially to mysteries of being while acknowledging each other to be worthy of respect partly because they are implicated in *this* common condition. A democratic ethos balances the desirability of governance through democratic means with a corollary politics of democratic disturbance through which any particular pattern of previous settlements might be tossed up for grabs again.

The ethos of democracy, understood in these terms, has territorial/ institutional conditions of existence, but it also embodies a crucial cultural disposition: at least a significant minority of those implicated in it understand that the porous understandings they share rest upon contestable foundations, that there are numerous differences among them grounded in a matrix of uncertainty, and that a laudatory way to respond to these uncertain commonalities and shared uncertainties is to cultivate respect for a politics of democratic governance and contestation that limits ways in which contested changes are to be initiated and disturbed traditions to be retained. The ethos of democracy both fosters a recurrent problematization of final markers (for they constantly tend to reinstate themselves) and foments a culture of agonistic respect among those who *affirm* this "alienated" world.

The key to a culture of democratization is that it embodies a productive ambiguity at its very center, always resisting attempts to allow one side or the other to achieve final victory: *its role as a mode of governance is balanced and countered by its logic as a cultural medium of the periodic denaturalization of settled identities and conventions.* In a world where the paradox of politics is perpetually susceptible to forgetfulness, there is a perpetual case to be made for the renewal of democratic energies of denaturalization.[29] For if the second dimension of democracy ever collapsed under the weight of the first, state mechanisms of electoral accountability would become conduits for fascist unity.[30]

The copulas in these formulations condense a host of contestable issues into the rhetoric of assertion. This is my condensation of the democratic imaginary in which we participate differentially. My formulation intersects with those that link democracy to political paradox in governance, to the problematization of final markers, and to maintenance of productive tension between the functions of governance and disturbance. It deviates from those that give singular hegemony to democracy as a mode of rule, sufficiently governed by shared understandings or timeless principles, confined within the borders of a sovereign state. In defense of my "is," I can say that these expectations float within the ethos of democracy wherever it has established a significant cultural presence and that, when they are thematized, these elements are likely to be appreciated by many for themselves and for their connections to other valued dimensions of democratic life.

To disaggregate the democratic imaginary is also to identify elements in it that can exceed its state territorialization. Territorial democracy and the pluralization of democratic spaces are drawn together today into mutual relations of dependence, but the scope of the second is not strictly confined by the state spatialization of the first. *Some elements of a democratic ethos can extend beyond the walls of the state.*

Take social movements. Gay and lesbian rights movements, for instance, challenge the dominant configuration of gender and sexual identity by striving to reconstitute definitions of difference through which those identities are secured. To the extent that they succeed, "heterosexuals" are less able to assume that their sexual orientation reflects nature or normality, more pressed to acknowledge the role of contingency in the formation of sexual identity, less able to find grounds for discriminating against gays or lesbians on a variety of fronts. A gay rights movement is not impelled to halt at the boundaries of a particular state. Activists may extend the movement beyond the state, establishing alliances with others of a similar political disposition in a variety of states, developing connections across state lines that exert pressure on states that imprison gays or treat them as psychologically abnormal or disqualify them as teachers, parents, soldiers, or intelligence agents. Such a movement might, for instance, press financial institutions that invest in homophobic states to divest those holdings. It might hold international conferences that expose globally homophobic state or corporate policies, publicizing the fragility of the evidence upon which these practices are based as well as the injuries and cruelties they impose and mobilizing new energies inside and outside particular states against these practices. It might exert pressure on a nonstate, cross-national organization such as Amnesty International to expand its scrutiny of states engaging in torture and political detention to include those that imprison, punish, or restrict individuals for homosexuality.

Or take state secrecy. To the extent that states classify political information, they deprive citizens of knowledge needed to hold officials accountable. But democratic pressures against secrecy inside any particular state are blunted by the state's monopoly over the classification process and political symbols of allegiance, danger, and security. Global, nonstate political organizations can increase knowledge of state secrecy and its effects by drawing together locals in a variety of states who are objects of these practices or witnesses to them. These cross-national, nonstate networks of information and leads dig global channels through which to publicize state practices of secrecy and manipulation, helping to delegitimize them in several states simultaneously. They crack through the walls of the state. Such a nonstate, international movement might help to invigorate democratic energies within states, exert external pressure upon the secret practices of states, and challenge the state's monopoly over the symbols of danger and security in the late-modern time.

And such issues can be proliferated indefinitely, engaging the state's monopoly over definitions of security and danger, gender rights, the rights of refugees, the need to expand the terms of plurality on a variety of territories, nuclear proliferation, the earth's ecological balances, the production of poverty, state immigration policies, and so on.

Cross-national, nonstatist democratic movements not only exert internal and external pressures upon states and corporations with respect to specific issues, they also challenge a state's monopoly over the allegiances, identifications, and energies of its citizens. They ventilate democratic politics inside the state by extending action beyond it. They complicate the constitution of the inside by extending constituency identifications inside the state to peoples and interests outside it. Most fundamentally, such movements contest the cultural assumption of alignment between a citizen's commitment to democracy and her commitments to the priorities of a particular state, thereby attenuating those exclusionary, nationalist sentiments flowing to the state as the legitimate site of democratic action through formal elections. To the extent such movements unfold—taking advantage of the globalization of markets, transportation, and communications that enable them to exist—a fundamental imperative of the late-modern time becomes more apparent to more people: today decent democrats must sometimes be disloyal to the state that seeks to own them morally and politically; and they must sometimes do so in the name of allegiances to a global condition that exceeds the confines of any state. As things stand now, corporate elites, military advisers, financial institutions, communication media, intelligence agencies, and criminal networks exercise considerable leeway in this regard. Only democratic citizens remain locked behind the bars of the state in the late-modern time. And even here there is already considerable movement, exemplified by disparate phenomena such as an international divestment movement in South Africa, Greenpeace, and Amnesty International, to pry open space between the bars.

But if the globalization of capital provides one condition of possibility for cross-national movements, doesn't the implacable logic of the global market render such movements permanently marginal? Certainly, recent examples of "downsizing" by international corporations suggests this possibility. Indeed, it might be argued that the dispersion of authority within the state is today matched by the consolidation of global market power over segments of labor within and across states. Put another way, the state may be losing its ability to shape its own fate even as it translates global economic pressures into losses, injuries, and exclusions imposed upon the most vulnerable constituencies within its boundaries.

There is surely something to these points. Others with more skills and knowledge in international political economy might be able to address this issue in the detail needed. But it does seem to me that the most promising way to respond to these effects is through the reorganization of capitalist labor movements. The old, national unions have faded under the pressures of internationalization. They cannot reach the forces that regulate and discipline them. But perhaps new labor movements, crossing state boundaries, can now be constructed along a variety of dimensions. Auto workers in Japan, Europe, and the United States have points of connection that crisscross their old divisions along state lines. It may be that only cross-national collaborative movements can speak to the current ability of international capital to isolate and discipline workers within separate states. And another example: regional alliances of workers stretching across the Rio Grande/Rio Bravo border may be needed to build more accountability into corporate movements across this border. The point is to resist translating earlier readings of implacable state/capital alliances into new readings of the implacable logic of global capital. And one point at which to test and stretch that logic may be through the consolidation of cross-national labor movements.

Another objection emerges, as it were, from the other side. If the democratic state does not form the only space of political allegiance and identification (*the* place of "belonging," *the* site of "shared understandings"), what else could? Timeless principles and standards seem too abstract and general to perform this function sufficiently. (These insufficiencies inspired the reformulations by Walzer and Herz.) An appropriate response requires first a critique of the question. Theories (and practices) of pluralism *within* the state acknowledge how loyalties move from one place to another as issues and concerns shift. You may be loyal to the faith of your church, but not necessarily to its legal proposals in the domains of capital punishment, abortion, the right to die, or gender relations. You may be loyal to your union with respect to the issue of dues checkoff, but not necessarily to its endorsement of political candidates. Similarly, with respect to the state, one might be loyal to its institutionalization of democratic elections and to many rights it endorses constitutionally, but not necessarily to its war policies, its strategic course, its classification practices, its resource dependencies, its constitution of criminality, or its ecological practices. Most pertinently, there is no a priori reason why deep differences with respect to these state priorities must be expressed only within the parameters of state politics. In a multidimensional, pluralist world, every particular allegiance is contingent because the occasion might occur when it collides with another you have found to be even more fundamental at this *time*.

But where is the *place* that might, if not supplant loyalty to the state, compete with it so that sometimes a new "we" finds itself bestowing allegiance on constituencies and aspirations in ways that contest the state's monopoly over political allegiance? There is no such place—at least if "place" is implicitly defined through the optics of political nostalgia. Today, though, a series of new we's might come to terms with limitations to democratic action generated by the demand for symmetry between state-territory and democratic institutions. We might extend political identifications to a distinctive *global time* that impinges upon us in fundamental ways even while it is not organized into a (non)sovereign political place. We match the understanding of how sovereignty has been traditionally overplayed as a coherent practice within the state to one that appreciates how it poses too stringent a limitation to identifications and loyalties extending beyond it.

Late modernity is a distinctive political time without a corresponding place of collective political accountability. It is a time of pluralization of political spaces of action. It is marked by the globalization of markets, communications, monetary exchanges, transportation, disease transmission, strategic planning, acid rain, greenhouse effects, resource depletion, terrorist activity, drug trade, nuclear threats to civilization, and tourism—just to list a familiar miscellany. Late modernity is not brand-new in these respects. Its distinctiveness is that in this time these interactions have become intensified, extended, and interlocked more tightly, while the speed at which the whole complex circulates has accelerated. The web of the world is spun smaller, tighter, closer, and faster than it used to be. We all impinge upon each other more densely and actively than our foreparents did, and the numerous networks of discordant interdependencies in which we are implicated generate aggregate effects with impressive consequences for the global future. Moreover, there are distinctive cultural developments that reach many areas of the world in the late-modern time with respect to the problematization of final markers, the generalization of the drive to economies of rapid growth, the spread of democratic aspirations, the rise of nationalist sentiments, the drives to universalize rights, the tendencies of states to monopolize symbols of danger and democracy, and so on. These trends intersect with those interdependencies densely enough to provide cross-national movements with convergent points of reference through which timely political issues can be defined and pursued. They provide the need for and the condition of possibility—not for the globalization of democratic elections or the liquidation of territorial democracy, but for the pluralization of democratic energies, alliances, and spaces of action through and above the territorial democratic state.

To refuse to develop political allegiances and identifications with this global time as a time would be to fail to elevate democratic sensibilities and spaces of action to the levels reached by other components of late-modern life. That would be unrealistic democratism. To define timely global and regional issues is to identify with others living in this time through political engagements that cross the boundaries of states. It is to recognize—and to legitimize the recognition—that today democratic politics flow below, through, and above the level of the state.

The extrastate pluralization of democratic spaces stands to the state today as state-territorial organization stood to city-states in sixteenth-century Italy or as feminism stood to the structure of gender relations as late as the early 1960s. It is protean, unformed, and unrealistic from the perspective of fixed identities and conventional boundaries. Epistemic realists will always find it difficult to participate in the activation of new energies if they demand the solidification of future possibilities into fixed objects prior to the representation of them.

The aura of unrealism in the extension of democratic energies resides in the inevitable inchoateness from which new formations are (sometimes) created out of old energies, identities, emergent spaces, and volatile energies. But one aspect of this cloudy condition can be addressed now. Culturally stabilized terms of comparison between territorial democracy and extrastate democratization can be revalued by coming to terms more bluntly with corollary limitations imposed upon democracy by the contemporary territorial state. For today statist democracy is pervaded by its own cloud of unreality. Its historically received mode of territorialization no longer responds multifariously enough to the complex democratic aspiration to have a hand in shaping corporate, strategic, distributive, ecological, and military practices that enable, discipline, and endanger our lives. Territorial democracy will become a late-modern anachronism unless it is compromised and exceeded by a new pluralization of democratic spaces, energies, and allegiances. And even that may not be enough.

Tocqueville, Religiosity, and Pluralization

THE AMBIGUITY OF BOUNDARIES

Boundaries abound. Between humanity and the gods. Between human and animal. Between culture and nature. Between life and death. Between genders, nations, peoples, times, races, classes, and territories. But boundaries have also become problematic today, perhaps more so than before. In a world experienced by many to be without a natural design to which they might conform, the function of boundaries becomes highly ambiguous. Boundaries form indispensable protections against violation and violence; but the divisions they sustain also carry cruelty and violence. Boundaries provide preconditions of identity, individual agency, and collective action; but they also close off possibilities of being that might otherwise flourish. Boundaries both foster and inhibit freedom; they both protect and violate life.

The political question is how to come to terms with the ambiguity of boundaries, how to fight against their sacrifices and violences without sacrificing their advantages altogether. The question poses endless difficulties, for each attempt to achieve the right balance erects a set of boundaries susceptible to the sort of interrogation that inspired it. The most tempting thing is to suppress the question itself.

Moses, in the J version of Exodus, struggles with the ambiguity of boundaries. He must respect the boundary between himself and Yahweh while bridging it to represent the word of Yahweh to his

163

people, indeed bridging the boundary in order to help constitute his people. And he must represent Yahweh authoritatively to consolidate his people. It seems clear that Yahweh too struggles with the ambiguity of boundaries, the boundaries between him and his people, between his people and other peoples, and between Moses and the people. Consider the threat to the pharaoh: "The houses of Egypt will be full, their floors will be one with the land: hidden under flies. That day I will distinguish the borders of Goshen—the land my people squat upon—to be untouched by flies, so you may know I am Yahweh, here on earth. I will put borders between your people and mine—by tomorrow this marking will be plain."[1] The flies at once mark the boundary between two peoples, the power of Yahweh over humanity, the Egyptians as a people selected for special punishment, and the Israelites as the people of Yahweh. Does the very awesomeness of the power required to establish these boundaries testify to the artificial, precarious, ambiguous character of the boundaries themselves?

The most dangerous moment for boundaries may occur when Yahweh descends to Mount Sinai and Moses ascends to meet him. A gift is being transmitted, but the very mode of transmission threatens to destroy it. The line between the giver and the recipient must be sacralized, for this is the source, the law of laws, upon which laws are grounded. But this division between the sacred and the mundane must also be breached if the sacred gift is to be transmitted. Yahweh becomes nervous and demanding:

> Descend, hold the people's attention: they must not be drawn to Yahweh to destroy boundaries. Bursting through to see, they will fall, many will die. Even the priests who approach Yahweh must be purified, so they are not drawn to destruction.

And again:

> The people will be a boundary, warn them to watch themselves, approach but not climb up, not touch the mountain. For those who overstep boundaries, death touches them, steps over their graves.[2]

After the tablets are carved, and Moses approaches Yahweh alone, Yahweh warns him against the temptations of other gods and the daughters of other peoples. And, later, when Moses approaches his people, bearing the gift, he is enraged to see "the calf" and that "dancing abounds": "His bitterness knows no bounds. He heaves the tablets from his hands, smashing them against the mountain."[3]

Clearly, Moses heaves the tablets because his people have crossed the boundary that enables them to be a people. But this rage may be aimed at the god as well as the people: the tablets are broken against the very mountain to which Yahweh has descended. Yahweh, the consummate source of boundaries, now becomes an object of rage. Moses, this ambiguous carrier of sacred gifts who speaks with a stammer and bears an Egyptian name, is well placed to appreciate the ambiguity of boundaries. Perhaps he hopes that the consolidation of this boundary will protect his people against the wildness of things and the aimlessness of life without identity, while he senses that these very boundaries carry their own violences and injustices within them. Moses responds to the ambiguity of boundaries first by accepting the gift, then by smashing it against the mountain, and then by accepting it again. He responds to his people first by leading, then by repudiating, and then by leading again. His recognition of ambiguity takes the form of three discrete acts separated by time, two for and one against. It is when we collapse this temporal boundary between acts that we can discern ambiguity in the reception of boundaries.

Rousseau, writing centuries later, honors Moses as one of three "legislators" in history who knew how to found a people (Numa and Lycurgus are the other two). Moses is the most admirable of the three, according to Rousseau's backhanded compliment, for he founded a people "out of a swarm of wretched fugitives" who did not yet inhabit a territory they could call their own:

> He founded the body of a nation, using for his materials a swarm of wretched fugitives who possessed no skills, no arms, no talents, no virtues and no courage, and who without an inch of territory to call their own, were truly a troop of outcasts upon the face of the earth. Moses made bold to transform this herd of servile emigrants into a political society, a free people; at a moment when it was still wandering about in the wilderness. . . . Even today, when that nation no longer exists as a body, its legislation endures and is as strong as ever.[4]

Rousseau, who recognizes the fundamental ambiguity involved in the founding of a people,[5] is nonetheless reluctant to emphasize its continuing effects once a good founding has occurred. His drive to political unity discourages him from politicizing the ambiguity he recognizes all too well. Indeed, in the essay on Poland where Moses is introduced, Rousseau is hell bent on separating the people now in question—the Poles—as thoroughly as possible from other peoples. He wants the strategies of Moses—roughly, weighing the people down "with rites and peculiar ceremonies" and "countless prohibitions"[6]—to be combined with the advantage of inhabiting a common territory. He wants, that is, to overcode the difference between the Poles and other peoples. To do so in order to make them a free people. It is good that the Poles have a large territory to themselves:

> But so large a country, and one that has never had much intercourse with its neighbors, must have developed a great many usages that are its very own, but are perhaps being bastardized, day in and day out, in line with the Europe-wide tendency to take on the tastes and customs of the French. You must maintain or revive (as the case may be) your ancient customs and introduce suitable new ones that will also be purely Polish. Let these new customs . . . even have their bad points; they would, unless bad in principle, still afford this advantage: *they would endear Poland to its citizens and develop in them a distinctive distaste for mingling with the peoples of other countries.* I deem it all to the good, for example, that the Poles have a distinctive mode of dress.[7]

The line of correspondences is tight: to be free you must belong to a people; to be a people you must have a common identity burned into you; to be a flourishing people you must exclusively inhabit a contiguous territory; to flourish freely as a territorialized people you must stringently define and exclude the foreign. Wandering and plurality must be repressed along a variety of dimensions. Rousseau underlines the centrality of territory to the constitution and protection of a people in *The Social Contract*:

> It is understandable how the combined lands of private individuals become public territory, and how the right of sovereignty, *extending from the subjects to the ground they occupy,* comes to include both property and persons. . . . This advantage does not appear to have been well understood by ancient kings who, only calling themselves kings of the Persians, the Scythians, the Macedonians, seem to have considered themselves leaders of men rather than masters of the country. Today's kings more cleverly call themselves Kings of France,

Spain, England, etc. *By thus holding the land, they are quite sure to hold its inhabitants.*[8]

A people, to be both a people and free, must inhabit a common territory, and the territory, somehow, must inhabit them spiritually. Their identity must extend "to the ground they occupy"; and sovereignty must come to include "property and persons," so that it holds the inhabitants by "holding the land" (and vice versa). This set of correspondences has been fractured in recent centuries through the international commerce of people, things, and ideas, but it has yet to be reconfigured significantly in either the dominant theories of politics circulating through Western states or in the political cultures prevailing in them. In fact, the accelerated circulation of people, communications, cultural dispositions, things, and currencies across state boundaries very often fosters reactive movements of nationalism and fundamentalism that are extremely violent toward heterogeneity inside and outside their regimes.

And even late-modern conceptions of democracy make a contribution to these effects. Late-modern ideals of democratic politics, while varying along several familiar dimensions, still revolve around the people, the territorial state, and the citizen, producing multiple sets of Others through this very line of correspondences. Modern political thought, in its general drift, celebrates the political advantages of overcoded boundaries by suppressing the violences accompanying these codes. It thus remains closer to my Rousseau than to my Moses, particularly with respect to the ambiguity of coding identity onto territory and politics onto territorial identity.

But evidence of the violence in these inscriptions keeps returning. It even returns in the etymology of *territory,* which derives from *terrere* and *territorium,* and insinuates a dim memory of violence into the boundaries of territory. Through Tocqueville, the classic defender of pluralism and territoriality, we might be able to bring this memory into more explicit focus.

THE CIVI-TERRITORIAL COMPLEX

Alexis de Tocqueville is a Rousseauian pluralist.[9] As pluralist, he celebrates an un-Rousseauian diversity. As Rousseauian, he insists that underlying this diversity must be a common identity, a fixed "civilization" burned into the mores of the people. As pluralist, he may be more alert than Rousseau to violences engendered by the boundaries he endorses; as Rousseauian, he becomes resigned to these violences by demoralizing them. Tocqueville in these ways registers latent ambiguities residing in several forms of pluralism preceding and succeeding him in the West.[10]

Let us concentrate on the "Indian" in Tocqueville's "America."[11] Tocqueville knows that the North American continent was not devoid of human life before Europeans arrived. Consider a few statements:

> These vast wildernesses were not completely unvisited by man; for centuries some nomads had lived under the dark forests or the meadows of the prairies.

> The Indians occupied but did not possess the land. It is by agriculture that man wins the soil.

> North America was only inhabited by wandering tribes who had not thought of exploiting the natural wealth of the soil. One could still properly call North America an empty continent, a deserted land waiting for inhabitants. . . . In this condition ["watery solitudes," "limitless fields never yet turned by the plowshare"] it offers itself not to the isolated, ignorant, and barbarous man of the first ages, but man who has already mastered the most important secrets of nature, united to his fellows, and taught by the experience of fifty centuries.[12]

If the nomads merely visited the land, if isolated tribes wandered on its surface under the forest wilderness, if they occupied but did not possess the land upon which they wandered, if they failed to win it through agri-culture, failed to master the land or to exploit its natural wealth, then it is *proper* to "call North America an empty continent, a deserted land *waiting* for *inhabitants*." Civilization and territory thus become intercoded through Tocqueville: agri-culture, mastery, possession, exploiting natural wealth, and applying the experience of fifty centuries to the land constitute crucial elements of civilization; and civilization establishes itself by taking possession of a contiguous territory and becoming possessed by it. Tocqueville registers, then, in carefully crafted language, the construction of "America," a civi-territorial complex in which the crucial dimensions of territory and civilization reinforce each other until they accumulate enough force together to propel the "triumphal progress of civilization across the wilderness."[13] What of those wandering nomads who are, well, not dispossessed from territory they never possessed but displaced from a wilderness upon which they wandered? Tocqueville disposes of them sadly and regretfully, for they are dead to civilization even before the advance of civilization progressively kills them off.

Once civilization is coded onto a contiguous territory—so that its occupants are occupied by the same culture—it is possible to strengthen both together. Christian monotheism provides the cultural glue binding the civi-territorial complex together. It does not really matter whether everyone truly believes the Christian faith; it only matters that it is professed generally and persistently enough so that it enters into the "reason" and "mores" that bind people together:

> In the United States it is not only mores that are controlled by religion, but its sway extends over reason. . . . There are some who profess Christian dogmas because they believe them and others do so because they are afraid to look as though they did not believe in them. So Christianity reigns without obstacles, by universal consent; consequently, as I have said elsewhere, everything in the moral field is certain and fixed, although the world of politics seems given over to argument and experiment.[14]

Tocquevillian pluralism floats on the surface of the civi-theo-territorial complex. There is a mild pluralization of ethnic groups, religious congregations within Christianity, local customs, and forms of governance. And democratic politics does form a positive nomadic element in the Tocquevillian world. But politics is free to dance lightly on the surface of life only because everything fundamental is fixed below it. The American imaginary is determined outside of politics:

> Thus while the law allows the American people to do everything; there are things which religion prevents them from imagining and forbids them to become. . . . Religion, which never intervenes directly in the government of American society, should therefore be considered as the first of their political institutions.[15]

Separation of church and state does not render the state neutral with respect to religion, nor does it sanction significant religious diversity. The superficial faiths of the nomads, for instance, remain outside this zone of tolerance. So does the profession of atheism, which, as Tocqueville notes without dismay, effectively rules one out of competition for public office, probably because those who contend "that everything perishes with the body . . . must be regarded as the natural enemies of the people."[16] Rather, the separation of church and state allows monotheism to install its effects in the hearts of the people and the presumptions of their institutions below the threshold of political debate. The mores of civilization precede, ground, pervade, and restrict politics. Removing them from the clash and clang of politics preserves the sanctity of civilized religion and sets the boundaries of pluralism in the civi-theo-territorial culture. Separation of church and state enables Christian monotheism to form the first "political institution" above the fray of politics.

Once patriotism is tracked onto religion, mores, reason, imagination, civilization, and territory, the terrain upon which pluralist democracy moves has been fixed. You can also locate the spaces through which democratic sovereignty circulates: "The principle of sovereignty of the people, which is always to be found, more or less, at the bottom of almost all human institutions, usually remains buried there."[17] In most cultures, prior to America, sovereignty appeared to reside in the king while it "more or less" flowed to the king from its hidden source in the people. Sovereignty, that is, was located nowhere exactly, but circulated secretly and uncertainly between its official site and its unofficial source. In the new American pluralism this uncertainty remains, but now sovereignty circulates uncertainly between the will of the people and the civi-theo-territorial complex that constitutes them. For "the people" can be officially sovereign in America only because those human beings who diverge from the essence of civilization have been displaced from the land they previously wandered over and because the territorialization of civilization itself sets the parameters of popular sovereignty. The exact site of sovereignty (the people or the civilization that shapes its imagination) remains as uncertain in Tocqueville's America as it does in every theory or culture preceding and succeeding him; it is the spaces through which this uncertainty circulates that have shifted.

The historical consolidation of the civi-territorial complex requires the elimination of the Indian. Since this complex sets conditions of possibility of morality itself, Tocqueville finds it impossible to judge the extermination or colonization of the Indian to be immoral. He has not acquired the powers of imagination, best exemplified by Nietzsche, to probe the "injustice in justice" or the "immorality of morality." How, then, does Tocqueville come to terms with violence that is undeserved and also exceeds the territory of morality? He implicitly struggles with this dilemma by repeatedly using phrases such as "ill-fated," "unfortunate people," and "unlucky people" to characterize the victims of cultural violence. He also repeatedly regrets the "inevitable destruction" bound up with the "stubborn prejudices" of the "savages" and the "chance" that "has brought" two diverse "stocks together on the same soil."[18] This slippery language of regret without moral indictment and, more significantly, of the recognition of undeserved suffering without any plan to curtail it in the future, places a heavy burden on this staunch defender of a civilization of moral uprighteousness, solid mores, and deep convictions. For this violence must not be defined as unjust even though it cannot be defined as just. Anything that sets the preconditions of moral virtue must not itself be immoral, according to the implicit dictum guiding Tocqueville's prose. The drive to struggle against the injustice in justice, at any rate, remains outside both the moral imagination of Alexis de Tocqueville and the culture registered through his imagination. The Indian is thus simultaneously the first Other of the civi-territorial complex, the first sign of violence inscribed in its boundaries, and the first marker of how violence is obscured or forgotten by the complex that requires it.

Tocqueville knows that the most pervasive violence against the Indian is not that of war and massacre, though that happens often enough. The very terms of settlement dictated by the extension of civilization—that is, of the civi-territorial complex—make it impossible for these nomads to live within a "hundred leagues" of the nearest new settlement. Each new settlement unsettles the ecology of nomadic life. Each new settlement impels nomads to wander further to the west. The most profound pattern of violence against the Indian is always revealed *retrospectively* in traces that can easily be ignored; it shows itself in the retreat of tribes from land they occupied, in the enervation of peoples already wrenched from the land, in "unprovoked" attacks by Indians on white settlements. This obscure violence, this violence that is repeatedly and belatedly recognized through traces and signs from the past, forms a constitutive element in the civi-territorial complex of America. The form it assumes is fugitive, deniable, and forgettable, more likely to be acknowledged tomorrow through regret over a past that could not have been otherwise than challenged today through a determination to change the future. These unfortunate effects on the Other are installed, again, in civilization itself, particularly and ironically, perhaps, in a Euro-American civilization that creates room for political pluralism. For "how could society escape destruction, if, when political ties are relaxed, moral ties are not tightened? What can be done with a people master of itself, if it is not subject to God?"[19] If you answer these questions in a Tocquevillian way, it becomes clear that the territorialization of pluralism requires the eradication of the Indian and that the presentation of pluralism as the highest ideal requires the demoralization of the violence upon which it rests. For "there are certain great social principles which a people either introduces everywhere or tolerates nowhere."[20]

Tocqueville, I have already suggested, cautiously vindicates a nomadic movement inscribed in the *politics* of pluralism itself. But before this modest nomadism can be installed, the fundamental nomadism of the Indian must be purged. What happens, though, when Tocqueville encounters new nomadic elements *within* the civilization he admires, modes of mobility that are both indispensable to the civilization he celebrates and dangerous to the boundaries it requires? What about money, goods, labor, capital, and entrepreneurial activity, for instance? These mobile media flow across territorial boundaries rather freely; they exceed the effective control of sovereign power, even while it depends upon them to provide material sustenance. I suspect that the very pressures toward centralization of the state Tocqueville decries so much in volume two of *Democracy in America* flow from attempts by the state to control those internal (and yet also external) nomadic elements it cannot expel from the civilization. And that Tocqueville's later pessimism about the future of democracy is bound up with his inability to imagine a viable response to forms of nomadism that cannot be eliminated by, nor are very consonant with, the civi-territorial complex he imagines. I will not pursue these suspicions here. Rather, I will ask, What orientation to the boundaries of pluralism and the pluralism of boundaries might be more responsive in the future to the nomadic element in politics? Is it possible to imagine boundaries to pluralism that are not impelled to eliminate the Indians they engender?

TOCQUEVILLE, THOREAU, APESS

Have I wrenched Tocqueville "out of context"? (As if a context were not always the dissonant conjunction of contemporary issues and the time and place interrogated.) Consider, in the context of my concerns, Henry Thoreau, a nineteenth-century eccentric residing in this same civi-mono-national-territorial complex. In "The Allegash and East Branch," written a couple of decades after *Democracy in America*, Thoreau reviews his canoeing trip with an Indian guide, Joe Polis. "Polis" and "the Indian"—the two labels through which Thoreau identifies the guide—seem to fit Tocqueville's characterization when Thoreau and he negotiate on the white man's ground. And Thoreau could still identify him in Tocquevillian terms once they arrived at "the wilderness." At first Polis appeared to be quiet, stolid, almost "mild and infantile." Then Polis became active, skillful, engaging, and indispensable to the project they pursued together.

Does Thoreau slip onto that familiar incline where the Indian as barbarian slides into the Indian as noble savage? Does he merely invert the valuation given to this figure of the European-American imagination? He can be read that way, as when he says that "nature must have made a thousand revelations to them which are still secrets to us."[21] But when such general statements are considered in relation to specific concerns shared by the three travelers (Thoreau's brother, identified only as a companion, accompanies him on this trip) about directions, medicine, signs, pests, game, and myths they encounter together on their journey, the faint light of another experience begins to glimmer through the stereotype.

Thoreau and Polis, meeting on an ambiguous space neither wholly within nor wholly outside Tocquevillian civilization, both work to extend the cultural imagination through which each engages the other. For example, when Thoreau, the naturalist, discovers the fluorescent light that "dwells in the rotten wood" of one kind of tree, the Indian tells him that the light is called *Artoosoqu'* and that "his folks sometimes saw fires passing along at various heights, even as high as the trees."[22] This leads to a discussion of Indian gods. Thoreau engages "the Indian" not as he might have been before the arrival of the "white man" (Polis's handle for Thoreau and his type) nor simply as he was constituted by the white man at that time. Rather, Thoreau engages Polis as the other whose mode of being crosses his own at crucial points and who is central to the ethical sensibility Thoreau himself seeks to cultivate. Polis turns out to be neither reducible to the cultural categories through which the Anglo-American culture receives him nor susceptible to a characterization that equates him to a white man with a "red skin." The white man and the Indian, on this journey on the edge of "civilization," forge an operational relationship of dissonant interdependence in which each maintains a certain pathos of distance from the other while selectively drawing sustenance from him.[23]

Once, as the conversation wanders toward religion, Polis professes to be a Protestant while nonetheless telling stories reflecting commitments from other times. Thoreau professes to be a Protestant too, while confessing (to the reader) that this profession is an exaggeration. It is the relation Thoreau seeks to establish that contrasts sharply with Tocqueville: "I have much to learn of the Indian, nothing of the missionary. I am not sure but all that would tempt me to teach the Indian my religion would be his promise to teach me *his*."[24]

The white man finds that the Indian brings out—through terse assertions that he doesn't "know" how he guides himself through the forest or stalks game—a strand of tacit skill also flowing silently through the white man's inventory of explicit, formal knowledge:

> Often when an Indian says 'I don't know,' in regard to the route he is to take, he does not mean what a white man would mean by those words, for his Indian instinct may tell him as much as the most confident white man knows. He does not carry things in his head, nor remember the route exactly, like a white man, but relies on himself at the moment. Not having experienced the need of the other sort of knowledge, all labelled and arranged, he has not acquired it.[25]

Thoreau, the naturalist who labels and orders everything, does so in part to encounter experiences that exceed his labels. He strives to *cultivate* a generous ethical sensibility that becomes an instinctive disposition to life; he strives to detach himself from a set of settled conventions to enable himself to recognize and resist hidden violences in them. Polis thereby helps Thoreau to recognize a subterranean, fugitive strain in his own culture and to modify the (socially crafted) instincts through which he engages difference. Thoreau, who seeks to become bicultural, eventually glimpses how bicultural Polis already is: Polis avails himself "cunningly of the advantages of civilization without losing any of his woodcraft."[26] And Thoreau conveys in his notebooks how the (Tocquevillian/American) perception of "the Indian" as nomadic hunter is belied by the agricultural traditions of many American peoples who grew corn, melons, squash, tobacco, and other crops. This white man draws sustenance from Polis by appreciating how his own categories of experience never suffice to grasp the other and by cultivating numerous connections enabled by the multiple friction points between them. The pathos of distance between Thoreau and Polis amplifies an important element in the ethical relation.

Still, Thoreau's engagements with Polis are limited. He relates to this individual as a distinctively bicultural being without digging deeply into the patterns of kinship, language, and myth of entire peoples.[27] And this connection occurs on the edges of "American" cultural space, making it difficult to translate its implications for conventional life. Moreover, the engagement with Polis is governed first and foremost by Thoreau's own desire to gain distance from the world into which *he* has been thrown. Finally, Thoreau's antipolitical stance, governed by fear that entry into politics would inexorably enable the they-world to overwhelm him, inhibits the political engagements he might have pursued in alliance with indigenous peoples struggling against the constraints of the American civi-territorial complex. Thoreau and Polis press against the Tocquevillian rendering of civilizational necessity without cracking its code. Indeed, it would be impossible for them to do so on this neoreservational space.

But what if Thoreau, while pursuing the trail we have reviewed, had encountered William Apess, the son of Pequot parents in New England, Christianized by a series of white couples who serially adopted and abandoned him? This ambiguous Pequot, educated briefly in New England schools, eventually became a leader and spokesman for the Mashpee, a small tribe fighting to protect its land and culture on Cape Cod during the 1830s. Apess, as we can belatedly see through Barry O'Connell's collection of his essays, was a fierce political leader and effective polemicist, drawing critical resources from the Christianity of his Christian oppressors. Apess crosses the border between two cultures residing on the same territory, revealing as he proceeds how these borders have already become blurred and how the dominant party in border building is hell bent on stopping the flow. Apess, and the peoples he draws sustenance from, disrupts the territorialization of civilization marked by Tocqueville; he crosses the border glimpsed by the Thoreau/Polis encounter.

In his essay "Indian Nullification of the Unconstitutional Laws of Massachusetts Relative to the Mashpee Tribe; or, The Pretended Riot Explained," Apess explains how he and his band were arrested and jailed for "rioting" when they prevented white poachers from taking wood from their land. He uses this event to publicize the case for a coalition of Indians and whites against the oppressive practices of the Commonwealth. Apess writes to at least three possible audiences: to Mashpee and associated peoples touched by this struggle; to a possible minority of white Christians (as he labels them) in New England who might respond to the justice of the Mashpee claims; and to a generalized posterity that might profit in yet unknown ways from the words of a literate, Christianized, politicized, Pequot, Mashpee not supposed to be able or willing to encompass such a combination. We can merely sample here the prose of this hybrid activist, writing and rebelling during the time of *Democracy in America*:

> I ask: What people could improve under laws which gave such temptation and facility to plunder? . . . If the government of Massachusetts do not see fit to believe me, I would fain propose to them a test of the soundness of my reasoning. Let them put our white neighbors in Barnstable County under the guardianship of a board of overseers and give them no privileges other than have been allowed to the poor, despised Indians. Let them inflict upon the said whites a preacher whom they neither love nor respect and do not wish to hear. Let them, in short, be treated just as the Mashpee tribe have been; I think there will soon be a declension of morals and population. We shall see if they are able to build up a town in such circumstances. Any enterprising men who may be among them will soon seek another home and society, which it is not in the power of the Indians to do, on account of their color. . . . The laws were calculated to drive the tribes from their possessions and annihilate them as a people.
>
> Why should not this odious, and brutifying system be put an end to? Why should not the remaining Indians in this Commonwealth be

placed upon the same footing as to rights of property, as to civil privileges and duties, as other men? Why should they not *vote*, maintain schools . . . and use as they please that which is their own? If the contiguous towns object to having them added to their corporations, let them be incorporated by themselves: let them choose their officers; establish a police, maintain fences and take up stray cattle. I believe the Indians desire such a change. I believe they have gone as far as they are allowed to introduce it. But they are fettered and ground to the earth.[28]

Suppose the contingencies of chance and timing had spawned an encounter between the Thoreaus and the Mashpee of this day (as well as with, in different combinations, say, the Cherokee in the south and the Sioux in the Midwest). Is it not *possible* that the former, with their fugitive attractions to "paganism," might have overcome their instinctive aversion to politics, and that the latter, with their ambiguous "Christianization," might have entered into a new political alliance? In this unactualized space of political conjunction between two types we know to have inhabited nineteenth-century America we glimpse unpursued political possibilities. As Apess shows, an immanent critique of Christianity goes part of the way in opening up this space. But it does not go all the way. A change in widespread cultural presumptions about the territorial preconditions of civilization is also needed, for instance. It is highly improbable, of course, that such a political assemblage could achieve much in that time, even if it were consolidated. It is, even, highly uncertain what terms it might have assumed and how persistent its pressures could have been. But such counterfactual assessments of historical *probability* do not exhaust the pertinent issues. For the very identification of this unpursued space of historical *possibility* begins to crack the Tocquevillian/American code of moral/civilizational/territorial *necessity*. It begins to set an agonizing pattern of Tocquevillian/American violence within a contingent constellation of institutional entrenchments rather than the intrinsic imperatives of civilization as such. These Tocquevillian/American entrenchments are doubtless terribly resistant to reconfiguration, but they are nonetheless ungrounded in the very necessity of morality, the requirements of civilization, or the ontological conditions of politics.

The hypothetical Apess/Thoreau conjunction drains the presumption of necessity from the historical options between assimilation of the Indian and exclusion of the Indian from civilized land. Identification of a possible conjunction between a few thousand "Thoreaus" and "Apesses" on the land of "New England" thus presses people today either to endorse those violences more nakedly or to respond affirmatively to struggles against their contemporary effects.

We indulge this critical nostalgia for a past that never was to fan sparks of possibility in the present. For more of the present than we normally think is bound up with circumstances that might have been otherwise. We are much more the result of contingent historical arrangements sedimented into complex contemporary constellations than of civilizational necessities set in the cement of intrinsic cultural identities. When we excavate past violences, pressing against the self-protective naturalizations and ontologizations in which they have been set, we may discern new possibilities of pluralization in the present. We may glimpse the outlines of a more rhizomatic pluralism.[29]

JUSTICE AND CRITICAL RESPONSIVENESS

In what follows I explore a contemporary pluralist imagination that scrambles and pluralizes the civi-territorial complex. The intention is not to focus on the economic conditions of pluralist politics, a task begun in chapter 3. Rather, I elaborate some of the ethicopolitical conditions of multifarious pluralism, reviewing a few themes introduced elsewhere in this study and linking them to a new discussion of the politics of enactment. This pluralization of pluralism does not usher in a pluralism without boundaries, for no such beast is possible. Nor does it dismantle in prose the territorial state. For such an intervention would be self-destructive even if it succeeded in the late-modern age. It does support, rather, a dis-nationalist, late-modern pluralism in which the overcoded boundary of the civi-territorial state is translated into multiple lines of division that do not correspond to one another on the same plane. We pursue, then, a more fluid and mobile pluralist imagination.

If you define the root idea of democracy—vaguely, as any root idea must be defined—to be *rule* by a unified *people* of *itself,* you bring under arrest twice the nomadic element circulating through the ethos of democracy. For that definition impels you to ask, first, How can a people become unified enough to rule itself? and, last, How can rule reproduce the unity of the people? Your thinking is likely to oscillate between the statist (im)possibilities of a general will, a rational consensus, a Schmittian decisionism, and the arboreal pluralism of Tocqueville, where diversity consists of several limbs stretching out from the (civi-territorial) trunk that provides them with support and nourishment. But if you treat democracy to involve the more protean idea that those affected have their hands and voices in modeling the multiple cultures that constitute them, the insufficiency of the politics of rule comes more prominently into view.

On this reading, political rule is always pertinent to a democratic ethos, but so is the question of how to loosen, challenge, or interrupt sedimented presumptions about identity, nature, gender, morality, nationality, divinity, civilization, and the global environment that enter into ruling. A democratic ethos now becomes, among other things, a setting in which nomadic *movements* periodically interrupt centered cultural presumptions so that the element of power, artifice, and contingency in these all too readily naturalized norms becomes more palpable, so that voices defined as (interior, internal, external) Others in the established order of things can locate cultural space to contest some of these definitions, so that new combinations emerging out of these disturbances can develop agonistic respect for one another in changing contexts of interdependency.

Tocqueville, in volume one of *Democracy in America,* appreciates the nomadic element in pluralist democracy. He says:

> That constantly renewed agitation introduced by democratic government into political life passes, then, into civil society. Perhaps, taking everything into consideration, that is the greatest advantage of democratic government, and I praise it much more on account of what it causes to be done than for what it does. . . . Democracy does not provide a people with the most skillful of governments, but does that which the most skillful government cannot do; it spreads throughout the body social a restless activity, superabundant force, and energy never found elsewhere, which, however little favored by circumstance, can do wonders. Those are its true advantages.[30]

The difficulty is that Tocqueville pretty much restricts the element of agitation, restless activity, and mobile energy to localities and, most fundamentally, *never encourages it to flow into the sacred trunk of civilization itself.* Tocqueville is too enamored with trees and agri-culture. He roots the tree of civilization so deeply into the soil of monotheism, territory, and governance that he is reluctant to ask how forces already there might contribute to the nomadic element he prizes within democracy. This tendency is consolidated in volume two, where Tocqueville codifies a normative divide between spirituality and materialism, in which the former is aligned with God, soul, immortality, permanence, the infinite, morality, and immovable nature, while the latter is aligned with restlessness, movement, egoism, greed, physical pleasure, the soulless, the mundane, emptiness, and madness.

When you attend to the productive role of nomadism in politics, it is possible to pursue it in a variety of directions. The politics of disturbance within the state, for instance, might grow into the formation of cross-national, nonstatist social movements that speak to particular issues within a state, between states, and in the global setting as a system. As we have already seen in chapter 5, such movements, in their cumulative effect, can compromise the state as the highest or final site of citizen identification. They can thus help to render the state more accountable to its members and the interstate system more accountable to constituencies affected by the global economy and interstate negotiations. Tocqueville never thought about how extension of the nomadic element above the level of the state as well could compromise the very tendency of the state to gain too much power over the allegiance of its members. That was reasonable enough, perhaps, in the context of early America. It is not today. The nomadic element can grow in another direction as well, as constituencies within states translate the politics of selective disturbance into the politics of enactment of new identities out of old differences, energies, and injuries. This is the dimension we will focus on.

The most fragile and indispensable element in a pluralizing democracy is an ethos of critical responsiveness to new social movements, an ethos that opens up cultural space through which new possibilities of being might be enacted. The politics of enactment applies new pressures to existing constellations of identity\difference by shaking the cultural ground in which they are rooted. But this is not all. It also presses hegemonic identities, which are always dependent upon the very differences they define, to translate this experience of disturbance into a will to modify *themselves* so that they no longer remain exactly what they were, so that they change enough to open up new possibilities of negotiation and coexistence with new claims to identity. The politics of enactment, therefore, is not sufficiently represented through the language of overcoming prejudice, promoting tolerance, extending diversity, or following a settled code of justice among preexisting subjects. Such portrayals not only underplay the constructed, relational character of what we are, they also conceal the precarious political process by which a new claim to identity is drawn onto the register of justice from a nether region residing below it.

Puritans (one of Tocqueville's favorite American/Christian sects),[31] participating in such an ethos of pluralization, might find themselves propelled to redefine their relational religious identity each time Catholicism engages Protestantism, Judaism engages Christianity, paganism engages monotheism, secularism engages theism, and nontheistic reverence for the ambiguity of being engages the twentieth-century hegemony of the sacred/secular pair. Puritan faith is not necessarily thinned out by the progressive appearance of new alternatives, though that is one of the directions it might take. Rather, new presumptions and contestable articles of faith in Puritanism are revealed by the enactment of each new cultural alternative. When a democratic ethos is operative, Puritans and their descendants are challenged each time to come to terms with the contestable character of sacred presumptions previously outside the scope of consideration; they are also pressed to modify the way they hold these now contested articles of faith. Some might become post-Puritans over time, either in the form of the faith they adopt or in the way they now articulate it. Or in both ways. Others may become more reticent to generalize what they are in the name of religious truth or (the secular variant of Christianity) moral universality.

The cumulative effect of such enactments, when a generous ethos is operative, links a growing number of constituencies to appreciation of the fundamental contingency of things; to acknowledgment by more people in more settings of the role power plays in the naturalization of cultural boundaries; and to enhanced cultural responsiveness to the call to open up room for positive identities to crystallize out of the energies and injuries of difference.

The politics of enactment is so fragile, risky, deniable, and crucial that it is necessary to revitalize periodically opportunity and responsiveness in this domain. The risk resides partly in the chance that a new enactment will eventually jeopardize the ethos of responsiveness itself, partly in the chance that it will be suppressed to protect the self-confidence of powerful identities disturbed by the threat it poses to their claims to self-certainty, but mostly in the probability that it will be defined automatically to fall into the first category by those whose self-certainty is shaken by its very appearance.

We caught a glimpse of the politics of enactment in the terms of interaction between Henry Thoreau and Joe Polis and in that hypothetical alliance between nineteenth-century Thoreaus and Apesses. We also saw through Tocqueville's dismissive delineation of the Indian how fragile such a possibility can be at its point of enactment, how vulnerable it is to reactive violence in the name of civilization or intrinsic morality or Christian universalism or consensual democratic rule or territorial integrity closed up beyond the (always debatable) point of necessity.

Numerous political movements pursuing new possibilities of being are discernible in America's recent past: in a thwarted black power movement that revealed an institutional racism running much deeper than prejudice; in a feminist movement that cracked open the existing rule of gender hierarchy; and in multiple ethnic movements forged out of the experience of devalued immigrant nationalities.

Perhaps the most revealing ethicopolitical moment occurs when a movement remains poised on that precarious threshold of enactment prior to its crystallization into a new form. This is the moment when it remains highly vulnerable to dismissal or repression by those responding to it through the very categories it seeks to contest. There are several recent or current examples of such moments in America: As when those who demand the right to doctor-assisted death for the terminally ill fight against the predominant Christian view that "suicide" is always a sin and the judgment lingering in some corners of secularism that death must come when nature wills it. As when sexual minorities fight through injuries imposed on them by sacralization and medicalization of the heterosexual/homosexual pair to generate lesbian/gay movements pluralizing the possibilities of positive sexual identity and extending the operational space in which rights may be claimed. As when feminists proceed through the fight against discrimination within gender duality to pluralize gender performance itself. As when citizens risk the charge of treason or irresponsibility by extending their political affiliations beyond the boundaries of the territorial state. As when carriers of postsecular, nontheistic reverence for the diversity of being struggle to pry open space between the conventional sacred/secular division, doing so to place a new ethical sensibility on the political scale.[32]

Each of these pluralizing movements is precarious at a critical historical moment. Each can all too readily be drawn back into the regulatory discourse of the divine/natural injunction against suicide, the hetero/homo pair, the divine/natural basis of gender duality, the nation-state/world anarchy combo, or the (Christian) sacred/secular division. Each, that is, is susceptible to recolonization by assumptions installed in the institutions of public communication, military life, church membership, marriage law, citizenship, teaching, intelligence agencies, and so on.

Such susceptibility occurs because the drive to crystallize a positive identity out of injuries buried within established constellations not only threatens the self-confidence of existing identities; at an early and vulnerable moment the new possibility has not yet achieved a sufficiently positive definition to pose a credible alternative to hegemonic definitions of what it is. A new "it" has not yet been formed. And the old institutionalized definition thereby retains considerable cultural resonance. The politics of enactment involves the struggle to cross both of these boundaries together—the barrier posed by the resistance of disrupted identities and that posed by difficulty the movement faces in clearing sufficient institutional space to articulate a positive identity.

An ethos of critical responsiveness, when it is operative, supports these boundary crossings. That is why such an ethos is critical to maintenance of the constitutive tension between pluralism and pluralization. But what shape does such an ethos assume? It is never entirely reducible to any fixed code or criteria of morality. For it provides the cultural reserve of care and generosity from which reassessment of the morality of existing moral codes is periodically renewed. It does not conform to the teleological model of virtue, even though it shares with that model the conviction that no ethics is reducible to the codes it authorizes and that cultivation of a generous sensibility is crucial to ethics. Nor does it conform to the model of paternal care for a child, which has traditionally been conceived as a relation in which the law of the father sets the ends into which the child grows, while the love of the mother motivates the child in the predetermined direction. Critical responsiveness, however, arises in settings where the end in question is often not yet clearly in view, either to the initiators or to the respondents.

The responsiveness in question, rather, is anticipatory, critical, and self-revisionary in character. It is *anticipatory* in that it responds to a movement to pluralize even before the constituency in question has become fully consolidated into a recognized, positive identity. For the positive identity is an effect at the end of a political struggle, not quite a fact or implicit concept at its beginning. It is *critical* in that it must consider, for instance, whether the new movement is relentlessly fundamentalist, whether it drives to impose its identity as the universal standard and to punish everyone who deviates from it. It is, most crucially, *self-revisionary* in that those on the responding end eventually must modify what they are, in form or content or both, if the new movement is to attain sufficient cultural space to crystallize a new identity. Critical responsiveness to the injuries of Otherness (e.g., to Indians, atheists, slaves, pagans, homosexuals, ladies, illegal immigrants) implies a comparative denaturalization and reconfiguration of hegemonic identities whose character depended on these specifications of difference.

Consider the ambiguous relation critical responsiveness bears to the discourse of justice. Each pluralizing movement, if and as it succeeds, migrates from an abject, abnormal, subordinate, or obscure Other *subsisting* in a nether world *under* the register of justice to a positive identity now *existing* on the register of justice/injustice. It is only after a movement crosses this critical threshold of identification that its injuries can acquire the standing of injustice or illegitimacy. This reveals the essential ambiguity of justice: the practice of justice is both indispensable after the crossing and a barrier to enactment before it. Critical responsiveness midwifes pluralizing movements across this critical threshold.

To encapsulate such a political migration under the radical theme of dialectical progression or the liberal theme of belated recognition of an implication of your own principles is not to misrecognize it altogether. To reduce the migration to these characterizations, though, is to miss the most critical and precarious moment in the *politics* of enactment. Those who do so place themselves in a position to celebrate previous crossings while remaining deaf to the claims of movements *now* pushed below the threshold of justice. Here is such a formulation, by Seyla Benhabib, who is criticizing the political ethics of François Lyotard and Jacques Derrida through reference to a historical "dialectic" built into the universal respect for persons in the American Declaration of Independence:

> For between the formal structure of the original act of identity constitution and exclusion and the normative content of the declarative which obliges us to obey certain laws *a contradiction exists*. Although it is "we," the white, propertied, Christian, North American male heads of household, who hold these truths to be self evident, 'that all men are created equal . . .', between our contingent historical identity which affirms these truths and the content of those truths a tension, a *dialectic* of momentous historical proportions exists.[33]

But there was not a *contradiction* between the general assertion by propertied white Christian North American males of the rights of man and their effective denial of particular rights to those placed below that threshold—women, slaves, and Indians—as long as the cultural constitution of the latter placed aspects of their lives under the threshold of candidacy for inclusion in the universal. Tocqueville shows us precisely how such a reduction works, through his rendering of the Indian. To fight against such a constitution, no new lessons in Aristotelian or Hegelian logic are needed. Participation in the ambiguous politics of enactment is needed.

The recourse to the dialectic obscures the most profound ambiguity inhering in universal rights. Universal human rights do set one condition of dignity; but the very closure of this universal into a sufficient moral condition sets up a barrier to new pluralizing drives. "Homosexuality," for instance, must break its cultural constitution as an "objective disorder" *before* the "dialectic" can take hold. So must the binary line of division between the sacred and the secular before postsecular care for the excess of life over identity can gain a cultural foothold. Otherwise it will simply be defined as "parasitical" upon true morality by happy secular rationalists and theistic universalists. It is exactly this powerful historical tendency toward closure in the structure of universals that renders deconstruction, genealogy, political disturbance, and the politics of enactment indispensable elements in the politics of pluralism.[34] For such interventions explore how the historical construction of minority formations (such as atheism, Indians, homosexuals, etc.) function to naturalize majority formations (such as theists, whites, heterosexuals, etc.) before the question of justice is brought into play. Is the recourse to the dialectic, then, a last-ditch effort to avoid the coils of genealogy? Probably. But its effect is to celebrate past achievements of pluralization by making critical responsiveness today less alert and energetic than it might be.

Benhabib's list of groups excluded by application of the universal in early America, for instance, includes Indians, slaves, and women, but it does not include new movements *now* poised on that precarious threshold of enactment. Why? Perhaps because the dialectic always functions best as a retrospective description of movements that have already migrated from a place under-justice to a place on the register of justice/injustice? When you acknowledge the ambiguous relation of enactment to justice you neither anticipate that day when the dialectic will have been fully realized nor pretend that it is pretty much completed now. You appreciate, rather, the crucial role of the politics of enactment in forming new identities out of old injuries, energies, and violences; and you affirm the supporting role played by an ethos of critical responsiveness in the politics of enactment. You invoke the universal. But you also invoke the politics of enactment and responsiveness to speak to the ugly underside persistently attached to any universal treated as sufficient and closed at any moment. Critical responsiveness speaks to those injuries residing under justice as obscure, unfortunate, or objective disorders in a way that invites comparison to Heidegger's exploration of untruth as the foreign residing below a historical regime of truth/falsity.[35]

As a movement struggles to cross the magic threshold of enactment, it may introduce a new right onto the register of justice. It thereby exposes retrospectively *absences* in a practice of justice recently thought by happy universalists to be complete. If and as the new movement becomes consolidated into a positive identity, it too becomes sedimented into the settlements of the newly configured pluralism. And its presumptions, too, may now constitute a barrier to the next drive to pluralization. If you anticipate, as I do, that such consolidations and retrospective disclosures recur indefinitely—that we never reach the point of justice without absence—you might acknowledge that the practice of justice and rights is indispensable to cultural pluralization *and* that justice itself depends upon cultivation of an ethos of critical responsiveness to difference that exceeds it.

You might acknowledge that each operative code of universal justice sets up barriers to pluralization by placing a series of injuries and grievance under justice. And these barriers are susceptible to dispute. Future (possible) gays are constituted as homosexuals; future (possible) carriers of nontheistic reverence as a-theists; future (possible) participants in cross-national movements as irresponsible citizens; future proponents of the right to die gracefully as doctors of death. The contemporary constitution of each places it—to varying degrees—under the regime of justice/injustice in a way inadequately captured by the retrospective discourses of dialectics and hypocrisy. Justice now trembles in its constitutive uncertainty, dependence, and ambiguity. And it is just that it so tremble.

To acknowledge these points is to say that the uncodifiable reserve of critical responsiveness is more fundamental than the universalizing codes of justice it exceeds. But this denies significance neither to moral codes in general nor to practices of justice in particular. Rather, it makes that significance ambiguous. Maintenance of dissonant interdependence between the practice of justice and the ethos of critical responsiveness is crucial to justice itself. And the relation goes the other way around. For once a constituency achieves a place on the register of justice by shifting the operational constellation of identities and differences, the practice of justice now becomes indispensable to its recognition and protection. This "place" provided by justice may itself incur injuries in need of critical attention. But such considerations do not render the practice of justice ethically dispensable. Justice and critical responsiveness are thus bound together in a relation of dissonant interdependence. Reforms in justice depend upon a more general ethos of critical responsiveness to new social movements, and the practice of justice invokes relations of agonistic respect between contending identities already on its register. The ethos and the code coexist in an asymmetrical relation of strife and interdependence.

The ethos of critical responsiveness is more fundamental than justice partly because its very shape calls into question the quest to find a solid ground of morality or justice. For critical responsiveness may flow from a care for the diversity of being irreducible to any more basic principle established by a contract, transcendental deduction, or rational consensus. If critical responsiveness exceeds the codes of justice nourished by it, it may be drawn from sources that escape the sort of solid, universal ground conventional theorists of justice often demand. To come to revere effervescent energies flowing through and over identity, the universal, and the real, to be moved by them partly because they do not embody commands from a transcendental god/principle or conform to an intrinsic design of being, is to draw upon an invaluable source of forbearance in the enactment of political initiatives and of critical responsiveness to pluralizing drives.

Does such a formulation deny the very possibility of progress in politics? No. It modifies the shape of what counts as progress. Progress, on this reading, occurs when a pluralist culture appreciates more profoundly this dissonant interdependence between justice and critical responsiveness. And when a larger number of constituencies come to terms with the relational character and element of contingency in what they are. The cultivation of critical responsiveness grows above all out of the appreciation that no culturally constituted constellation of identities ever deserves to define itself simply as natural, complete, or inclusive. For it is this fugitive, always underdeveloped, experience of contingency in what you are that taps into the ethical capacity to respond to injuries shuffled under justice by the practice of justice.

Does the moralist's demand for a secure ground of morality, then, contribute to the immorality of morality? Perhaps.[36] But this "perhaps" must place itself on that ontological register, where alternatives contend with each other while, hopefully, acknowledging the fundamental and reciprocal contestability of these contending articles of faith. For it is precisely when such acknowledgments become reciprocal that it becomes most feasible to respond *ethically* to the Nietzschean question of what kind of ethical relations to establish between alternative readings of ethical sources.[37]

RECONFIGURING THE SACRED/SECULAR DUOPOLY

Let us trace one possibility of pluralization, even before it has reached that point where retrospective appraisal is feasible. Suppose a political movement is launched, looking as arbitrary, capricious, or indulgent to many in its initial formation as the Mashpee demands did to nineteenth-century Angloids, as feminism did to most American men and women in the early 1960s, and as gay/lesbian movements still do to many today. It strives to *pluralize* the existing division of the sacred and the secular. It thereby strives to pluralize further the cultural field of faith, which is marked by fundamentalist Christianity; moderate Protestant, Catholic, and Jewish mono-theisms; post-Christian moral secularisms such as neo-Kantianism and utilitarianism; agnosticism and atheism. (But, of course, this field delineation is *already* retrospective, already formed from a per-spective that marks its boundaries in a specific way. You always run ahead of yourself in telling this kind of story.)

Initially, those challenging the established field of sacred/secular discourse resist conventional definitions of themselves as relativistic, anarchistic, nihilistic, a-theistic or (merely) textualistic, insisting that these very articulations function to fundamentalize the very histori-cal division they seek to pluralize. The *seculere,* after all, emerged historically within North African and European Christian culture as a subordinate space in which the mundane and the material could be given due attention. Even after the secular established a degree of in-dependence from its founding fathers—establishing a precarious space to adjudicate disputes between Christian sects so as to avoid their degeneration into destructive civil wars—it retained certain affinities to the Other it defines itself against. For example, conven-tional secular doctrines tend to *naturalize* the identities they endorse, while Christian doctrines tend to *transcendentalize* them. Moreover, powerful parties in both traditions often seek a secure "ground" for morality, either in the commands/purposes of a god or in commands/purposes of a natural or rational subject. Even the mod-ern contract tradition of morality consists of a series of modest revi-sions in the Augustinian reading of Genesis. Many secularists who have lost confidence in a god replace it with an overweening confi-dence in the power of logic, reason, or nature as a guide to life. Sometimes these assumptions are explicit. At other times they are ex-pressed through the hostility selected secularists display to practices of genealogy, deconstruction, political disturbance, and political en-actment, that is, through hostility to the very practices by which de-naturalization of dogmatic identities is fomented. Finally, contempo-rary carriers of the sacred and the secular often converge in thinking that only a god is worthy of reverence. The former invest reverence in a god; the latter tend to invest it nowhere. Carriers of these two intercoded traditions thus have a difficult time even recognizing an impious reverence aimed at that which exceeds identity but is not shaped like a god. And whatever they say in unison about such an alien perspective almost goes without saying. Tocqueville concurs in several of these points. He merely places a different ontological spin on them.

With these points of affinity and complementarity forming the background of their relations, each of these two constituencies tends to reinforce the presumption of the other that together they exhaust the range of viability in the domain of ethics. But suppose that eventually, through a series of distinctive political interventions into issues of gender, race, sexuality, and ecology, numerous agents of resistance to the monotheisms and monosecularisms now define themselves—retrospectively, as it were—as carriers of nontheistic gratitude for the rich diversity of being. They ground a positive ethos of critical diversity in appreciation of a world governed by no prior design or sufficient universal. These postsecularists, as we may now call them, open up ethical space between monotheism, mono-Kantianism, and monosecularism, a space that heretofore existed pretty much as a mélange of official absences and negations (marked by accusations of nihilism, amoralism, etc.), obscure experiences of injury and limitation, and neglected minority reports *within* the two major moral encampments.

These monsters, fools, mystics, or carriers of freedom through cultural pluralization—take your pick—now advance a possibility of ethical pluralization against which established forms of intrinsic identity, command morality, purposive nature, contractual ethics, and arboreal pluralism can be assessed. They prize the excess of life over identity; they embody the sense, experienced again and again retroactively as new identities are propelled into being, that life, bodies, and the earth exceed cultural articulations of them. They refuse to devalue these fugitive experiences by investing a commanding god, law, primordial contract, or intrinsic purpose into them. They insist upon a postsecular *recovery* of love for life and the earth that is not reducible to a set of divine commands, a fundamental design, or traditional piety.[38]

If and when postsecular care for the diversity of being becomes an active competitor on the cultural field of ethics, the old cultural duopoly (as you could now call it) will find itself faced with new ethical questions and challenges. And many of these moral duopolists will appear, from this perspective, to be too complacent in what they are: too exclusionary in their universalism; too inattentive to injuries lodged in the paradoxical relation between hegemonic identities and the differences through which they become solidified; too oriented to political condensations from the past in their appreciation of contemporary possibilities of pluralization; and too tone deaf to muffled cries of arbitrariness circulating through (Christian) sacred/secular practices of morality. The issue for moral duopolists will be not so much whether they concur with this unwelcome pluralization of the ethical field, though that may become an issue for some. *The issue will be what ethical relationship they seek to establish to a perspective that pluralizes the sources and codes of ethics while acknowledging the contestability of its own presumptions.* Will they struggle to exclude this third position? Will they forcefully reimpose the conventional sacred/secular division as if it were grounded in nature or divinity? Will they recognize *this* alternative while celebrating retrospectively the "dialectic" that made this recognition possible, thereby failing to place themselves in a position to practice critical responsiveness to the *next* social movement? Or will they enter into relations of agonistic respect with a perspective that, like theirs, is distinctive and contestable?

The introduction of such a third term might, over the long run, bring out more palpably the historically constructed character of the conventional secular/sacred division. And it might open up new negotiations between and across these two traditions, connecting with each on some points while calling into question complementary presumptions they share. Could postsecular care for the rich diversity of things draw sustenance from American peoples who preceded Christian/secular America? Would its enactment disclose strains in pre-Christian conceptions of gods, life, and the earth heretofore underappreciated within the (Christian) sacred/secular complex? Perhaps. But we have already proceeded further down this hypothetical trail than we are now justified in going. The politics of enactment in this domain, after all, *is barely off the ground.* We can only say that the contemporary promise of such a politics of ethical pluralization is to open up possibilities closed down by the Tocquevillian constellation. For it is, historically, when official representatives of secular reason and the Christian sacred come together that the most powerful barriers to pluralization have been posed.

The risk of the drive to pluralize the sacred/secular division is that it might spur fundamentalist reactions among secular/religious in-heritors of the Tocquevillian model of civilization who insist upon the right to duopolistic control over the currency of ethics. Its con-temporary promise is that it might give life to minority voices trans-lated into background noise by politically dominant parties within the two major traditions. Such risks and promises often accompany the politics of enactment.

The element of paradox in the politics of enactment, then, is that before success the new movement is likely to be judged in those terms through which it is already depreciated, and after success a new identity emerges that exceeds the very energies and identifica-tions that spurred it into being. The paradox of enactment of a new possibility within a pluralist ethos thus repeatedly reenacts at a mi-crocosmic level the macroparadox Rousseau identified in the politics of founding a republic.[39] Such a paradoxical element creates political binds that a pluralizing culture seeks to stretch and loosen.

We are primed to expect a new identity to precede our recogni-tion of it; and we tend to judge inchoate claims upon us now through terms of recognition already installed in the culture. An ethos of critical responsiveness to the politics of enactment relaxes this expectation and ambiguates that standard of judgment. It appre-ciates how something new and admirable can be enacted out of ob-scurity, where obscurity signifies not a void but a set of injuries, en-ergies, and desires yet to be crystallized into a positively valorized identity actively engaged with the differences through which it re-ceives specification.

To become implicated in the ambiguous politics of pluralization is, then, to respond to civilizational stresses, exclusions, and vio-lences that may be less necessary than they seem. That is why geneal-ogy, deconstruction, political disturbance, and the micropolitics of desire are important components in the life of a pluralizing culture. Cultivation of responsiveness to the binds of political enactment, to binds that show the options between discovery or creation to be too crude to capture their shape, forms the linchpin of a democratic, plu-ralizing ethos. Those who affirm the politics of pluralization to be crucial will seek to enliven the awareness of contingency within es-tablished constellations of identity and difference; to subdue the sense of threat arising when a new movement disrupts the sense of completeness, naturalness, or necessity in what you are; and to cultivate new possibilities of collaboration and coexistence between new formations and old forms shaken and moved by them.

It is when numerous constituencies in a culture appreciate simultaneously inchoate currents of energy flowing through its solid formations, the value amidst risk of new enactments, and the inability of new enactments to represent perfectly the energies that propelled them into being that a democratic politics most actively embodies a pluralizing ethos. In a democratic, pluralizing ethos, agents of enactment would exercise a certain *forbearance* in pressing their claims, and agents of reception would exercise a reciprocal *generosity* in responding to productions that disturb what they are. This agonistic reciprocity *is* the pathos of distance in politics. The historical difficulty is that agonistic respect grows out of the pluralistic culture that precedes it, while a pluralist culture is also a precondition of that respect.[40]

Once a new social identity is consolidated, its indebtedness to cultural differences that endow it with specificity, and its attunement to traces of difference that flow through it, can engender a certain empathy for what is not. This element of empathy across the space of difference, contestation, and collaboration provides the cultural currency of a democratic, pluralizing ethos. Such an ethos, in turn, sets one condition for the mobilization of political assemblages to enact the economic conditions of cultural pluralization.

The combination of presumptive forbearance and presumptive generosity that constitutes the pathos of distance in politics, then, gains its power from political interruptions of established economies of identity\difference, from critical responsiveness to new drives to pluralization, from reciprocal cultivation of agonistic respect between interdependent identities that have already crossed the threshold of enactment, and from prudence today toward the adversary you may need to align with tomorrow.

THE BORDERS OF PLURALIZATION

Limits—that is, exclusions, restrictions, and boundaries—must be drawn around the ethos of pluralization. These limits sustain its conditions of existence. Economic inequality cannot be allowed to become too extreme, for instance. And a democratic, pluralizing regime should tolerate a fundamentalist constituency, but it must resist the drive of such a constituency to impose its exclusionary norms upon the entire culture. The problem is that any constituency might be overtaken by the drive to condemn difference in order to naturalize itself. This problem of evil in pluralist politics is particularly pertinent today because the cultural conditions of possibility for the politics of pluralization also create temptations for the politics of fundamentalization. The fundamentalist drive to exclusive identity proceeds by translating cultural differences against which it defines itself into intrinsic evils to be punished or needy beings to be reformed. The Augustinian translation of Greek cosmologies into paganism and of alternative versions of Christianity into heresies presents a well-entrenched paradigm of such a politics.

There are several risks and dangers in a pluralizing culture, but the one that requires the most sensitive political response is the tendency by established identities to fundamentalize what they are by demonizing or rendering needy what they are not.[41] For when the contest between contending identities degenerates into a cultural war, the ethos of critical responsiveness becomes an early casualty. And, as a corollary, if you respond to the imperative to restrain fundamentalism as fundamentalists would respond to you, you risk recapitulating the form of the evil you are mobilized against.[42]

There are other limits to pluralization as well. They include, for instance, general civilizational values, including the protection of life, respect for privacy, the appreciation of diversity, and protection from undeserved suffering. Tocqueville is right to invoke civilizational values, even though his reification of civilization constricts the possibilities of plurality too narrowly. When you deconstruct the Tocquevillian model you realize that such civilizational limits can seldom be reduced to *criteria* through which to include or exclude practices. The five contemporary exemplifications of pluralization reviewed earlier reveal how the demand to freeze temporarily defined limits into a set of fixed criteria all too readily inflicts the sort of injuries it purports to insure against. The same point can be made with respect to the public/private distinction. Provisional lines of division between the public and the private are important to the vitality of pluralism, but these crooked lines require periodic renegotiation as new movements expose through their enactments systematic injuries previously hidden in the private sphere.

There is a deeper reason why the appreciation of limits and the delineation of criteria are not synonymous. It involves the complex relation between a pattern of cultural norms and the shape of corpo-real experience. Thus, sex between Catholic priests and adolescent boys in the United States differs significantly from the pleasures of *aphrodisia* between aristocratic adult men and adolescent boys in classical Greece. This is partly because the first relation is defined by its participants as a transgression of the natural order, while the sec-ond is surrounded by an ethic of restraint and taken to reflect nat-ural human desires.[43] But it is also because these respective under-standings have become *corporealized* by the parties implicated in them. The corporealization of culture shapes to a significant degree experiences of exploitation or reciprocity, injury or gratification, degradation or respect, naturalness or disorder.

Those who roundly condemn "cultural relativism"—an unlikely stance usually attributed to those who do not affirm it themselves—do not appreciate how violent it is to treat cross-cultural differences as if they were different "values" painted on the surface of the same acts and identities. They thereby fail to appreciate how dicey and permeable the boundary is between the positive corporealization of cultural norms and the infliction of injury through cultural imposi-tion. Since all of us are pressed into making such judgments, and since we are also implicated in specific conjunctions between culture and corporeality, we are never in a perfect epistemological position to draw the line at which corporeal flexibility ends and universal in-jury begins. I would place clitoridectomy on the injurious side of that line, without being able to delineate the exact shape of the line itself. But the recent history of pluralization suggests that a whole host of other established judgments in this domain will eventually undergo reassessment in response to reflective experiences opened up by new drives to pluralization. Critical responsiveness seeks attunement both to the need for civilizational limits and to the persistent possi-bility that established lines of demarcation inflict unnecessary in-juries and closures. It respects the ethical complexity of political judgment by adopting an ambiguous orientation to moral codes.

A related limit to the politics of pluralization flows from the need to honor the constitutive tension between pluralism and pluraliza-tion. Pluralism, configured at any time as the ethical condensation of previous settlements, both enables drives to pluralization and poses barriers to their success. If we have attended recently to the latter ef-fect, it is now timely to recall the former condition. A pluralist/

pluralizing culture is one in which people participate to varying degrees in multiple identities and in which, therefore, several alter identities reverberate in them as differences regulated to be what they are. These subterranean connections across the lines of difference provide handholds for new drives to pluralization. Moreover, preexisting pluralist stabilizations enable such drives to gain the visibility they need to become enacted. If every settlement came up for grabs at the same time, then a sustaining condition of pluralization itself would self-destruct. There would be nothing to pluralize nor any connections to draw upon in doing so.

In this domain, too, no formula, code, fixed set of criteria, theorem of justice, or settled procedure *suffices* to determine in advance just what the operational balance must be between pluralism and pluralization. But maintenance of this constitutive tension does often become a pertinent issue of political judgment: the balance regularly inclines in one direction when hegemonic identities impose heavy burdens upon the differences through which they are consolidated; it occasionally inclines in the other when pressures to rapid pluralization become intense in several contexts simultaneously.

One additional limit that is commonly invoked, however, must now be reconfigured. It is typically advanced as a question with a self-evident answer: "How much diversity and fragmentation can the order tolerate if it is to promote the common good through collective action?" (This question has been addressed to me each time I have delivered this chapter as a paper.) But its form already confines too narrowly the range of possible answers. First, its invocation of "fragmentation" misrecognizes the interdependence between identity and difference; second, it projects the arboreal presumption that a thick trunk (a sequoia tree) must set the common base from which stubby limbs of social diversity might branch out. The question identifies extensive cultural *diversification* with the loss of cultural *connections*.

This equation between diversification and fragmentation does hold when competing cultural identities are organized as intrinsic, exclusionary forms, with the consolidation of any single set posing intractable barriers to the activation of others. Perhaps theorists who translate the politics of diversification into social fragmentation do so because they assume that every identity *must* be organized in a dogmatic way. The violence in such an assumption is brought out effectively by the Tocquevillian rendering of the Indian. But what if you lived in a pluralizing culture where economic inequalities have been reduced, where many have come to grips with the ironic connection between the consolidation of identity and the constitution of difference, and where appreciation of the previous history of pluralization has generated a cultural ethos of critical responsiveness? To the extent these achievements were attained, new drives to pluralization would foster multiple, shifting *connections* between a variety of interdependent constituencies.

Cultural pluralization, critical responsiveness, and complex networks of interconnection grow together. It is important to emphasize this point, even if it applies to a possible world a little distant from the actual world of culture wars. For it translates the dogmatic presumption of a strict *ontological* limit to pluralization into the contestable enunciation of historically entrenched barriers to its effective operationalization. Those who find such a translation credible will chip away at the historical limits to pluralization, one of which is the drive to set these contingent limits in ontological cement.

It is often more feasible, say, for gays and straights to enter into alliances with respect to health care, taxes, marriage laws, the rights of free speech, state consumption policies, alimony, and the rules of military service than it is for heterosexuals and homosexuals to do so. This is so because neither constituency, in the first set, is constituted as intrinsically unnatural, abnormal, or immoral by the other. The same holds when the conventional sacred/secular division is pluralized through introduction of a third disposition communicating with elements on both sides of that divide. *When the cultural conditions of pluralization are reasonably intact, differentiation along some lines opens up multiple possibilities of selective collaboration along others.* To pluralize, therefore, is not to fragmentize. To dogmatize is to fragmentize. This finding discloses how self-appointed opponents of fragmentation so often work on its behalf.

Boundaries abound. So do the ambiguities traversing them. We may experience the ambiguity of boundaries more actively today because of the acceleration of speed in so many domains of life. This effect accentuates the issue of boundaries in democratic politics. Once you acknowledge the difficulty of defining in advance precisely when, where, and how democratic exclusions must be enforced, the foremost challenge today becomes to multiply boundaries in imperfect correspondence with one another—so that lines of division across one dimension do not correspond too closely with those across others, so that multiple cultural spaces for political enactment are opened up, so that a pathos of distance often links intersubjective differences to intrasubjective differences, and so that political negotiations between numerous constituencies connected by threads of identity, difference, responsiveness, interest, justice, and agonistic respect can forge majority assemblages supporting the conditions of pluralism.

These are impossible conditions of democratic pluralism and pluralization, in that they have never been fully intact anywhere and never could be combined perfectly in any specific spatiotemporal context. When conditions are favorable, multivalent pluralism is always coming into being across one dimension or another. It never simply *is,* intact in all respects. This is so because the interdependent elements from which the regulative ideal is composed are punctuated by necessary dissonance. To pursue the ideal, for instance, is to focus on a drive to pluralization at one moment and to consolidate recent settlements of pluralism at another. Similarly, it is to apply a standard of justice at one time and to modify its scope at another. Something significant must often be sacrificed or deferred to enable pursuit of another priority important to the ideal.

Critical pluralism thereby honors politics as the multifaceted medium through which the multiple dissonances within it are exposed and negotiated. A tragic element resides within the regulative ideal itself. Its proponents, though, resist that resignation to immovable fate Nietzsche so effectively identifies, criticizes, and supplants in the tragic tradition. Rather, in affirming a multifarious condition always coming into being along one dimension or another, the pluralist temper foments multiple possibilities of micropolitics, collective assemblage, cross-national movements, pluralization, and responsiveness. The constitutive tension between pluralism and pluralization implies that there is always more political work to be done.

Notes

INTRODUCTION: THE PLURALIST IMAGINATION

1. The most impressive and prescient work here was by Ernesto Laclau and Chantal Mouffe, *Hegemony and Socialist Strategy: Towards a Radical Democratic Politics* (London: Verso, 1985). It is impressive that this reworking of Marxism precedes the downfall of the Soviet Union, prefiguring later currents within socialist politics as recovering Marxists reconstruct their ideals while striving to retain valuable kernels of critical insight from Marxism. The irony is that Laclau and Mouffe launched a reconfiguration of pluralism from a post-Marxist perspective even before many pluralists had perceived the need to rethink pluralism.

2. For thoughtful exemplifications of this trend, see the recent book by Charles Taylor, with commentaries by Amy Guttmann, Steven Rockefeller, Michael Walzer, and Susan Wolf, *Multiculturalism and "The Politics of Recognition"* (Princeton, N.J.: Princeton University Press, 1993). I respond to Taylor's version of multiculturalism in "Pluralism and Multiculturalism," a paper delivered at the Bohen Foundation Symposium on Diversity, Citizenship, and Democracy held in New York in February 1994. This paper, along with those of the other participants, will be published by a book of approximately the same title as the symposium. I do not engage the individualist/communitarian debate actively in these essays. For interrogations of complementary presumptions between these disputants from a democratic perspective emphasizing the positive value of agonistic respect between interdependent and contending identities, see William E. Connolly, *Politics and Ambiguity* (Madison: University of Wisconsin Press, 1987) and *Identity\Difference: Democratic Negotiations of Political Paradox* (Ithaca,

N.Y.: Cornell University Press, 1991), especially chapters 1 and 5. Bonnie Honig, in *Political Theory and the Displacement of Politics* (Ithaca, N.Y.: Cornell University Press, 1993), addresses this issue by defining both individualists and communitarians to be carriers of "virtue" politics challenged by the politics of "virtu." And *In the Nature of Things: Language, Politics, and the Environment*, edited by Jane Bennett and William Chaloupka (Minneapolis: University of Minnesota Press, 1993), contains a series of essays that explore complementary assumptions about nature and ecology in this debate, offering alternative conceptions to challenge the presumptions of nature as plastic material to be used or as the source of an intrinsic purpose to be realized.

3. An individual is the site of multiple identifications, and those identifications themselves often embody a struggle between the identifications the individual seeks and those different constituencies are willing to bestow. I use the language of "constituencies" to emphasize how discussion of identity is not simply about discrete individuals, but about collective identifications through which they are marked. I prefer the language of individuality to that of the individual because the former suggests the uniform standard of the normal individual while the latter suggests the value of diversity across and within selves. Maintenance of the tension between pluralism and pluralism is one of the conditions of individuality. Finally, I think that individuality is never exhausted by the social stock of identifications applied to any self. A fugitive fund of diference, as we shall see, exceeds identity\difference relations.

4. Hegel offers a famous account of such a relation in the dialectic of lordship and bondage. I recommend against absorbing this account within Hegel's scheme, however. For my scheme emphasizes how the paradoxical character of this relation is never dissolved or overcome but is subject to a variety of negotiations and permutations. It finds the nonteleological excess of being over identity to provide a valuable source of innovation in moral and political life. And it thereby values relations (depending on the circumstances) such as critical responsiveness, agonistic respect, the pathos of distance, and studied indifference over those of obedience to fixed roles set by the substance of the state embodied in Hegel's highest ideal. My affinities here are more to Nietzsche than to Hegel, more to Foucault than to Rawls, more to Judith Butler than to Carol Gilligan, and more to Barney Frank than to Bill Clinton. Given a chance, however, I would vote for any of the above for public office—*except* Hegel.

5. A particularly egregious example of this occurs in Richard Rorty's *New York Times* op-ed piece of February 13, 1994. Rorty juxtaposes national identity to "the politics of difference" peddled by the academic left in the American academy: "If in the interests of ideological purity, or . . . the

need to stay as angry as possible, the academic left insists on a 'politics of difference,' it will become increasingly isolated and ineffective. . . . A left that refuses to take pride in its country will . . . eventually become an object of contempt." Rorty, whose critical explorations of truth and contingency have inspired recent reflections about identity\difference relations and ethics, nonetheless retains a flat conception of identity\difference relations. He thereby contributes to the contempt for the academic left he seeks to protect.

6. Friendship at micropolitical levels and agonistic respect and critical responsiveness at macropolitical levels mediate these relations in ways most compatible with maintenance of the constitutive tension between pluralism and pluralization.

7. Such a conception is pursued most actively in chapters 1 and 6 of this book. For an essay that sets the groundwork for these formulations, see "Beyond Good and Evil: The Ethical Sensibility of Michel Foucault," *Political Theory*, August 1993, 365-90. I tend to call a normative orientation a morality when it claims to be anchored in a transcendental system of command or a world of intrinsic design. Also, that word seems suitable for those perspectives that give priority to a code over an ethos and to obligation over the good. The teleological tradition is, thus, a morality on one of my registers and an ethic on the other. That's okay by me. But it may foster a little confusion. The ethic I endorse is an ethic of cultivation that finds no code to be sufficient to it and seeks to respond to a fundamental contingency of things recurrently naturalized by social practices. It is not that such naturalizations are despicable or entirely eliminable. They are, rather, often ambiguous developments, and the ethical task is to bring out the side of the ambiguity that is currently occluded.

8. An amplified sense of the disconnections as well as the connections between the source of an ethic and its mandates is developed by Jane Bennett in "Toward a Genealogical Idealism," forthcoming in *Journal of Politics*. I am indebted to Bennett's reading of this relationship.

9. Etienne Balibar and Immanuel Wallerstein, *Race, Nation, Class*, trans. Chris Turner (New York: Verso, 1991), 213.

10. Gilles Deleuze and Félix Guattari, *A Thousand Plateaus*, trans. Brian Massumi (Minneapolis: University of Minnesota Press, 1987), 214-15.

11. I do not suggest, of course, that the "center" or the "right" is inhabited only by fundamentalism, just as I concur that the "left" certainly can be. I suggest, rather, that any position on the hemisphere of recognized political positions might be. A fundamentalist of the center first acts as if centrist identities are incontestable and then builds an exclusionary logic around the practices of agency and rights endorsed.

12. Contemporary liberals who contend against these tendencies in liberalism most effectively, I think, are Isaiah Berlin in *The Crooked Timber of*

Humanity (New York: Vintage, 1992); Richard Flathman in *Toward a Liberalism* (Ithaca, N.Y.: Cornell University Press, 1991); Stuart Hampshire in *Innocence and Experience* (Cambridge, Mass.: Harvard University Press, 1991); and George Kateb in *The Inner Ocean* (Ithaca, N.Y.: Cornell University Press, 1992). I dissent from the conceptions of politics in these perspectives, but these disagreements do not impugn their admirable efforts to strip themselves of the fundamentalist tendencies they resist in others. My critique of George Kateb's conception of politics, placed alongside my preference for his conception of *individuality* over the unconscious Rawlsian strategy to protect the *normal individual*, appears in chapter 4, "Liberalism and Difference," of *Identity\Difference*. An exemplary effort, by one who does not call herself a liberal, to engage the dangers of identity politics, to fend off drives by her own allies to fundamentalize the stance she endorses, and to construct an affirmative political sensibility is now available; see Judith Butler, *Bodies That Matter* (New York: Routledge, 1993).

13. Nothing in this last sentence implies that moralities of god, home, and country are to be excluded from this imagination. That would depluralize this model of pluralism, rendering its own imagination a mirror of the monisms it opposes. Only a decisionist logic of either/or would be compelled to read the formulation in that way: "If transcendental violence is said to inhabit practices of God, home, and country, that implies that all forms of each must be expunged. But what would life be like without faith, houses, countries? It would be nihilistic and anarchistic. Hence these guys are nihilists." Such a reading, however, misrecognizes the logic of the formulation. A plurality of imaginations is possible in these domains. Some moralities grounded in a god, for instance, diffuse the god of unilateral command by treating divinity as a site of alterity that exceeds every human representation of it. This results in a divinely sanctioned morality of pluralism. It is beautifully portrayed by Emmanuel Levinas in *Totality and Infinity,* trans. Alphonso Lingis (Pittsburgh: Duquesne University Press, 1969). It is not exactly the moral source I endorse, though. I draw my ethic partly from a (Nietzschean) nontheistic appreciation of the abundance of being, partly from concern that the long historical record of Western monotheism *and* secularism requires articulation of a nontheistic ethic of pluralization to contest tendencies to violence within both. These two orientations contain important points of overlap and collaboration with the Levinasian model they resist along some dimensions. Critical responsiveness may draw sustenance both from (Nietzschean) care for the "abundance of being" and from the (Levinasian) experience of indebtedness to the alterity that reveals the constitutive incompleteness of your own subjectivity. There is tension between these two sources as well. But I suspect an ethic of critical responsiveness requires both. It requires the first because the Levinasian call to responsibility

to difference may well draw blanks if it does not draw upon an *abundance* in those called to responsibility; and the second because the Nietzschean ethos of generosity between contending equals is insufficiently responsive to the regular suffering of subordinates upon which existing structures are built. The Levinasian attention to suffering lacks a genealogical strategy to expose the artifice and contingency flowing through forms of life now presented as fixed or necessary. Such an ethic could profit considerably from Nietzschean genealogy, for its paradigmatic examples of alterity (the widow, the poor man, the stranger) do not emphasize negated identities (e.g., the homosexual, the woman, the foreigner) whose negative social construction is concealed until a genealogy of the heterosexual, the man, and the citizen has been negotiated.

A pluralizing culture pluralizes *sources* of ethics as well as *models* of what is ethical; several parties to this ethical pluralism then engage each other across relations of agonistic respect and selective collaboration. In doing so they strive to become more alert to drives in themselves to fundamentalize what they are. If they have enough political clout, they *tolerate* spaces for fundamentalisms to be, at least when the latter do not compel the universalization of what they are. These preliminary formulations merely start us down the trail pursued here.

1. NOTHING IS FUNDAMENTAL . . .

1. This theme is most reflectively developed in Hans Blumenberg, *The Legitimacy of the Modern Age*, trans. John Wallace (Cambridge, Mass.: MIT Press, 1983).

2. John Rawls, "Justice as Fairness: Political Not Metaphysical," *Philosophy and Public Affairs*, Summer 1985. Richard Rorty, *Contingency, Irony and Solidarity* (Cambridge: Cambridge University Press, 1989). See also my review of Rorty in *History of the Human Sciences*, February 1990, 104-8.

3. Martin Heidegger, "The Essence of Truth," in *Heidegger: Basic Writings*, ed. David F. Krell (New York: Harper & Row, 1977). For an "Anglo-American" essay that moves in the same direction, see Ian Hacking, "Language, Truth and Reason," in *Rationality and Relativism*, ed. Martin Hollis and Steven Lukes (Cambridge, Mass.: MIT Press, 1982), 48-66.

4. Charles Taylor, "Overcoming Epistemology," in *After Philosophy*, ed. Kenneth Baynes, James Bohman, and Thomas McCarthy (Cambridge, Mass.: MIT Press, 1987), 464-88. I discuss the linkage between this conception of responsibility and a vengeful element in the logic of punishment in "The Desire to Punish," chapter 2 of this book, and in "Responsibility for Evil," in *Identity\Difference: Democratic Negotiations of Political Paradox* (Ithaca, N.Y.: Cornell University Press, 1991), chapter 4.

5. Michael Shapiro, *The Politics of Representation* (Madison: University of Wisconsin Press, 1988), examines how the rhetorical structure of Wilson's text secures the fundamental pattern of identity and responsibility it endorses and then distributes responsibility among its subjects according to this prearranged and undefended pattern.

6. Roberto Unger, *Social Theory: A Critical Introduction to Politics, a Work in Constructive Social Theory* (Cambridge: Cambridge University Press, 1987). See my review of Unger, "Making the Friendly World Behave," *New York Times Sunday Book Review*, February 19, 1988.

7. Jon Elster, *Sour Grapes* (Cambridge: Cambridge University Press, 1983), 1.

8. Michel Foucault, *The Order of Things* (London: Tavistock, 1970), 211.

9. This formulation is designed to call attention to the juncture where Derrida meets the Foucault of *The Order of Things,* for example, in Derrida's "Différance," *Margins of Philosophy,* trans. Alan Bass (Chicago: University of Chicago Press, 1982), 1-29, and also "The Force of Law: The Mystical Foundation of Justice," in *Deconstruction and the Possibility of Justice,* ed. Driscilla Cornell, Michael Rosenfeld, and David Gray Carlson (New York: Routledge, 1992). There are two strategic points where these thinkers point in different directions, with each, as I now see it, in need of support from the other. The first: Derrida's presentation of the play of *différance* on a linguistic register complements and presupposes Nietzschean/Foucauldian/Deleuzian presentations of the compelling, elusive flow of "life" and "force" on a corporeal register. Derrida once emphasized this interdependence, as when he says, "*différance* appears almost by name in their [Nietzsche's and Freud's] texts, and in those places where everything is at stake. I cannot expand upon this here; I will only recall that for Nietzsche 'the great principal activity is unconscious,' and that consciousness is the effect of forces whose essence, byways and modalities are not proper to it. Force itself is never present; it is only a play of differences and quantities." Then he quotes Deleuze: "'Quantity itself, therefore, is not separable from the difference of quantity. The difference of quantity is the essence of force. The dream of two equal forces . . . is an approximate and crude dream, a statistical dream, plunged into by the living but dispelled by chemistry.'" The second: that crucial intersection where the movement of the *symbolic,* through which, for instance, the experience of the law insinuates itself into subjectivity, encounters "*real practices*" applied by disciplinary authorities to the body. I explore this intersection— this intersection at which Derrida and Foucault can draw sustenance from the other—in the next chapter.

10. Foucault, *The Order of Things,* 327. As will emerge later, I pursue a version of "straining to catch its restless murmur," doing so to call into

question the demand to render things transparent or to become attuned to an intrinsic purpose in being. Some of Foucault's formulations seem compatible with such a project; others seem less so.

11. Foucault, *The Order of Things*, 341.

12. Ibid., 41.

13. Taylor, "Overcoming Epistemology," 480-81; italics added.

14. Foucault, *The Order of Things*, 248.

15. Just so no one concludes that I claim that this matrix exhausts the possibilities of thought today, consider a short list of social and political thinkers, even in the Anglo-American world, who press against its boundaries in one or more ways: Keith Ansell-Pearson, Jane Bennett, Wendy Brown, Judith Butler, David Campbell, Bill Chaloupka, Romande Coles, Bill Corlett, Simon Critchley, James Der Derian, Michael Dillon, Fred Dolan, Thomas Dumm, Kathy Ferguson, Richard Flathman, Michael Hardt, Ernesto Laclau, Kirstie McClure, Bill Martin, Anne Norton, Shane Phalen, Michael Shapiro, Rob Walker, Bernard Williams. Rather, the matrix functions as a set of interlocking positions that tend to converge in the way they read theorists like those listed above and to be pleased with this convergence.

16. Martin Heidegger, "The Age of the World Picture," in Heidegger, *The Question Concerning Technology* (New York: Harper & Row, 1977), 127-28.

17. Sometimes proponents of the communion orientation insist that their position cannot be stated as the communion with a higher purpose in being. It cannot precisely because the higher purpose is above any human comprehension of it. When this theme is pushed very far, however, proponents of this perspective risk becoming operational Nietzscheans. For it is the latter view that dissonances, resistances, surpluses, contingencies, and differences are signs of an excess of being exceeding every human organizational scheme. The Nietzscheans refuse to project a god into this excess because that projection encourages too many to think they can read a higher purpose in it. My reading of the communion perspective is influenced by how its representatives interpret Nietzsche. If they read him reductively, this may be a sign that they project purpose, harmony, and direction into being, and that the reductive reading of Nietzsche is needed to maintain space for their favorite position.

18. The recent collection edited by Jane Bennett and Bill Chaloupka is relevant here, for most of the essays challenge both conceptions of nature that have heretofore contended for primacy in social and political theory. See *In the Nature of Things: Language, Culture, and the Environment* (Minneapolis: University of Minnesota Press, 1993).

19. Of course, its outlook *can* be translated back into these vocabularies. We might develop the shared understanding that identities are contingent,

relational formations, dependent upon the constituencies against which they are defined, etc. I would not object to such a translation, as long as the translator, after showing me that I too presuppose some such notion of shared understandings, did not surreptitiously then slide the term back into the old consensual frame it was nested in all along.

20. Charles Taylor, in *Sources of the Self: The Making of the Modern Identity* (Cambridge, Mass.: Harvard University Press, 1989), admirably reviews a variety of "moral sources" that have contended for attention in the history of the West. His reading of the evanescent and irreducible role of sources informs my defense of a Nietzschean/Foucauldian ethic in "Beyond Good and Evil: The Ethical Sensibility of Michel Foucault," *Political Theory,* August 1993, 365-90.

21. Friedrich Nietzsche, *Twilight of the Idols,* trans. R. J. Hollingdale (Middlesex: Penguin, 1969), 44. I do not deny, of course, that other sentiments can be culled from other sentences by Nietzsche. I merely support *these* Nietzschean sentiments, suggesting that they grow out of his fundamental reading of being and that they can stand alone without necessarily being drawn into Nietzsche's aristocraticism.

22. To anticipate a question. "Isn't your post-Nietzscheanism a lot like the liberalism of John Stuart Mill? Why not forget Nietzsche and reread Mill?" It is something like the perspective of Mill. The points of contact between Nietzsche and Mill are well worth pursuing. But so are the points of difference. Mill presupposes a unified subject that is treated more ambiguously in this alternative perspective. Mill lacks, crucially, a genealogical disposition, a disposition that encourages us to probe the contingent bases of contemporary unities of self, truth, morality, and sovereignty and to encounter arbitrary violences and exclusions in them. And Mill's conception of "civilization" as presented in *Considerations on Representative Government* (New York: Liberal Arts Press, 1958) is far too close to the conception offered by Tocqueville and criticized in the last chapter of this book.

23. See William Connolly, *Political Theory and Modernity*, 2d ed. (Ithaca, N.Y.: Cornell University Press, 1993), the last chapter and the epilogue to the second edition.

24. Friedrich Nietzsche, *Beyond Good and Evil,* trans. Marianne Cowan (South Bend, Ind.: Gateway, 1955), 100.

25. Ibid, 60. This formulation is clarified by the following: "What is amazing about the religiosity of the ancient Greeks is the enormous abundance of gratitude it exudes; it is a very noble type of man that confronts nature and life in *this* way" (ibid., 58).

26. Bernard Williams, *Shame and Necessity* (Berkeley: University of California Press, 1993), 163-64. Williams's point is that while Sophocles and Thucydides disagree, the first emphasizing cosmic interests that are hostile

to human hopes and the second the fundamental contingency and indifference of the world, they come together by comparison to the first set of thinkers on the list. And, as Williams makes abundantly clear, he concurs with the Sophocles/Thucydides picture, particularly with the Thucydides version of it.

27. Michel Foucault, in *Foucault Live,* ed. Sylvere Lotringer, trans. John Johnson (New York: Semiotexte[e], 1989), 267.

28. It would be fascinating to detail the shifts that have occurred in Anglo-American critiques of Foucault between, say, 1978 and 1994. You would encounter the following, roughly in the order of their appearance: (1) Foucault's assertion of radical discontinuity in history makes it impossible to even identify these discontinuities. (But then it turns out that even *The Order of Things* contains continuities, with minor literatures in each "episteme" challenging dominant tendencies of the episteme.) (2) If power is everything, it is impossible to evaluate one regime of power as superior to another. (But then it turns out that power is everywhere, not everything, and that reciprocal power is ethically superior to subjugating power.) (3) Foucault lacks the ability to engage in moral judgment because of (1) and (2) and, additionally, because he treats the subject of morality as a fiction. (But the Foucauldian subject is a complex cultural formation, neither an originary source nor a fiction.) (4) Foucault makes moral judgments, but these judgments are "parasitical" upon the necessary presumptions of morality as such that he undermines through genealogy. (5) Foucault only supports the politics of resistance; he makes no contribution to a positive ideal toward which we could strive. (6) Foucault *is* (now) an ethicist, but his ethics is sunk in an aestheticism that plays up style over substance and opens itself to stylized violence; it never offers any *criteria* of moral judgment. (Foucault in fact emphasizes the importance of the intersection between a code of morality [criteria] and an ethos in his work on ethics. And do you notice how the charge of Foucault as amoral agent of resistance has faded here?) (7) Foucault's stylistics ignore the class basis of modern society and the role of institutional power in constraining the ability of many to style themselves. (But it turns out that Foucault repeatedly makes this point about the effects of class society himself, while articulating an *ideal* of the self as variable work of art that breaks with the ideal of collective unity critical theorists of class often invoke.) (8) To focus on the "arts of the self" is to ignore our responsibilities to others, let alone our differential relations to power. (But this forgets both that care of the self opens it up to care for others, according to Foucault, and that Foucault's disciplines of the self are presented as *one* of the means through which to respond to the pressures of a normalizing, disciplinary society.) (8) Foucault's life reveals one who transgressed social standards to test the limits of life itself. His texts reduce to this narcissistic adventure.

And though it has never been proven that Foucault killed anybody by infecting them with AIDS, one book on Foucault is structured around the presumption of the very rumor it fails to confirm.

It is fascinating how old, definitive criticisms fade from view as new, definitive criticisms are introduced. Indeed, many critics silently fold dimensions from the Foucault they earlier refuted into their later work, even while introducing new, definitive objections against the whole corpus. Part of this (say, 33 percent) is because of Foucault, whose distribution of emphasis did shift over time. But the rest is a result of the insistence of several critics on *reducing his thought to the one dimension in it that troubles them the most at the moment.* They treat a disturbing element in his thinking as if it did not exist in critical relation to numerous other elements. And when the thought is so reduced, it does become susceptible to those eliminative critiques a certain kind of philosopher loves to deliver. So, let us anticipate a couple of future criticisms. Foucault, it will be said, was *too* concerned with the ethical dimension of life. He was not realistic. Or he did not pay attention to how so many people are ground down by the necessities of daily life. And how ethics is a luxury available to academics, but unavailable to many others. (Could I suggest a rereading of the texts on power here?) And, finally, it may be said that Foucault ignored the extent to which the inner city and the Third World have become deinstitutionalized. For the accentuation of disciplinary society in some domains correlates with the deinstitutionalization of life in the inner city. There is something to this latter point, though it is more accurate to treat the "deinstitutionalization" of the inner city as a politics of internment.

And those criticisms in which I concur? I find Foucault to be an important ethicist whose distinctive contributions to ethics are closely bound up with his distinctive explorations of power. But his later emphasis on the elaboration of a distinctive, positive ethical ideal never sufficiently connects the ethics of the self to the reconfigurations of social pluralism it supports and is supported by. And his later concession that critical attention to the extremities of the social order must be connected to the state and the pursuit of reforms through the state was not pursued far enough either. Hence, there is something for others to do. I also suspect that Foucauldians and post-Soviet Marxists need each other, with the former exploring the logic of disciplinary power while pursuing a social ideal that significantly corrects the Marxian ideal of community, and the latter focusing critically on the dynamics of capital, commodification, and differential labor power in ways that remain highly pertinent.

29. *Michel Foucault: Politics, Philosophy and Culture*, ed. Lawrence D. Kritzman (London: Routledge, Chapman and Hall, 1988), 328.

30. In chapter 5 of *Identity\Difference* I explore Nietzsche's engagement

with the limit experience of death. The way you engage that limit prior to succumbing to it is crucial to the sort of ethical sensibility you develop, according to Nietzsche. Foucault displays a similar attentiveness in *The History of Sexuality*, vol. 1 (New York: Pantheon, 1978), chapter 5.

31. *Foucault Live*, ed. Sylvere Lotringer, trans. John Johnston (New York: Semiotext[e], 1989), 79.

32. Foucault, "Truth, Power and Self: An Interview with Michel Foucault," *Technologies of the Self*, ed. Luther H. Martin, Huck Gutman, and Patrick H. Hutton (Amherst: University of Massachusetts Press, 1988).

33. When I informed Joan Kleinman, a Chinese anthropologist, that the assertion "nothing is fundamental" invokes for me a protean fullness *enabled* by the absence of any fundamental purpose or principle in being, she suggested that this fugitive thought is more overt in the Chinese term *hsu*, meaning empty, hollow, void, open, shapeless, full, and groundless in some complex pattern of interdependent determinations. I have profited, I hope, from our discussion of this word. Nietzsche's way of putting this thought is to say that the abyss and the abundance are the same.

34. A word of friendly advice to the fundamentalist. You will want to ask, "Do Nazis count then?" Etc., etc. But the form of your question fails to grasp the formulation, returning us to a fundamentalism the formulation is designed to contest. You demand a formula in place of a formulation. A hint: Is not Nazism exactly the doctrine that denies that almost everything counts for something?

2. THE DESIRE TO PUNISH

1. This is not the case, however, in the recent work of critical legal theorists, as Tom Dumm has kindly pointed out to me. Two very salient and illuminating examples are Robert M. Cover, "Violence and the Word," *Yale Law Journal* 45 (June 1986): 1601-29, and Austin Sarat and Thomas R. Kearns, "A Journey Through Forgetting: Toward a Jurisprudence of Violence," in *The Fate of Law*, ed. Sarat and Kearns (Ann Arbor: University of Michigan Press, 1993), 209-73. Cover explores gaps between judicial decision and institutional enactment of legal violence, and between the perspective of the judged and that of the judge, gaps that judges often refuse to consider in settling upon one interpretive possibility and in sentencing the agent found guilty. Sarat and Kearns, working similar terrain, say that "of course uncertainty in law is most visible when officials render conflicting judgments or when they openly confess or contend that the rules conflict or have a gap or are simply silent on the matter at hand. But this kind of difficulty is easily masked by a boldfaced refusal to acknowledge the latitude that system of rules makes available" (238-39). I will continue down this trail, presupposing this latitude in rules and exploring how vengeful violence infiltrates into

these spaces. The terrain we are running over is treacherous and fraught with unexpected bogs and precipices.

2. See "What Calls for Punishment?" in *Foucault Live,* ed. Sylvere Lotringer (New York: Semiotext[e], 1989), 280-92.

3. *Baltimore Sun,* June 9, 1993, sec. B, 1, 3. This case, among the thousands like it, initially attracted my attention because I am an upper-middle-class white male with a pretty decent Toyota Camry living in Baltimore. I was relieved when Carter was caught, but unnerved by the progression of his case through the court.

4. I have traced some of these developments in the epilogue to the second edition of *Political Theory and Modernity* (Ithaca, N.Y.: Cornell University Press, 1993), 176-97; the epilogue is entitled "Modernity, Territorial Democracy and the Problem of Evil." The crucial case of Augustine is considered in *The Augustinian Imperative: A Reflection on the Politics of Morality* (Newbury Park, Calif.: Sage, 1993). Michel Foucault was a master at uncovering actual cases that confound the categories designed to govern them. See, for instance, *I Pierre Riviere, Having Slaughtered My Mother, My Sister and My Brother,* ed. Michel Foucault, trans. Frank Jellinek (Lincoln: University of Nebraska Press, 1975). Perhaps it should be said that I do not draw from the problematical character of existing conceptions of responsibility the conclusion that responsibility must be scrapped in favor of a causal or therapeutic code. Responsibility, I want to suggest, is both *indispensable* to the culture in which we participate *and deeply problematical.* If many repress this ambiguity, forgetting the difficulties to affirm the indispensability, it is of little help to reverse that procedure. The dilemma itself must be kept alive, informing the forbearance with which we attribute responsibility and opening us up to more critical responses to the politics through which the ambiguity of responsibility is suppressed. The practice of responsibilities, as I will discuss later, needs to be tempered and balanced by critical responsiveness.

5. I do not deny a distinction between stable and unstable conduct. What is questionable is to conclude that the contingent etiology of desire that fosters a rough fit between the contingent code of many and the institutional imperatives of a particular social order means that the carriers of correspondence are therefore responsible agents. Even when the dominant norms through which such a fit is celebrated are not in question, the claim to correspondence between stability and responsible agency has never been proven to the degree, or with the cleanliness, that the confident judgment suggests. Hence the absence of a stable fit in some does not prove the responsible agency of those in whom it is present. The claim that it does, though, enables those so characterized to give themselves credit by claiming responsibility for what they already are while simultaneously condemning

others to irresponsibility or the lack of a normal capacity for responsibility. Responsibility is better conceived as something overlaid precariously on a contingent pattern of desire through cautious work by the self on itself than as something possessed by responsible agents as part of their being.

6. Friedrich Nietzsche, *Human All Too Human,* trans. R. J. Hollingdale (New York: Cambridge University Press, 1986), 45.

7. Ibid., 313.

8. Here I concur with Jack Katz, who, in *Seductions of Crime* (New York: Basic Books, 1988), concludes that structural accounts of crime are highly deficient: "The statistical and correlational finds of positivist criminology provide the following irritations to inquiry: (1) whatever the validity of the hereditary, psychological, and social ecological conditions of crime, many of those in the supposedly causal categories do not commit the crime at issue, (2) many who do commit the crime do not fit the causal categories, and (3) and what is most provocative, many who do fit the background categories and later commit the crime go for long stretches without committing the crimes to which theory directs them" (3-4). I am indebted to the Katz study, as will become clear, for its portrait of the role of desire in criminal violence. But Katz (1) underplays the background role of structural elements in setting contexts out of which particular patterns of identity and desire are constructed and (2) pays no attention to the role played by revenge in conventional practices of punishment. These deficiencies in an otherwise innovative study render it easily colonizable by those who want to add another arrow to their quiver of revenge against minority criminality. For this reason, it might usefully be read in conjunction with Patricia Williams, *The Alchemy of Race and Rights* (Cambridge, Mass.: Harvard University Press, 1991). Among other things, Williams strives to express and render problematical the subject position from which she (as a "female," "black," "lawyer" and "teacher" of future corporate lawyers) engages legal discourse while exposing how the corollary subject positions of conventional lawyers, judges, and juries typically become universalized and objectified through readings of precedent, judicial rules of evidence, the impersonal voice, the reasonable person, etc. To place these elements in quotes is to call attention to their relevance to the interpretations advanced, to indicate how the positions they invoke never exhaust the energies and perspectives flowing through them, and to suggest that there are always more dimensions of a subject position beyond the laundry list conventionally considered pertinent. I will offer a laundry list of my own later, as it bears upon my responses to the Dontay Carter case. But in this case, I am poignantly aware of how crude and misleading its delineation is. And you, Katz?

9. Sigmund Freud, *Moses and Monotheism,* trans. Katherine Jones (New York: Vintage, 1969). According to Freud, Moses, an Egyptian rebel who

brings a new religion to the people of Israel, is killed first and honored later. Freud rewrites the story of Exodus so that none of the religions of the West can claim a pure, singular standing, untouched by its origins in the others. This is not the "self-hatred" of a Jew. Rather, Freud's appreciation of contingency and dependence in the identity he admires and endorses provides an excellent source from which an admirable ethic might emerge.

10. René Girard, *Violence and the Sacred,* trans. Patrick Gregory (Baltimore, Md.: Johns Hopkins University Press, 1972), 144.

11. Ibid., 145; italics in original.

12. "No eroticism is possible for a couple without the addition of a third party. It's true that the third party is nearly always there! If not in person, at least in the mind of one of the partners. While making love, haven't you ever been visited by the image of someone other than the person whose caresses you're savoring? Isn't your husband's hard flesh made softer when, at the same time, your closed eyelids give you in imagination to one of his friends, the husband of one of your friends, a man you passed in the street, a screen hero, your childhood lover."(Emmanuelle Arsan, *Emmanuelle*, trans. unlisted [New York: Grove, 1971], 159). This book would repay extended treatment with respect to a couple of issues pertinent to this essay. First, the story is set in Bangkok during a period of colonial dependence. This foreign, exotic, provincial setting allows the author to project the desired erotic atmosphere onto it. Servants and bystanders, for instance, provide the main French characters with chances to expose themselves in unthreatening contexts and to discover erotic secrets in a magical setting unencumbered by the reader's independent experience of everyday life. So the book opens this question: How do triangular codes of desire reflect differential codes of right, subordination, and exchange, say, in the domains of self-exposure and enforced visibility? Second, while Emmanuelle's erotic adventures range across men and women, male figures set an authoritative context of prohibition, instruction, confession, and daring within which the action proceeds. A masculine system of property rights over erotic pleasure shapes the market of regulated exchange and delicious duplicity.

13. Girard, *Violence and the Sacred,* 145-46.

14. But what drives the subject to project wholeness into the model? Here Girard's account may presuppose Jacques Lacan's theory of the mirror image, where the infant of five to seven months perceives itself through a mirror as more complete and in charge of its motor capacities then it feels itself to be. See Jacques Lacan, "The Mirror Stage," in *Ecrits,* trans. Alan Sheridan (New York: Norton, 1977). Lacan says: "What I have called the mirror stage is interesting in that it manifests the affective dynamism by the subject who originally identifies himself with the visual gestalt of his own body: in relation to the still very profound lack of coordination of his own

motility, it represents an ideal unity, a salutary imago; it is invested with all the original distress resulting from the child's intraorganic and relational discordance." This "will crystallize in the subject's internal conflictual tension, which determines the awakening of his desire for the object of the other's desire" (18). This is the point, so to speak, where Girard steps into the picture. Luce Irigaray, in *This Sex Which Is Not One,* trans. Catherine Porter (Ithaca, N.Y.: Cornell University Press, 1985), offers a compelling critique of the masculine version of "the real" and "the symbolic" in which Lacan's theory of the imaginary is placed, without, I think, dropping the significance of the imaginary itself. Her analysis is pertinent to Girard as well.

15. In a fascinating essay connected to issues posed here and inspiring some of its themes, Thomas Dumm considers how a masculine code of desire in this culture draws the politics of George Bush, Gary Gilmore, Philip Abbott, J. Edgar Hoover, and Roy Cohn together across the legal boundary that divides them. What they share is the insistence that the feminine position in sex is both the receiving one and the inferior one, while the male position is both penetrating and superior. This explains why most in this group are vehemently antigay, including covert gays such as Hoover and Cohn who publicly despise homosexuals. And it is implicated in the violent code of politics they endorse. The code of desire they share across the conventional divide between official lawfulness and official lawlessness propels a lot of violence in public life. I want to suggest that Dumm's essay is both illuminated by one strain in Girard's analysis and capable of challenging another strain in it. See Thomas Dumm, "George Bush, or Homosocial Politics," in *Body Politics: Disease, Desire and the Family,* ed. Avery Gordon and Michael Ryan (San Francisco: Westview, 1993).

16. Have I "misrecognized" Lacan, since he is the one who locates the source of the demand for fullness in the imaginary and the possibility of displacements in the symbolic? Yes and no. Yes, he drives past the imaginary in his reading of identifications, but, no, the Lacanian symbolic reintroduces a law of desire that is not itself subject to significant modification. I would try to argue that there are possibilities of modulation between, say, a Deleuzian model of desire and a Lacanian model that are not now recognized by either party.

17. But, crucially, not resentment. Ressentiment is stored resentment that has poisoned the soul and migrated to places where it is hidden and denied. Agents of ressentiment often express love for the beings they injure. Resentment, though, might arise when someone has injured you unjustly, and you call that person on it, or when you are enraged by lies another tells about you and gets away with it. Nothing said here about ressentiment implies that it is never appropriate to act out of *resentment.* Moreover, one who resents another might come to see that the feeling proceeds from a judgment that is

214 NOTES TO CHAPTER 2

false or inflated. Perhaps the judgment of responsibility is too strong for this case, etc. There is good reason for the widow of Dontay Carter's victim to resent him. But her insinuation of that feeling into the categories of legal judgment deserves critique, and, particularly, the judge's drive to vindicate that process requires critique. Ressentiment is the thing to struggle against, then, particularly when it becomes folded into established practices of law. So laugh off those fools who think they have "caught you in a contradiction" if you resent their misrepresentations of their beliefs. Laughing here can both express resentment and fend off its tendency to flow into the form of the ressentiment you resist. Bestow cautious respect upon the element of resentment in desire. The goal is not to purify desire, for, verily, purification, pursued relentlessly on all fronts, dissolves desire.

18. I am both impressed with the way in which, say, Augustine, Girard, Freud, and Lacan show how the experience of the law returns onstage as you fight against its arbitrariness onstage and wary of the necessity each tends to impose upon this pattern; Freud is perhaps the most open to the play of other possibilities. Foucault and Deleuze, you might say, acknowledge these forces and constantly work on them *as if* they were subject to significant modification. This approach seems viable to me.

19. Wendy Brown, "Wounded Attachments," *Political Theory*, August 1993, 394.

20. Michel Foucault, "On the Genealogy of Ethics: An Overview of Work in Progress," in *The Foucault Reader*, ed. Paul Rabinow (New York: Pantheon, 1984), 369.

21. Michel Foucault, "About the Beginning of the Hermeneutics of the Self," two lectures delivered at Dartmouth College in 1980, transcribed by Thomas Keenan and edited by Mark Blasius, *Political Theory*, May 1993, 200. I attended these lectures by Foucault in 1980 with members of a graduate seminar at the University of Massachusetts who were studying his work. Tom Keenan, an undergraduate at Amherst College at the time, was a member of that seminar. Many of us are grateful that he took the time and effort to record and transcribe these lectures, which might not otherwise have been available now. The lectures mark a transition, but not a fundamental shift, in Foucault's work. For he here moves from accounts of how discipline is installed through the institutional techniques of normalizing society to an exploration of tactics on the self by the self through which these institutional effects may be modified. These lectures altered my reading of Foucault significantly. I remain "astonished" that so many have still not perceived the poverty in the charges that Foucault "lacks an ethic" or "lacks a conception of self" or "celebrates transgression for the sake of transgression," etc. Perhaps a few cold showers, right after reading key sections from the pertinent texts aloud, would help.

22. Gus Frias, *Barrio Warriors: Homeboys of Peace* (n.p.: Diaz Publications, 1982), 21. Quoted in Jack Katz, *Seductions of Crime: Moral and Sensual Attractions in Doing Evil* (New York: Basic Books, 1988), 88.

23. I doubt that this appearance of fullness always operates; certainly it is not the universal shape models assume after one's childhood years. The variations here are probably significant within a life cycle and across time, but, still, it does seem likely that the very young project such fullness into their initial models.

24. One of the most compelling defenses of the model of responsible agency is by Peter Strawson, "Freedom and Resentment," in his *Studies in the Philosophy of Thought and Action* (New York: Oxford University Press, 1968), 71-96. Strawson defends presumptions of agency and responsibility inside the reactive attitude of resentment by (a) showing the difficulty, perhaps the pragmatic impossibility, of imagining a world where these attitudes of resentment, indignation, and the like were absent; (b) claiming it would be humanly contradictory to deny the viability of agency and responsibility while continuing to express these presumptions in conduct; and (c) comparing this model to an impossible alternative of determinism that collapses the reactive attitudes into a causal matrix. He then says, in collaboration with the general cultural disposition identified here, "that the participant attitude, and the personal reactive attitudes in general, tend to give place, and it is judged by the civilized world should give place, to objective attitudes, just insofar as the agent is seen as excluded from ordinary adult human relationships by deep seated psychological normality" (81). I would contest this argument, not by asserting the truth of the contrary proposition Strawson criticizes, but, first, by emphasizing the numerous uncertainties and problematical presumptions in both positions; second, by interrogating the place and role of the "we" in these articulations of "our" assumptions; and, third, by commending acceptance of a more ambiguous stance that affirms an element of social indispensability in invoking this uncertain model of agency while seeking to find ways to respond to probable injustices built into the assumptions it makes about those judged by it. The persuasive power of Strawson's argument depends upon a prior, unproven demand that governing social concepts *must* be clean and coherent. Of course, I previously agreed with Strawson on these matters, drawing sustenance from his argument even in a book designed to bring out the "essential contestability" of cultural concepts. See William Connolly, *The Terms of Political Discourse* (Princeton, N.J.: Princeton University Press, 1974; 3d ed., 1993), chapter 5.

25. This is a propitious moment to call attention to a thoughtful essay by Richard Wollheim that supports one of the central claims of this essay. In "Crime, Punishment and 'Pale' Criminality," an essay in his *The Mind*

and Its Depths (Cambridge, Mass.: Harvard University Press, 1993), 132-44, Wollheim treats the pale criminal as one whose illegal desire has become imperious. I disagree only with his assumption that the etiology of desire in the pale criminal is unique. I would suggest, rather, that (1) certain general tendencies built into desire are exacerbated in the case of the pale criminal; (2) the contingent objects of imperious desire of the pale criminal involve it in illegal, violent acts where similar patterns of imperiousness in noncriminals, where they arise, are attached to less violent or more legal objects or both; and (3) Wollheim's admirable call to reconsider the connection between current practices of punishment and current celebrations of state violence in other domains involves him too with the question of how to modify patterns of desire in normalized, noncriminalized subjects. These statements may exaggerate the points of difference between us amidst the crucial point of agreement. Here is the latter point: "To grasp the non-voluntariness of the action, we need more information that turns up on the agent's desire-belief schedule. . . . When an agent does something which he couldn't help doing or which he had to do, what is at stake is not just the desires he had, it is the hold that these desires had over him. It is not to the desires, it is to their imperiousness, that we should look, though it may well be that . . . certain kinds of desires, desires with certain histories, have a tendency to acquire the required imperiousness" (120).

26. Actually, I bypass the general version of this question too, namely: "How could the spirit of revenge be drained from modern Western culture?" Friedrich Nietzsche responds to this question powerfully in *Thus Spoke Zarathustra,* trans. Walter Kaufmann (New York: Penguin, 1978). He decides that only a few can face up to what it takes. I consider the relation of one Nietzschean strategy for subduing ressentiment, preparing to die at the right time, to the spirit of agonistic respect in a democratic culture in *Identity\Difference: Democratic Negotiations of Political Paradox* (Ithaca, N.Y.: Cornell University Press, 1991), chapter 6.

27. See Judith Butler, *Gender Trouble: Feminism and the Subversion of Identity* (New York: Routledge, 1990). With respect to the naturalness of gender duality and heterosexuality, Butler says, "The critical task is, rather, to locate strategies of subversive repetition enabled by those constructions, to affirm the local possibilities of intervention through participating in precisely those practices of repetition that constitute identity and, therefore, present the immanent possibility of contesting them" (147). In her new book, *Bodies That Matter: On the Discursive Limits of Sex* (New York: Routledge, 1993), Butler stresses more the extent to which patterns become corporeally entrenched and the limits set by these entrenchments upon the possibilities of performativity.

28. The type of techniques pertinent here are explored extensively in Jane

Bennett, *The Nature Effect: Reading Henry Thoreau against the Grain* (Newbury Park, Calif.: Sage, 1994).

29. I consider the relation between affirmation of the relational and contingent character of identity and cultivation of an ethos of critical pluralism in "Beyond Good and Evil: The Ethical Sensibility of Michel Foucault," *Political Theory*, August 1993, 365-89.

30. Critics of the perspective I am developing often treat the refusal of the intrinsic model of identity to imply that you endorse the model of the self as a self-*chosen* self. But these two theories, let us call them the Taylorite and the Sartrean models, are mirror images of each other. And the model pursued here endorses neither.

3. DEMOCRACY, EQUALITY, NORMALITY

1. Arnold Kaufman, *The Radical Liberal: The New Man in American Politics* (New York: Atherton, 1968). The affinity between Kaufman and Macpherson can be marked by a seminar I took with Kaufman during the early sixties entitled "Human Nature and Participatory Democracy." The organization of that seminar tracked pretty closely the four "models" of democracy later discussed in print by Macpherson. And Kaufman's ideal of "participatory democracy" set part of the agenda for the 1962 "Port Huron Statement"; Tom Hayden, the leading architect of that statement, also was a student in this seminar. Kaufman's essay is printed in *The Bias of Pluralism*, ed. William Connolly (New York: Atherton, 1969).

2. Macpherson, *The Life and Times of Liberal Democracy* (New York: Oxford University Press, 1977), 34.

3. Ibid., 43.

4. Ibid., 42.

5. Mill, quoted by Macpherson. Ibid., 45.

6. Ibid., 51, 48.

7. Ibid., 49.

8. Ibid., 70.

9. Ibid., 79.

10. Robert Dahl, quoted by Macpherson. Ibid., 82.

11. Ibid., 86.

12. Ibid., 100. Rousseau's own version of the paradox is: "In order for an emerging people to appreciate the healthy maxims of politics, and follow the fundamental rules of statecraft, the effect would have to become cause; the social spirit, which would be the result of the institution, would have to preside over the founding of the institution itself; and men would have to be prior to the laws what they ought to become by means of laws." Jean-Jacques Rousseau, *On the Social Contract: With Geneva Manuscript and*

Political Economy, ed. Roger Masters, trans. Judith Masters (New York: St. Martin's, 1978), 69.

13. This distinction between exclusive and inclusive goods is elaborated and exemplified in Michael Best and William E. Connolly, *The Politicized Economy* (Lexington, Mass.: Heath, 1976; 2d ed., 1982). It is elaborated further in terms of its implications for the Democratic Party in the United States in my "Civic Disaffection and the Democratic Party," *Politics and Ambiguity* (Madison: University of Wisconsin Press, 1987), 31-41.

14. It might seem that this example is simply Bill Clinton's proposal for health care. Actually, it breaks with his in that it is built around the generalization of health maintenance organizations, but it does share a common objective. This version was first worked out in the 1970s as part of a more general pursuit of an infrastructure of consumption built around generalizable goods. See the references in the previous note.

15. C. B. Macpherson, *Democratic Theory: Essays in Retrieval* (Oxford: Clarendon, 1973), 53-54.

16. Ibid., 54-55; italics in original.

17. In *Political Theory and Modernity* (Oxford: Basil Blackwell, 1988) I give a reading of Hobbes in which the self-interested self is a social construction rather than the fundamental datum upon which society is built. This Hobbesian formation is designed to convert an unruly, irascible, and volatile being into a calculable, predictable, governable, individual. So the Hobbesian individual is not simply the problem a sovereign must cope with or the restraint against sovereign power the individualist can celebrate; it is also a site of order and governance. See chapter 2 and the First Interlude. Macpherson makes Hobbes into more of an atomist than he is, and in that way becomes diverted from seeing certain affinities between his position and that of Hobbes.

18. There are a lot of presumptions packed into the adjective *modern* in this sentence. It can be argued that the issue of identity does not really arise in a culture in which the members belong to a common life that is experienced as being set in a cosmic order not to be called into question. That is perhaps true, for the politics of identity arises in a culture in which individuals and groups seek modes of recognition that others may be inclined to withhold. Identity is a relational formation, and it involves the response of others to a particular constituency, as much as the claims of those seeking recognition. However that may be, it does seem that something like the politics of identity reaches at least as far back in "Western" culture as Augustinianism. And probably much further than that.

19. Gilles Deleuze and Félix Guattari, *A Thousand Plateaus,* trans. Brian Massumi (Minneapolis: University of Minnesota Press, 1987), 6-7, 15. Emphasis added.

20. See Claude Lefort, *Democracy and Political Theory,* trans. David Macey (Minneapolis: University Of Minnesota Press, 1988). I discuss the Lefort position in chapter 5.

21. The issue of speed in politics deserves more attention. For, in the late-modern time, speed overwhelms distance, calling into question traditional verities of territorial integrity, sovereignty, and security. This issue is explored by Paul Virilio, *Speed and Politics,* trans. Mark Polizzotti (New York: Semiotext[e], 1986). But Virilio, while he recognizes the effects of acceleration upon cultural space, particularly the effects posed by the acceleration of military speed, also yearns for a time when things moved slowly. A political culture that becomes more open to the play of contingency and difference in the identities inhabiting it is one in which things move faster than they did in premodern times but not so fast that they wipe out the possibility of politics itself. Deleuze and Guattari, in *A Thousand Plateaus,* seem more alert to this issue to me. For a thoughtful exploration of political speed that pays attention to the effects of speed on the course of international relations, see James Der Derian, *Anti-Diplomacy: Spies, Terror, Speed and War* (Oxford: Basil Blackwell, 1992).

22. Michel Foucault, "Politics and Ethics: An Interview," in *The Foucault Reader,* ed. Paul Rabinow (New York: Pantheon, 1984), 377-79.

23. In an essay on the Mitterrand government, Foucault identified specific reforms he would support through state action in the domain of sexuality. "But, in the end, I've become rather irritated by an attitude, which for a long time was mine, too, and which I no longer subscribe to, which consists in saying: our problem is to denounce and criticize: let them get on with their legislation and reforms. That doesn't seem to me like the right attitude." Lawrence D. Kritzman, ed., *Michel Foucault: Politics, Philosophy, Culture,* trans. Alan Sheridan (New York: Routledge, 1988), 209.

4. FUNDAMENTALISM IN AMERICA

1. My colleague Dick Flathman called attention to this Bushism and its relation to the war during a talk at Johns Hopkins just prior to the American attack against Iraq.

2. "Morality and Homosexuality," *Wall Street Journal,* February 24, 1994. The signatories include Hadley Arkes, Amherst College; Gerard Bradley, Notre Dame Law School; Rabbi David Dalin, University of Hartford; Ernest Fortin, Boston College; Jerry Muller, Catholic University of America; Richard John Nehaus, Institute on Religion and Public Life; and Max Stackhouse, Princeton Theological Seminary.

3. Harold Bloom, *The American Religion* (New York: Simon & Schuster, 1992). A compelling essay by Susan Harding, "If I Die Before I Wake: Jerry Falwell's Pro-Life Gospel," in *Uncertain Terms: Negotiating Gender in*

American Culture, ed. Faye Ginsburg and Anna Lowenhaupt Tsing (Boston: Beacon, 1990), 76-97, is also very pertinent here. Harding appreciates the ambiguities and attractions of a position that is also threatening in obvious ways. She recognizes the presence of a fundamentalist strain in every orientation, even while struggling to loosen its hold. Listen to her summary of how a Baptist preacher embeds antiabortion politics in "the greatest story ever told": "The stories [of the abortion temptation] do not represent 'preexisting' asymmetries as fixed-eternal truths that must be swallowed whole, but reconstitute them. They transfer these new configurations from author to reader, with tremendous force and tenderness. . . . Repeatedly, superior persons (Falwell), terms ('male', spiritual, second birth, saved), stories (Gonophore's arrival at LGH, Falwell's listening to her Memorial Day Speech), and discourses (born again) incorporate and arise out of the transcendence of inferior persons. . . . The logic binding inferior and superior is neither literary nor causal, but divine; foreordained and indelibly written by God. If Isaac, then Christ. If 'female' then 'male', if Gonophore then Falwell-cum-maternity-home-maker" (93).

4. Quoted in Bloom, *The American Religion,* 178.

5. Quoted in Bloom, *The American Religion,* 226.

6. The most compelling presentation of the working-class ideology of sacrifice is Richard Sennett and Jonathan Cobb, *The Hidden Injuries of Class* (New York: Random House, 1973).

7. It found earlier expression in my work in an essay (written with Michael Best) entitled "Beyond the Economics of Environmental Management," in *Public Policy Evaluation,* ed. Kenneth Dolbeare (Beverly Hills, Calif.: Sage, 1975), 41-74. The theme was pursued further in Best and Connolly, *The Politicized Economy* (Lexington, Mass.: Heath, 1976). For example: "With nowhere else to go, the hostility to liberalism finds expression in spontaneous, unorganized ways—as in support for George Wallace, in the growing number of non-voters, in tax revolts at the lower levels of government, in minority support for a new party on the right, or in an uneasy withdrawal from the political arena altogether. . . . The present period, defined politically, is one of unrest, uncertainty, and ambivalence in the subordinate classes. Trapped within the limited electoral options available, distressed citizens might eventually move in surprising directions" (179).

8. This constitution of the masculine and the feminine is not to be compared to a stable, natural base from which it deviates. I doubt that there is such a place of stability at the bottom of things. The point here is to explore the forces that intensify that exclusionary logic of the masculine while searching for ways to turn it around. For this constitution of the masculine cannot be without a corollary constitution of the feminine that places both men and women so defined in demeaning, subordinate positions. For an im-

pressive study that considers how capital, the state, and masculinism converge in the American political economy, see Wendy Brown, *Wounded Politics: Essays on Power and Freedom in Late-Modernity* (Princeton, N.J.: Princeton University Press, forthcoming).

9. James Kurth, "The Post-Modern State," *The National Interest*, Summer 1992, 26-36.

10. Ibid., 29.

11. Ibid., 33.

12. Ibid., 35.

13. A letter from "Ollie North" inviting potential supporters to join his "Advisory Board," undated but mailed in March 1994, during his run for the Republican nomination for senator of Virginia. It says in big print, "THE PEOPLE REJECT LIBERALISM, HIGH TAXES AND WILD SPENDING!" "Wild spending," of course, is the traditional province of working-class wives and mothers, while their husbands spend on sober things such as beer, sports, cars, and snowmobiles. And North attacks "liberal Democrat Senator Chuck Robb, who is Lyndon Johnson's son-in-law": "Robb supported higher income taxes, higher gas taxes, higher business taxes, higher social security taxes, more pork barrel wasteful spending, more welfare spending, lifting the ban on homosexuals in the military, more power for left-wing union bosses, more red tape and regulations for small business."

14. It might be pertinent to call attention to the formulation of liberalism by Richard E. Flathman, *Willful Liberalism: Voluntarism and Individuality in Political Theory and Practice* (Ithaca, N.Y.: Cornell University Press, 1992). While this liberalism is not mine, it does actively resist the strain of fundamentalism recognizable in other variants. The most suggestive recent history of what I am calling liberal fundamentalism and its political effects is provided by E. J. Dionne, *Why Americans Hate Politics* (New York: Simon & Schuster, 1991). This thoughtful book reviews attempts within the left in the late sixties and early seventies to maintain contact with the white working class, and it develops a history of the fundamentalism that followed the failure of this effort. I do not mean to imply that it is easy to succeed on this terrain.

15. Ronald Dworkin, "Liberalism," in *Public and Private Morality*, ed. Stuart Hampshire (Cambridge, Mass.: Cambridge University Press, 1978), 127.

16. David Johnston, review essay, *Political Theory*, November 1993, 698-701; quotes from 700 and 701.

17. Michel Foucault, *The Use of Pleasure*, trans. Robert Hurley (New York: Pantheon, 1985): "If it is true, in fact, that every morality, in the broad sense, comprises . . . codes of behavior and forms of subjectivation; if it is true that they can never be entirely dissociated, though they may de-

velop in relative independence from one another—then we should not be surprised to find that in certain moralities the main emphasis is placed on the code, on its systematicity, its richness, its capacity to adjust to every possible case. . . . With moralities of this type the important thing is to focus on the instances of authority that enforce the code. . . . On the other hand, it is easy to conceive of moralities in which the strong and dynamic element is to be sought in the forms of subjectivation and the practices of the self" (29–30). I pursue the relation between code and ethos in the last chapter of this study, drawing it into an effort to maintain critical tension between pluralism and pluralization.

18. Would not such a postmodern liberalism undermine its own moral agenda by depriving itself of the fundaments on which it must be based? This is the anxiety underlying many of the charges against that diverse crew called "postmodern." I would argue, though, that it is when you cultivate an ethic that refuses to ground itself on a fictive Law of laws or intrinsic design of being that the greatest possibility of generosity in the competition between contending identities is present. An ethical sensibility of agonistic generosity, Nietzsche might say, requires conversion of the anxiety within contending fundamentalisms into a reciprocal "pathos of distance." I pursue this theme in *The Augustinian Imperative* (Beverly Hills, Calif.: Sage, 1993).

19. Perhaps this is a place to compare my thinking to that of Chantal Mouffe in *The Return of the Political* (New York: Verso, 1993). There is considerable overlap between my position and Mouffe's study, which appeared while this one was going into production. Mouffe is admirable in contesting the presumed "fact" of pluralism in contemporary political theories, in engaging the irreducible element of antagonism in politics, and in emphasizing the necessity of exclusion in every political order. But her critique of "essentialism" comes too close to replicating the form of the position she opposes. While "essentialism" can be criticized, while its underlying assumptions in its different versions can be shown to be deeply contestable, I doubt very much that the faith governing it can be definitively refuted. There is no place itself free of faith from which to do so. And while an "antiessentialist" position can be invoked (though not without drawing upon assumptions that are in tension with it), it too reflects a contestable interpretation of things. My concern is that an essentialist critique of essentialism risks recapitulating the form of the position it resists. That is why genealogy is such an important component in the position I endorse. Genealogy forces into view tendencies in your thought to naturalize the perspective you endorse.

Second, while one must grant Mouffe's claim about the necessity of political exclusion in every political order, when you pay attention to the way in which identities are indebted to the differences through which they are specified, when you explore how an *ethos* of critical responsiveness can translate some relations of antagonism into relations of agonistic respect, and when you explore how strains of absolutism within liberalism may contribute to the fundamentalism they abhor, rich *possibilities* of renegotiating fundamentalisms open up. This, of course, does not settle the probability of success, but it does open *one* window for the translation of antagonism into agonistic respect. Exploration of an *ethos* conducive to the politics of pluralization is the crucial move. And Mouffe does not actively engage this issue.

Third, one of the ways to challenge the fundamentalism of the nation-state is to legitimize and participate in cross-national, nonstatist movements that put pressure on states and the interstate system in the domains of ecology, national security, gender politics, labor policies, refugees, and so on. Mouffe confines pluralization to the boundaries of the territorial state. With these three points made, however, there is still considerable overlap between my effort to "convert an antagonism of identity into an agonism of difference" (*Identity\Difference: Democratic Negotiations of Political Paradox* [Ithaca, N.Y.: Cornell University Press, 1991], 178) and Mouffe's ideal of "agonistic pluralism."

5. DEMOCRACY AND TERRITORIALITY

1. Jean-Jacques Rousseau, *On the Social Contract: With Geneva Manuscript and Political Economy*, book 1, ed. Roger Masters, trans. Judith Masters (New York: St. Martin's, 1978), 46. I discuss this quotation in the context of Rousseau's general thought in chapter 3 of *Political Theory and Modernity* (New York: Basil Blackwell, 1988).

2. Paul Ricoeur, "The Political Paradox," in *Legitimacy and the State*, ed. William E. Connolly (New York: New York University Press, 1984), 254.

3. Ricoeur deals with these issues more extensively in *The Symbolism of Evil* (Boston: Beacon, 1967). Here he examines the "tragic myth," the "Orphic myth," and the "Adamic myth" comparatively to explore what together they tell us about the human experience of evil. He privileges the Adamic myth, but he also opposes the conception of original sin Augustine draws from it, in which there was initially a pure act of will by Adam followed by the history of human beings with divided wills. He also folds elements from the other two myths into the Adamic myth, claiming that they complete the insights built into it. Thus he makes a lot of the role of the serpent, a being that represents the anterior presence of evil even in the original condition. It is uncertain (to me) whether this tragic structure is retained once "Christology" is introduced into the picture by Ricoeur. To keep the issues as well defined as possible, I will simply say that I would give priority to

the tragic myth and try to build a vision of democratic politics around appreciation of that experience.

4. The classic response here is advanced by Peter Bachrach, *The Theory of Democratic Elitism: A Critique* (Boston: Little, Brown, 1967). Other critiques can be found in William E. Connolly, ed., *The Bias of Pluralism* (New York: Atherton, 1969), especially the essays by Arnold Kaufman and David Kettler.

5. Joseph Schumpeter, *Capitalism, Socialism and Democracy* (New York: Harper & Row, 1942), 257.

6. Ibid., 295.

7. Ibid., 292.

8. Ibid., 254, 263.

9. It is sometimes suggested that the class structure of contemporary capitalism is concealed by the politics of identity. Yes and no. Large numbers of people inhabit a plurality of class positions at the same time, being workers, consumers, owners, savers, and investors to varying degrees. And in each of these domains our class identifications are influenced by how our current position is interpreted in relation to future aspirations. The politics of class revolves around which positions assume primacy in the identity of particular constituencies. The politics of economic equalization depends upon success in modifying the actual and aspirational identifications of many who are dependent workers, middle-class consumers, aspiring homeowners, and hopeful investors. So it would be unwise to overturn the politics of identity in the name of the politics of class. Each is implicated in the other.

10. "Liberalism and the Art of Separation," *Political Theory,* August 1944, 321.

11. Michael Walzer, *Spheres of Justice: A Defense of Pluralism and Equality* (New York: Basic Books, 1983), 289.

12. Thomas L. Dumm has advanced this effort impressively in *Democracy and Punishment* (Madison: University of Wisconsin Press, 1987). I try to open it up in chapter 2 of this study.

13. *Spheres of Justice* continues this politics of concealment in the way it interprets the work of Michel Foucault. The Walzerian reading of *Discipline and Punish*, trans. Alan Sheridan (New York: Pantheon, 1970), construes Foucault to say that a series of bureaucratic elites have acquired unaccountable power over prisons (and other institutions), while I read it to say that disciplinary power operates through and over these agents as well. Moreover, for Foucault, recurrent cycles of prison discipline and prison reform contribute to the "success" of the prison.

14. Near the end of the book, this uninterpreted formulation appears: "Social meanings need not be harmonious; sometimes they provide only the intellectual structure within which distributions are debated" (314). Assum-

ing that "social meanings" correspond to "shared understandings," and that "sometimes" means more than rarely this concession, pursued closely, would require the text to move onto a plane it tries to avoid. One could continue to use the warm Walzerian language once that concession is made, but to do so the text would have to move onto a metaphysical plane and endorse a teleological philosophy. Walzer, though, signals in the preface that he does not want this book to move onto the ontological plane. After announcing how the book coheres with arguments by William Galston and Nicholas Rescher, Walzer says, "But, in my view, the pluralism of these two arguments is vitiated by Galston's Aristotelianism and by Rescher's utilitarianism. My own argument proceeds without these foundational commitments" (xviii). The upshot of the preceding critique is that the Walzerian argument expresses its social ontology in the political vocabularies it selects; it then conceals the contestable character of these presumptions by attributing them to "our shared understandings."

15. William Connolly, *Identity\Difference: Democratic Negotiations of Political Paradox* (Ithaca, N.Y.: Cornell University Press, 1991). Quotations are drawn from pages 31-34.

16. There is a crucial proviso to this, one that links politics and the "connected intellectual" to issues in other states. One might, Walzer knows, have identifications that bind one to another state, as a Jewish-American might be tied to Israel, an Irish-American to Ireland, a French-Palestinian to the idea of Palestine, etc. Walzer extends connectedness beyond the state. But even here the lines separating connected intellectuals from those unconnected to the issues in question are drawn too tightly. In an exchange between Walzer and Edward Said over the Israeli treatment of Palestinians inside Israel, Walzer uses the rule of connectedness to make this *his* issue: "The battle over the Jewish tradition is my battle; in that sense I am a parochial intellectual. But it is also a *battle*; it doesn't involve, as Said charges, 'just going along with one's own people for the sake of loyalty and "connectedness"'" ("An Exchange: 'Exodus and Revolution,'" *Grand Street*, August 1985, 250). It *is* Walzer's battle, and he is an effective warrior in it, ready to oppose those traditions that subvert other understandings he takes to be fundamental. But if the battle involves the way Israel treats Palestinians, it is equally Said's battle too. Just as Said's battles are also Walzer's. The way each connected intellectual is also implicated in the connections of the others helps to explain why the debate between these two is so vitriolic and how its terms may embody a tragic dimension detectable to those listening to them together. If those battles impinge upon contemporary considerations of peace and justice that implicate a large variety of others, then we others, too, are implicated in them, though to different degrees. The appropriate distinction here is not between the connected and the "unconnected" intellectual, with

the former having rights and obligations and the latter stuck in an abstract world of empty formulations. We are all connected, in a large number of domains. Connectedness, in the late-modern world, is a series of complex relations, embodying variable degrees of implication and distantiation. It is because Walzer underplays the global interconnectedness of peoples, issues, and contingencies in the late-modern world that he is tempted by dichotomies where complex gradations are needed. This is not to vindicate Said's closing comments in that exchange. They sink to a level that is unacceptable within an ethic of agonistic respect in intellectual engagement.

17. Michael Shapiro and Deanne Neaubauer explore these connections/disconnections effectively in "Spatiality and Policy Discourse: Reading the Global City," in *Contending Sovereignties: Redefining Political Community,* ed. R. B. J. Walker and Saul H. Mendlovitz (London: Lynne Refiner, 1990). The essays by Walker and Warren Magnusson in that collection are also pertinent to themes developed here. Walker poses a series of dilemmas surrounding "spatiotemporal" definitions of politics, and Magnusson explores how a variety of social movements trangress the boundaries of the state.

18. John H. Herz, *International Politics in the Atomic Age* (New York: Columbia University Press, 1959). By "epistemic realism" I mean (a) a mode of analysis that gives (putative) privilege to independent objects not deeply contaminated by ideas, beliefs, and ideologies and (b) a model that treats things to have greater causal efficacy the more "material" and the less "ideational" they are. By "political realism" I mean a normative conception of politics that treats as most real/normal/necessary those entities epistemically endowed with primacy and that adjusts its political imaginary to correspond to these real forces. In the first study Herz's epistemic and political realism coalesce; in the second, he retains the semblance of political realism by giving up large chunks of epistemic realism.

19. Ibid., 40.

20. There are several issues posed by this quotation that I bypass. One of them is a corollary issue involving models of interpretation such as rational choice theory and discursive theory that do incorporate ideational dimensions into their accounts of practice. They then silently dematerialize these practices, treating them as if they were constituted simply as conversations rather than as discursive practices that have become *materialized* in bodies, territories, dispositions, habits, identities, unconscious presumptions, institutional intersections, etc. These two typologies constantly seem to reproduce each other.

21. Herz, *International Politics,* 40-41.

22. Ibid., 57.

23. "In particular, it made it easier for the members of the family [of sov-

ereign states] to observe self-denying standards 'at home' by providing them with an outlet for their warlike and expansionist inclinations in the vast realm outside Europe" (ibid., 67).

24. Ibid., 104.

25. Ibid., 108.

26. John Herz, "The Territorial State Revisited: Reflections on the Future of the Nation-State," *Polity*, Fall 1968, 15.

27. Ibid., 21, 24, 25.

28. A presentation of the cultural "problematization of final markers" must be balanced eventually by one that explores how the politics of naturalization is always in the process of reconsolidating itself in the face of these pressures. This second dimension is explored more actively in chapters 4 and 5. Nietzsche is the hero here. He does not, as some of his critics suggest, contend that the self can simply create itself out of nothing once the challenge to old "idols" or "markers" has taken hold. For the density of linguistic abbreviations, the dictates of social coordination, the small size of the human "chamber of consciousness," psychic pressures to consolidate identity, and the fact that an identity is impressed upon one before one has the resources to examine it genealogically often work against the pressures to dissolution. That is why genealogy is ethically necessary.

29. The closely related phrase "dissolution of final markers" is coined by Claude Lefort in *Democracy and Political Theory*, trans. David Macey (Minneapolis: University of Minnesota Press, 1988). I am indebted to LeFort. But I prefer the "problematization of final markers," first, because these markers have not been dissolved but have become both more actively questioned and fundamentalized in modern life and, second, because my conception of democracy celebrates the *contestation* of markers you may take to be final, but not their final *elimination*.

30. One way to test what happens when the sovereignty side of democracy suffocates the disturbance side is to examine a theory of democracy that gives full priority to the first. Carl Schmitt, in *The Crisis of Parliamentary Democracy* (Cambridge, Mass.: MIT Press, 1988), made this implication clear while he was (in 1922) still a theorist of democratic sovereignty: "Every actual democracy rests on the principle that not only are equals equal but unequals will not be treated equally. Democracy requires, therefore, first homogeneity and second—if the need arises—elimination or eradication of heterogeneity" (9). The text makes clear that it does not take much for the need to arise in Schmitt's mind.

6. TOCQUEVILLE, RELIGIOSITY, AND PLURALIZATION

1. *The Book of J*, trans. David Rosenberg and interpreted by Harold Bloom (New York: Grove Weidenfeld, 1990), 149. I select the Rosenberg

translation partly because, as the latest in a very long line of translations, it calls our attention to the unavoidability of translation in this domain and the incorrigible moment of interpretation in every translation, and partly because it highlights the question of boundaries I want to consider. Robert Alter, in *The World of Biblical Literature* (New York: Basic Books, 1991), 153-61, argues that the Rosenberg translation is defective and that its attribution of some sections to "J" is questionable. I am sure he is right about the second point, and I am unqualified to judge the first. But Alter's critique seems to presuppose the the availability of a neutral translation not itself deeply invested with particular interpretations. This seems dubious to me. And his critique of Bloom's projection of "J" as a woman with an ironic sensibility forgets how this very projection functions in Bloom's reading. Bloom projects "J" as an aristocratic woman, partly to give coherence to his reading and *partly to underline the inevitability and contestability of some such set of projections in every reading of this text.* Bloom's ironic projection insinuates modesty into the indispensable practice of interpretation.

2. *Book of J,* 159–60.

3. Ibid., 162.

4. Jean-Jacques Rousseau, *The Government of Poland,* trans. Willmoore Kendall (New York: Bobbs-Merrill, 1972), 6.

5. See chapter 5, where I discuss Rousseau's recognition of the "paradox of politics."

6. Rousseau, *Government of Poland,* 6.

7. Ibid., 14; emphasis added.

8. Jean-Jacques Rousseau, *On the Social Contract,* trans. Roger Masters (New York: St. Martin's, 1978), 130; emphasis added.

9. While Rousseau is not a pluralist in *The Social Contract,* he becomes one of sorts in *The Government of Poland.* The first ideal, Rousseau suggests, may be actualizable nowhere, while the ideal projected for Poland might be approximated somewhere. The Rousseauian element in Tocquevillian pluralism is suggested in the following formulation: "the laws of a democracy tend toward the good of the greatest number, for they spring from the majority of all citizens, which may be mistaken but which cannot have an interest contrary to its own" (*Democracy in America,* trans. George Lawrence [New York: Anchor, 1969], 234). My reading of Tocqueville has affinities to those by Thomas Dumm, *Democracy and Punishment* (Madison: University of Wisconsin Press, 1987), chapter 5, and Stephen Schneck, "Habits of the Head: Tocqueville's America and Jazz," *Political Theory* 17, no. 4 (November 1989): 638-62. I am also indebted to participants in a fall 1992 seminar David Campbell and I taught at Johns Hopkins entitled "Sovereignty and Democracy." Tocqueville's *Democracy in America* was a central object of discussion. Those who have encountered Campbell's *Writing*

Security (Minneapolis: University of Minnesota Press, 1992) will detect similarities between this presentation of Tocqueville's "America" and Campbell's presentation of how contemporary foreign policy helps to constitute American political identity.

10. An earlier reading of Tocqueville by another Connolly was intent on showing how his appreciation of early American pluralism discloses the thinness of contemporary ideals of pluralism. For when you compare his model to contemporary conditions of class inequality, military organization, corporate hegemony, and micromanagement of cultural identities, several contemporary celebrations of pluralism look rather thin. But that essay slips over the way Tocqueville vindicated a set of violences and exclusions to protect the vision of civilization in which his pluralism was set. That Connolly was too much of an arboreal pluralist. See William E. Connolly, ed., *The Bias of Pluralism* (New York: Atherton, 1969), "The Challenge to Pluralist Theory."

11. I will continue to use the term *Indian* throughout this chapter, partly to follow Tocqueville's usage, partly to emphasize how this diverse set of indigenous inhabitants is presented to *us* by a European theorist and a European civilization.

12. Alexis de Tocqueville, *Democracy in America,* 2 vols., trans. George Lawrence (New York: Harper & Row, 1969), 27, 30, 280.

13. Ibid., 280.

14. Ibid., 292.

15. Ibid., 292.

16. Ibid., 543–44.

17. Ibid., 58.

18. The last formulation comes from page 317 of *Democracy in America.*

19. Tocqueville, *Democracy in America,* 294.

20. Ibid., 586.

21. Henry David Thoreau, "The Allegash and East Branch," in *The Maine Woods,* ed. Joseph J. Moldenhauer (Princeton, N.J.: Princeton University Press, 1972), 181. I am indebted to Mike Shapiro and Jonathan Boyarin for thoughtful critiques of an earlier version of this section.

22. Ibid., 182.

23. This journey is completely male, and the larger world Thoreau and Polis evoke together seems to be male centered as well. The pathos of distance they engender together may produce another other, but that remains a topic for another discussion.

24. Thoreau, "The Allegash and East Branch," 181.

25. Ibid., 185. For the role such a tacit knowledge plays in the ethical sensibility Thoreau himself develops, see Jane Bennett, *Thoreau's Nature: Ethics, Politics and the Self* (Newbury Park, Calif.: Sage, 1994). My reading of Thoreau is indebted to this study.

26. Thoreau, "The Allegash and East Branch," 201.

27. Robert F. Sayre, in *Thoreau and the American Indians* (Princeton, N.J.: Princeton University Press, 1977), explores Thoreau's trajectory as he moves from an early idealization of the savage to a later perspective that presses against this boundary itself. Thoreau, Sayre says, never really crossed the boundary he began to recognize. The essay I landed upon, to find a counter to the Tocquevillian reading set in the same approximate time, turns out to be the latest and most thoughtful probing by Thoreau of his own earlier perspective.

28. *On Our Own Ground: The Complete Writings of William Apess, A Pequot,* ed. Barry O'Connell (Amherst: University of Massachusetts Press, 1993), 212, 216. O'Connell's introduction is invaluable.

29. "A rhizome as subterranean stem is absolutely different from roots and radicles. Bulbs and tubers are rhizomes. . . . A rhizome ceaselessly establishes connections between semiotic chains, organizations of power, and circumstances relative to the arts, sciences, and social struggles. A semiotic chain is like a tuber agglomerating very diverse acts, not only linguistic, but also perceptive, mimetic, gestural and cognitive. . . . To be rhizomorphous is to produce stems and filaments that seem to be roots, or better yet connect with them by penetrating the trunk, but put them to strange new uses. We're tired of trees. . . . They've made us suffer too much" (Gilles Deleuze and Félix Guattari, *A Thousand Plateaus: Capitalism and Schizophrenia,* trans. Brian Massumi [Minneapolis: University of Minnesota Press, 1988], 6, 7, 15).

30. Tocqueville, *Democracy in America,* 243–44.

31. There are fascinating ambiguities in Tocqueville's reading of Puritanism. Puritanism set the basis for the American republic through its deep faith, its love of equality within that faith, and its commitment to the soil. But it is the evolution from Puritanism that Tocqueville seems to admire the most. Tocqueville, though, is extremely hesitant to trace failures in Puritan attempts to assimilate the Indian to elements in the doctrine of Puritanism. Two citations express these two themes: The first Americans "bequeathed to their descendants the habits, ideas, and mores best suited to make a republic flourish. When I consider all that has resulted from this first fact, I think I can see the whole destiny of America contained in the first Puritan who landed on those shores, as that of the whole human race in the first man. . . . Their fathers gave them love of equality and liberty, but it was God who, by handing a limitless continent over to them, gave them the means of long remaining equal and free" (*Democracy in America,* 279). "There have been several attempts to bring enlightenment to the Indians, leaving unchecked their vagabond mores; the Jesuits attempted it in Canada, and the Puritans in New England. Neither achieved any durable result. . . . The great mistake

of these lawgivers for the Indians was that they did not understand that to succeed in civilizing a people it is above all necessary to get them to take root, and that can only be done by cultivating the soil" (*Democracy in America,* 327).

32. Numerous other candidates could be added to this list. Take, for instance, the "minor" movement, discernible today in every health club in America, for a new virilization of men and women. Such a movement, located outside channels ordinarily characterized as political, nonetheless carries political implications because it scatters the presumed relations between manhood, masculinity, activity, and virility on one side and womanhood, femininity, receptiveness, and weakness on the other. It can feed into broader movements to pluralize possibilities of gender performance and sexuality. Of course, it too, like every movement, could adopt either the form of a dogmatic, universal identity or one that ironizes its relations to itself and appreciates other possibilities for others even as it sculpts a particular relation between bodily form and cultural identification. This movement merely underlines the corporeal dimension of identity production that is always present. Is the male academic, for instance, who presents himself as a disembodied intellectual unconcerned about body definition any less implicated in the connection between bodily presentation and cultural identification?

33. Seyla Benhabib, *Journal of Political Philosophy,* February 1994, 85, emphasis added. Benhabib's essay is admirable in several respects, particularly in the way she distinguishes between *ethnos* and *demos,* so that unity in religious, ethnic, cultural, or linguistic identity is not a precondition of political democracy. Here she concurs with Lyotard and Derrida. And Benhabib's introduction of a dialectic of development proceeds beyond tendencies in Walzer and Rawls to submerge the politics of becoming under shared understandings and the matrix of justice. If we engaged that tendency in Walzer in chapter 5, it is even more prominent in the Rawlsian drive to base justice on the flat combination of an "overlapping consensus" and "the original position." See John Rawls, *Political Liberalism* (New York: Columbia University Press, 1993). But Benhabib does not appreciate how the politics of enactment (or becoming) depends upon political challenges to established practices irreducible to a dialectical logic. Derrida, for example, both embraces universal rights and deconstructs closures in contemporary presentations of the universal. And Benhabib's critique of Lyotard, Derrida, and Honig for concentrating on ambiguities and exclusions lodged in "the formalism" of political *foundings* overlooks how this point of focus enables them to come to terms critically with silent, often less dramatic, recapitulations of such violences in everyday politics *after* the founding. Even Benhabib's example, the intervention of abolitionists into the issue of slavery, overlooks how most editorialists immediately after the attack at Harper's

Ferry defined John Brown as either an irresponsible offender or a "monoma-
niac" (the legal category at the time for an unresponsible agent of violence).
It was the political disruption of this double constitution of the white, radical antislave Other, in which Thoreau participated, that improved the
prospects of responding affirmatively to Brown's intervention. The most
fundamental difference between us, perhaps, is that Benhabib seeks to
ground morality on a solid universal that can realize itself dialectically, while
I pursue an ethic of cultivation that appreciates the fugitive abundance of life
over identity, attends to the paradoxical element in enactment, and is never
entirely reducible to the moral codes it admires. It is always possible to interpret politics dialectically; it is indeed very difficult not to do so as you look
back on developments that have already succeeded. But the debate between
democratic neo-Hegelians and democratic post-Nietzscheans may revolve
around whether recourse to the dialectic invokes fundamental assumptions
about being that pose unnecessary constraints to the politics of becoming
when it is *in* the process of becoming (rather than after the fact of its success). I concur with Gilles Deleuze, who says somewhere that "the dialectic
fits being like baggy clothes." You can wrap a world in which things are inherently *mobile* in such clothing, but the nuances of difference get lost in the
process. Of course, Benhabib would contend that logic (and concepts and
arguments) is indispensable to social explanation and critique, etc., etc. True
enough. The point, for us, is to deploy these indispensable elements while
also struggling against becoming captured entirely by the moral limitations
they produce. That is where genealogy, deconstruction, and critical responsiveness come in as indispensable counterpoints to existing codes of morality
and justice. These comments abbreviate a critique of an earlier version of
Benhabib's essay I gave at the 1992 meeting of the American Political Science Association.

34. Derrida, thereby, is more alert to this constitutive ambiguity than
Benhabib. He is specifically in favor of rights in the face of this ambiguity
but, more significant yet, is also committed to a responsiveness that speaks
to the constitutive ambiguity of rights. Derrida: "No cultural identity presents itself as the opaque body of an untranslatable idiom, but, always, on
the contrary, as the irreplaceable *inscription* of the universal in the singular,
the *unique testimony* to the human essence and to what is proper to man."
And then, when responsiveness is cultivated, "it has begun to open itself, or
rather to let itself open, or better yet, to be affected with opening without
opening *itself* onto an other, onto an other that the heading can no longer
even relate to itself as *its* other, *the other with itself*" (*The Other Heading:
Reflections of Today's Europe,* trans. Pascale-Anne Brault and Michael B.
Naas [Bloomington: Indiana University Press, 1992], 73, 76; emphasis in
original). I would rephrase Benhabib's objection to Derrida as a reservation,

for his very attempt to avoid implication in suffering or injustice at all may have the effect of disabling him from ethically responsive *action* in morally ambiguous contexts—that is, in most contexts. On *this* register I find Foucault to be more balanced than Derrida.

35. See the discussion of the Heideggerian relation of truth/falsity to "untruth" in the first chapter of this study.

36. Familiar objections are rather predictable at this point. Here is one: "If you say that, retrospectively, the new formation is better than the old one, then you are *implying* that there is a true set of identities toward which humans aim. Hence, da da da, da da da . . ." But this correction misses the point. What is relieved is a previously underappreciated mode of suffering or injury. That does not mean that the new identity is natural or true, but, rather, that in coming more closely to terms with its own contingency and contestability, both it and its alter identities are in a better position to fend off violent exclusions by making room for new possibilities. Similar responses are available to the all too familiar charge that this perspective reduces morality to "preference," or that it takes itself to be true while criticizing other perspectives for making such claims, etc. What we wish to say to moral fundamentalists is this: "Quit attacking us for endorsing an ethic that is not groundable in the certainty of a final command or design. We do so because *you* have never succeeded, after all these centuries, in proving one. If and when you succeed, we might come around. Until you do, we fear that the air of desperation in your search fosters the effect you purport to oppose. Indeed, the bellicose way you sometimes define those who challenge your claim to find a solid ground suggests that *you* would be unethical unless you could pretend to have secured a compulsory basis for ethics. We think an ethical sensibility is to be cultivated *because* there is no compulsory basis for ethics." There, that should settle matters between us.

37. Does this enhanced appreciation of contingency require "heroism"? Or does it appeal to privileges of leisurely reflection available only to a few political theorists? Such an appreciation will seem heroic to any perspective or group that insists upon the dogmatism of identity and the necessity of a solid ground of morality. Indeed, that demand provides the source of the question. But, when you think about this question comparatively and historically, the pretense of heroism drifts away. Many men, in a variety of subject positions, today experience masculinity rather differently than they did in the 1950s. Many previous "heterosexuals" now constitute themselves as straight, signifying a certain shift in the understanding of their own sexuality and of the coercive, degrading relation that the naturalization of heterosexuality established to sexual difference. Such a shift is even more discernible among feminists, gays, and lesbians, who provided the political initiative for most of these developments. In all these cases a shift, even if it is partial and

restricted to a minority, is discernible in the self-identity of the parties in question. It takes work, but not heroism, to make such adjustments. Indeed, given the general conditions of contemporary life enumerated elsewhere in this text, it *also* takes considerable work upon oneself to respond to these conditions as a conventional liberal, conservative, or fundamentalist. The self is always engaged in work on itself. This condition of life is not dispensable, even if it has been forgotten or occluded in a variety of academic theories of morality. The key questions are, in what directions, for what ends, by what means? As for political theorists, it has not been my experience, at least, that they are notably more or less effective in these respects than the members of numerous other social groupings.

38. There is indeed a series of divisions within this broadly defined grouping that eventually requires critical reflection. To schematize, thinkers such as Nietzsche, Foucault, and Deleuze emphasize, first, how goodness comes out of abundance, second, the significance of generosity in relation to intrasubjective and intersubjective difference, and, third, the productivity of tactics on the self by the self in cultivating virtues such as generosity, agonistic respect, critical responsiveness, passing by, and studied indifference. Thinkers such as Levinas and perhaps Lacan emphasize the incompleteness of the subject, its indebtedness to the Other it cannot fully comprehend, and the role of obligation in ethics. Derrida struggles to bridge these two traditions, though he does not pay enough attention to the centrality of techniques of the self in the Nietzschean tradition. I pursue some of these questions in "Beyond Good and Evil: The Ethical Sensibility of Michel Foucault," *Political Theory*, August 1994. Two impressive studies that focus on post-Kantian ethics from a Levinasian perspective, broadly defined, are John D. Caputo, *Against Ethics* (Bloomington: Indiana University Press, 1993), and Zygmunt Bauman, *PostModern Ethics* (Oxford: Blackwell, 1993). The followers of Levinas concentrate on our *obligations* to victims of suffering, while the Nietzscheans focus first on the cultivation of generosity to difference. To feel *one* of the effects of this differential emphasis, consider one of Bauman's formulations: "The Other is not a force, but a face: the Other . . . does not oppose me by her resistance (resistance is something I am prompted to fight against and overcome; it is the lack of resistance that truly disarms)" (79). I would say that in politics it is precisely relations of resistance that must be appreciated and infused with an ethos of agonistic respect (between rough equals) and critical responsiveness (between an oppressed constituency and its respondents). If you think an *ethics of engagement* between constituencies locked into relations of interdependence and strife is the key, a post-Nietzschean perspective has much to offer.

39. That paradox, where effect must precede cause and cause must precede effect, is discussed more extensively in chapter 5 of this study. I first explored it in *Political Theory and Modernity* (Oxford: Basil Blackwell, 1988),

now published with a new epilogue by Cornell University Press (1994). An excellent discussion of the paradox of founding, developed through readings of Arendt and Derrida, is Bonnie Honig, "Declarations of Independence: Arendt and Derrida on the Problem of Founding a Republic," *American Political Science Review,* November 1986. The seminal article by Derrida is "Declarations of Independence," *New Political Science,* Autumn 1986. A thoughtful dissertation on this general topic has been written by Alan Keenan (Johns Hopkins University, 1994). In "The Democratic Question: On the Rule of the People and the Paradoxes of Political Freedom," Keenan explores how a series of identifications and concealments of the paradox of democratic rule appear in works by Rousseau, Hannah Arendt, Ronald Dworkin, Stanley Fish, and Ernesto Laclau/Chantal Mouffe.

40. I discuss "agonistic respect" and its role in relations between constituencies connected by relations of strife and interdependence in *Identity\Difference: Democratic Negotiations of Political Paradox* (Ithaca, N.Y.: Cornell University Press, 1991). If critical responsiveness is an ethical relation a privileged constituency establishes with culturally devalued constituencies striving to enact new identities, agonistic respect is a relation between two contending constituencies, each of which has gained a fair amount of recognition and power in the existing order.

41. The production of a disposable welfare class enables political parties to perpetuate the debate over whether to treat them as needy or undeserving. The hegemony of this debate in turn allows both major parties to ignore underlying sources of poverty. See my *Identity\Difference,* chapter 6, for a discussion of this dynamic and its effects.

42. The issue can become a paradox under unfavorable conditions: if you do not set limits to the culture of pluralization, pluralism itself might become undermined; but if you respond to its fervent opponents as they would respond to you, pluralism might be defeated by the means through which it is saved. This combination registers the fragility of pluralism.

43. "The young man—between the end of childhood and the age when he attained manly status—constituted a delicate and difficult factor for Greek ethics and Greek thought. His youth with its particular beauty (to which every man was believed to be naturally sensitive) and the status that would be his . . . formed a 'strategic' point around which a complex game was required. . . . For him there was a test in all this, one that demanded diligence and training; there was also, for others, an occasion for care and concern" (Michel Foucault, *The Use of Pleasure,* trans. Robert Hurley [New York: Pantheon, 1985]). Foucault's reservation about this erotic model is not linked to its justification of male/male relations but to the effects upon women and male youths of the general distinction it draws between the virile, active partner and the passive, receptive one. For an excellent account of

how the Greek ideal of "sexuality" provides the model from which Pericles' ideal of reciprocity between citizen and polis is drawn, see S. Sara Monoson, "Citizen as *Erastes*: Erotic Imagery and the Idea of Reciprocity in the Periclean Funeral Oration," *Political Theory,* May 1994, 253-76.

Index

Agonistic respect: and critical responsiveness, 234, 235; and tolerance, xvii, 92. *See also* Ethics; Responsiveness, critical

Apess, William: and the Mashpee rebellion, 175-78

Baptists, Southern: and the fundamentals, 110-12; renegotiating the fundamentals, 129-31; and soul competency, 109-10

Bauman, Zygmunt: obligation to the other, 234

Benhabib, Seyla: and the dialectic of justice, 184-86; and the enactment of new identities, 231-32

Bennett, Jane, 201, 229

Berlin, Isaiah, 201-2

Bloom, Harold: on American religions, 109-12

Blumenberg, Hans: on history of ontologies, 2-3; and mastery, 24; and secularism, 3

Bodies: and cultural corporealiza-tion, 24, 56-58, 194-95; and Habermas, 13; and Nietzsche, 13

Boundaries: ambiguity of, 163-67; of pluralism, 193-98. *See also* Identity, Territory

Brown, Wendy: and displacement of class politics, 55-56

Bush, George, 107

Butler, Judith: the constitutive outside, v; on repetition, 25, 68, 216

Campbell, David: and the foreign, 228-29

Carter, Dontay: crime of, 43; desire of, 58-62; my relation to, 71-72; as responsible offender/racial monster, 45-46; sentencing of, 44; statement of, 43-44

Church and state: renegotiations of, 130-31, 188-93; Tocqueville on, 169-70. *See also* Sacred, Secularism

Collective assemblages: and connections across difference, xx, 96, 196-97; and dedogmatization of identity, 96-97; rhizomatic ideal of, 93-97

Connolly, William E.: on cold showers, 214

Consumption: exclusive and inclusive goods, 82-85

Contingency: and desire, 50-54; domestications of, 21-25; globalization of, 22-23

Correctness, political, xxvi-xxvii

Dahl, Robert, 79

Deconstruction: in relation to positive interpretation, 36-40; as strategy of disruption, 36

Deleuze, Gilles: and the dialectic, 232; and micropolitics, xxv-xxviii; and the rhizome, 94-96; and speed, 219; on trees, v

Democracy: ambivalence of, 97-104, 153-55; and belonging, 135-37, 158-60; and citizenship, 100-4; disaggregation of, 153-61; and displacement of revenge, 83; and economic equality, 80-85; and electoral accountability, 140-43, 153-55; ethos of, 101-4, 154-57, 178-81; and globalization, 131-33, 157-61; models of, 75-80; and normalization, 85-93; and the paradox of sovereignty, 137-40; and territory, 135-37, 146-53, 155-61

Der Derian, James: and speed, 219

Derrida, Jacques: and deconstruction, 36-40; and diference, 89, 99-100; and moral sources, 204, 232-33, 234

Desire: and abundance, 55; of Dontay Carter, 58-62; character of, xxv-xxvi, 50-51; Girard on, 51-58; imperious forms of, xxv, 71-72, 215-16; masculinization of, 60-61, 113-14; and micro-politics, xxv-xxviii, 65-70; and models of, 51-53, 59-60; opacity of, 10-11, 61; and quest for transcendence, 59-60; resistance to theorization, 49-51; and revenge, 55, 63-65

Difference: and connections, xx-xxi, 197-98; and the dialectic, 184-86, 231-32; and diference, 89, 99-100, 104, 107; and the ethics of cultivation, 27-30, 180-88; and fragmentation, 89-93, 194-98; and normalization, 85-93. See also Identity

Dumm, Tom: on masculine desire, 213; on punishment, 209-10; on Tocqueville, 228

Dworkin, Ronald, 124-25

Elster, Jon: on the thin theory of rationality, 8

Emmanuelle: and the triangle of desire, 212

Enactment: and critical responsiveness, 180-88, 190-93; and nontheistic reverence, 190-93; paradox of, xiv-xv, 182-84, 192-93; politics of, xiv-xvi, 59-60, 113-14. See also Identity

Epistemology: nonprimacy of, 5-6

Equality, economic: and collective assemblages, 93-97; and democracy, 75-80; and inclusive goods of consumption, 81-84

Ethics: of cultivation, xxiv, 27-30, 174-75, 202-3; as ethos, xv-xix, 26-30, 180-88, 190-93; and genealogy, 33-36, 203; and morality, xxvii-xviii, 126-28, 201, 221-22, 233, 234; multiple sources of, xxiv, 27-30, 104, 191, 204-6; and nontheistic reverence, 30-31; and teleological morality, xxiii-xxiv; without guarantees, 40. *See also* Morality, Responsiveness

Fascism: micropolitics of, xxvi-xxvii
Foucault, Michel: and the ambivalence of democracy, 101-4; and the anthropological sleep, 12; brief history of critiques of, 207-8; on code morality and ethos, 126-28, 214; on corporeal practices and symbolic codes, 56-58; on dogmatism and fragmentation, 26; on man and his doubles, 10-12; and "Nothing is fundamental," 31; and the state, 103-4; on transcendental arguments, 15-16, 35-36; and Bernard Williams, 31-34
Fragmentation: and fundamentalism, xxi-xxii, 26-27; inverse relation to pluralization, 196-97; and the rhizome, 93-97
Freud, Sigmund: on Moses, 211-12
Fundamentalism: and command morality, 108; defined, 105-6, 120-22; elite formations of, 107-9, 115-18; and fragmentation, xxi-xxii, 26-27; and fundamentals, 105; and individualism, 106; and nature, 108-9; political formula of, 118-22; possibilities of renegotiation, 128-33; and postfundamentalist liberalism, 125-28; and postmodernism, 119-20; and Southern Baptist Convention, 110-11;

and white male workers, 111-14

Genealogy: character of, 34-36; and the micropolitics of desire, 66-72
Girard, René: and desire, 51-58, 62
Globalization: and the ethos of democracy, 131-33, 154-60

Habermas, Jürgen: and the body, 13
Harding, Susan: on fundamentalism, 219-20
Hegel, G. W. F.: on lordship and bondage, 200
Heidegger, Martin: on the subjective/objective pair, 18-19; on truth and untruth, 5-6
Hermeneutics: pastoral form, 13-16
Herz, John: and the territorial state, 149-53
Heterosexuality: denaturalization of, 233-34; and the micropolitics of desire, 67-69; naturalization of, 185-86, 234-37; and the Ramsey Colloquium, 107-9
Honig, Bonnie, 200, 232

Identity: and class, 224; and diference, 89, 99-100; and difference, xvi, xx-xxi, 89-90, 193, 233-34; and normalization, 85-90; political enactment of, 59-60, 113-14, 116, 180-88, 190-93. *See also* Desire
Indian, the: and Apess, 175-78; and Thoreau, 173-75; and Tocqueville, 167-73
Individual: and collective identification, 200; fundamentalization of, 106-7

Johnston, David: critique of Foucauldianism, 126-27, 221-22
Justice: and critical responsiveness,
180-88

Kateb, George, 202
Katz, Jack: on criminal desire, 211
Kaufman, Arnold: and participatory democracy, 217
Keenan, Alan: and the paradox of
democratic rule, 235
Kleinman, Joan: and nothingness,
209
Kurth, James: and culture wars,
117-18; and the postmodern
state, 115-18

Lacan, Jacques: and René Girard,
212-13; and the symbolic, 213
Lefort, Claude: and the dissolution
of markers of certainty, 227
Levinas, Emmanuel: and moral
sources, 202-3, 234
Liberalism: ambiguous relation to
fundamentalism, 122-25; and
postfundamentalism, 125-28;
variants of, 123; and white male
workers, 111-14, 128-29
Locke, John: and the anxiety of
freedom, 126-27

Macpherson, C. B.: and contestable
postulates, 87-88; and democratic consensus, 101-4; and
economic equality, 80-82; and
models of democracy, xxvii,
75-80; and normalization,
85-93
Masculinity: codes of, 59-60, 113-
14, 116, 118, 141-42; instability
of, 220-21

Mehta, Uday, 126-27
Micropolitics: of desire, 65-70; and
fascism, xxv-xxviii
Mill, John Stuart, 78
Monoson, Sara, 236
Morality: as code, 126-28, 221-22;
as command, xxiii-xxiv; as
communion, xxiii-xxiv; and
critical responsiveness, xvii-xviii,
180-88, 201, 221-22, 233,
234
Moses: and the ambiguity of
boundaries, 163-65
Mouffe, Chantal: on pluralism,
199, 222-23

Nation: and fundamentalism, 117-
18; and the postmodern state,
115-18; and territory, 135-37,
165-67, 169-73
Nietzsche, Friedrich: critique of
mastery and attunement perspectives, 20-25; critiques of, 25-30;
and little deviant acts, 68; and
moral sources, 202-3; and nontheistic gratitude for being, 31;
and post-Nietzschean thought,
25-32, 36-39; and punishment,
47-48; and self as art work, 30-
31, 69-70; and spiritualization of
enmity, 28-29
Normalization: and alienation, 88-
93; and democratic theory, 85-
93; and the production of deviations, 89-91
Nothing: ambiguity of, 32-33, 39-
40; and diference, 89, 99-100;
and ontology, 1-2

O'Connell, Barry: on William
Apess, 175

Ontology: and compensatory
strategies, 19-26; contestability
of, 10-12, 15-16, 21; and epistemology, 5-7; and ethics, 26-30;
and Foucault, 10-13; and ontopolitical interpretation, 1-9,
16-19, 32-39; unavoidability of,
1, 4

Ontopolitical matrix: alternatives
to, 22, 24-25, 37-40; reductions
of, 25-32; structure of, 16-19

Pluralism: and the ambivalence of
democracy, 93; constitutive tension of, xv, 195-98; conventional
conceptions of, xiv-xv, xix, 133;
and critical responsiveness, 180-
88; and elitism, 76-77; imagination of, xiii, xix, xxx; limits to,
193-98; and pluralization, xi-
xiii, xiv, 180-88; and Schumpeter, 140-42; and territory, xxii-
xxiii, 137-49, 146-53, 168-73;
and Tocqueville, 169, 172-73;
and Walzer, 142-49

Pluralization: and critical responsiveness, xiv-xviii, 180-88; and
fragmentation, 26-27, 93-97,
196-97; and fundamentalization,
xxi-xxii, xxvii; and pluralism,
xiv-xvii, xix, 193-98; of the
sacred/secular duopoly, xxix-
xxx, 188-93; and territorial
identifications, xxii-xiii, 131-33,
155-60, 163-67

Politics: and boundaries, 163-67,
193-98; of disturbance and governance, 101-4, 153-55, 178-80;
of enactment, xiv-xv, 59-60,
113-14, 180-88, 190-93; and
globalization, xxii-xxiii, 131-33,
155-60; and micropolitics, xxv-

xxvii, 65-72; multiple dimensions of, xxi

Progress: as pluralization, 188,
195-98

Public: and private, 130-31, 169-
70, 194. *See also* Sacred, Secularism

Punishment: and astonishment, 47-
48, 61; the call to, 41-43; and
class/race relations, 43-46, 56,
73-74, 113-15; and responsible
agency, 46-48; and revenge, 45-
46, 48-49, 63-65, 113-15; shared
understandings of, 144-46

Puritanism: Tocqueville on, 230-31

Ramsey Colloquium of Christian
and Jewish Scholars: and homosexuality, 107-9; on morality
and nature, 108-9

Rationality: and ontology, 8; strategies of elaboration, 140-42; thin
theory of, 8-9

Rawls, John: and overlapping consensus, 3-4

Representation: and collective assemblages, 93-97; and ontology,
6-9

Responsibility: indispensability of,
210, 215; murkiness of, 45-47,
64-65; and normalization, 90-
91; and punishment, 45-47, 63-
65; and responsiveness, 70-72,
180-88

Responsiveness: and agonistic respect, xviii, 92, 234; as anticipatory, 184; and constituency self-
modification, 184; critical,
xv-xviii, 184; ethos of, xv-xix,
195; and justice, 180-88; and the
micropolitics of desire, 64-72;

sources of, 24-25, 27-30, 190-93, 202-3; and tolerance, xvii

Ressentiment: and resentment, 213-14; and revenge, 45-49, 55, 63-65, 67, 110-15

Revenge. *See* Ressentiment

Rhizome: and the arboreal imagination, 94-95; and a democratic ethos, 95-96

Ricoeur, Paul: and the paradox of politics, xxviii-xxix, 138-40, 223-24; and the territorial state, xxviii-xxix

Rorty, Richard: and the politics of difference, 200-201

Rousseau, Jean-Jacques: and national identity, 166-67; and the paradox of sovereignty, 137-40; and territorial boundaries, 165-67

Sacred: and secular, xxix-xxx, 31-32, 188-93

Sade, Marquis de: and desire, 10

Said, Edward: and the critical intellectual, 225-26; and identity, v

Sarat, Austin: on punishment, 209-10

Sartre, Jean-Paul: and the ontopolitical matrix, 19

Schumpeter, Joseph: and democratic realism, 78-79, 140-43

Secularism: legitimacy of, 2-3; and monomorality, xiii-xiv; and pluralizing the sacred/secular divide, 26-30, 130-31, 188-93

Shapiro, Michael, 204, 226

Sovereignty: and globalization, 157-61; paradox of, 137-40, 170-71; and pluralism, 140-49; and territory, 149-53

Speed: effects on identity, xi-xii, 100-101, 159-61, 219

State: and fundamentalization, 115-18, 131-33; and multiple sites of political action, xxi, xxv-xxviii, 65-72, 131-33, 156-61; and nation, 135-37; and sovereignty, 115-18, 137-40; and territory, 131-33, 149-53, 156-61

Strawson, Peter: and the indispensability of responsibility, 215

Swaggart, Jimmy, 110

Taylor, Charles: and Foucault on consensuality, 101-4; and multiculturalism, 199-200; and pastoral hermeneutics, 14-16; and the primacy of epistemology, 4-7

Territory: and the civi-territorial complex, 167-73; and the democratic ideal, 135-37, 163-67; and pluralism, xxi-xxiii, 137-49; and security, 149-53; and sovereignty, 137-49; and *terra*, xxii; and *territorium*, xxii

Thoreau, Henry: and William Apess, 177-78; and Joe Polis, 173-75

Tocqueville, Alexis de: and church/state relation, 169-70; and the civi-territorial complex, 167-73; and democratic agitation, 179-80; and fundamentalization, xxvii-xxviii; and the Indian, 168-73; and the pluralist imagination, xxix-xxx, 169, 172-73; and Puritanism, 183; and sovereignty, 170-71

Transcendental argument: paradox of, 11-13, 15-16

Truth: Heidegger on, 5-6; and untruth, 5-6

Understandings, shared, 145-46
Unger, Roberto: and the ontopolitical matrix, 7-8, 19

Walzer, Michael: and connectedness, 225-26; and criminal punishment, 144-46; and ontology, 224-25; and pluralism, 142-49; and the territorial state, xxviii, 146-49

Williams, Bernard: and Foucault, 31-35; and the tragic conception, 32-34, 206-7
Wilson, James Q.: on crime, 7
Wollheim, Richard: on imperious desires, 215-16
Workers, male and blue-collar: and claims to dignity, 111-12, 129, 131; and cross-national labor movements, 132-33; and fundamentalism, 111-14, 128-29; and hypermasculinization, 113-14, 116

WILLIAM E. CONNOLLY teaches political theory at Johns Hopkins University, where he is a professor of political science. He has served as the editor of *Political Theory* and is now the series editor of *Contestations: Cornell Studies in Political Theory*. He has been a fellow at Nuffield College, Oxford, the Institute for Advanced Study, Princeton (1986–87), the European University Institute, Florence (1990), and the Center for Advanced Study in the Behavioral Sciences, Stanford (1993–94). His publications include *The Terms of Political Discourse* (1974, 1983, 1994), *Politics and Ambiguity* (1987), *Political Theory and Modernity* (1988, 1993), *Identity\Difference: Democratic Negotiations of Political Paradox* (1991), and *The Augustinian Imperative* (1993). His essays have been published in *Political Theory; Millennium; Theory, Culture and Society; Philosophy and Social Criticism;* and *Polity*.